POKÉMON CROCHET SQUARES

Bring Pikachu and friends to life with over 30 cute Pokémon granny squares

Ira Rott

DAVID & CHARLES
— PUBLISHING —

www.davidandcharles.com

Contents

Introduction . . . 3
Tools and Materials . . . 4
How To Use This Book . . . 6
Basic Shapes . . . 8

THE SQUARES . . . 10
- Pikachu . . . 12
- Poké Ball . . . 14
- Piplup . . . 16
- Fuecoco . . . 18
- Mudkip . . . 20
- Cyndaquil . . . 22
- Oshawott . . . 24
- Oran Berry . . . 26
- Quaxly . . . 28
- Master Ball . . . 31
- Chespin . . . 32
- Pecha Berry . . . 35
- Grookey . . . 38
- Great Ball . . . 41
- Froakie . . . 42
- Litten . . . 44
- Treecko . . . 48
- Sitrus Berry . . . 50
- Popplio . . . 52
- Ultra Ball . . . 54
- Turtwig . . . 55
- Squirtle . . . 58
- Tepig . . . 60
- Sprigatito . . . 62
- Chimchar . . . 65
- Rowlet . . . 68
- Fennekin . . . 71
- Scorbunny . . . 74
- Totodile . . . 77
- Tamato Berry . . . 80
- Torchic . . . 82
- Chikorita . . . 84
- Sobble . . . 87
- Charmander . . . 90
- Bulbasaur . . . 92
- Snivy . . . 94

THE PROJECTS . . . 97
- Lap Blanket . . . 98
- Pillow . . . 100
- Banner . . . 104
- Mug Rug . . . 106
- Play Cubes . . . 108
- Wall Hanging . . . 110

Techniques . . . 112
Working With Felt . . . 122
Finishing . . . 124
About The Author . . . 126
Thanks . . . 126
Suppliers . . . 126
Index . . . 127

Introduction

Step into the enchanting world of Pokémon crochet, where majestic Pokémon come to life in a brand-new way! From Pikachu to Fennekin, and everything in between, get your hooks and yarn ready, it's time to crochet some Pokémon!

Pokémon Crochet Squares includes adorable Pokémon, powerful Poké Balls, and nutritious berries. You can easily decorate your room with an array of Pokémon accessories by following the bright and colorful project ideas. Make a snuggly blanket with coordinating pillow for resting on to read Pokémon stories, and a mug rug for keeping your favorite beverage by your side. A handy wall hanging with pockets will make any space a little more lively, and it is perfect for storing small items. Add a touch of fun to your Pokémon parties with a stylish banner and a few play cubes. They will catch your guests' attention and set the mood for a playful celebration. This book has everything you need to create your own unique projects using 36 Pokémon-inspired granny squares.

Happy crocheting!

Tools and Materials

Having the right tools and materials will help you achieve the best results when creating your Pokémon squares. Don't worry–we've got you covered with everything you need to know when selecting your supplies.

Yarn

All of the projects in this book were made from Stylecraft Special DK—a super soft and naturally anti-pilling, 100% premium acrylic yarn, with 322yds (295m) per 3½oz (100g) ball. This yarn comes in a fabulous range of colors to meet all of your needs when creating Pokémon crochet squares. To make one square you will need a small amount of each listed color, or approximately ¾–1oz (20–30g) combined weight.

In addition, you will need a slightly thinner yarn to stitch small details on some Pokémon squares, such as thin black lines for facial features and white highlights. I used Stylecraft Special 4-ply, a fingering-weight yarn with 462yds (422m) per 3½oz (100g) ball.

Some extra thin lines are stitched with three strands of DMC embroidery floss (thread).

Craft Felt

Choosing the right felt is crucial to the success of cutting and handling small pieces, such as Pokémon eyes, smiles, and patches. Good quality felt will also improve the durability of your final project. Therefore, opt for a thin (1–1.2mm) and dense wool felt as it will be pressed with a hot iron. For the projects in this book, I used Wool Blend Felt Sheets from Canadian Felt Shop. This felt is soft, strong, and resistant to pilling.

For the Play Cubes project you will also need thicker, medium-weight felt (3–4mm) to stabilize their shape.

Other Materials

For some of the Pokémon squares you will need Mill Hill glass beads in sizes 6 (4mm) and 8 (3mm). Alternatively, you can used DMC embroidery floss for stitching tiny details, like freckles and fruit pores. You will also need some stitch markers, tapestry needles, straight pins, fabric snips, freezer paper, and Quick Bond Fabric Fuse (white fabric glue). Polyester stuffing is also required for some projects.

Crochet Hooks

You will need a set of crochet hooks ranging in size from 2.5mm (B/1 closest match) to 5mm (H/8). The metric sizes are listed with the project instructions, but you will find a hook conversion on each square as well as in the chart below, which is a quick reference for converting hook sizes to other standards.

Metric	US	UK	Japan
2.5mm	-	12	4/0
3mm	-	11	5/0
3.5mm	E/4	9	6/0
3.75mm	F/5	–	–
4mm	G/6	8	7/0
4.5mm	G/7	7	7.5/0
5mm	H/8	6	8/0

Safety

Please note that the projects with small parts, such as beads, felt, and glue, should not be used by young children without supervision.

Yarn and Felt Colors

All of the yarn and felt colors used in this book are abbreviated using numbers or letters and are listed alongside the projects. For instance, rectangles with numbers indicate the yarn colors (Stylecraft Special DK), and circles with letters indicate the felt colors (Wool Blend Felt Sheets from Canadian Felt Shop). Simply refer back to this page when you need to decode the colors.

Yarn

1	White (1001)
2	Cream (1005)
3	Black (1002)
4	Graphite (1063)
5	Silver (1203)
6	Hint of Silver (1807)
7	Matador (1010)
8	Tomato (1723)
9	Claret (1123)
10	Dark Brown (1004)
11	Walnut (1054)
12	Gingerbread (1806)
13	Mocha (1064)
14	Camel (1420)
15	Buttermilk (1835)
16	Stone (1710)
17	Clementine (1853)
18	Jaffa (1256)
19	Spice (1711)
20	Gold (1709)
21	Dandelion (1856)
22	Saffron (1081)
23	Citron (1263)
24	Lemon (1020)
25	Apple (1852)
26	Lincoln (1834)
27	Grass Green (1821)
28	Bright Green (1259)
29	Spring Green (1316)
30	Aspen (1422)
31	Spearmint (1842)
32	Kelly Green (1826)
33	Petrol (1708)
34	Empire (1829)
35	Turquoise (1068)
36	Sherbet (1034)
37	Cloud Blue (1019)
38	Aster (1003)
39	Denim (1302)
40	Royal (1117)
41	Lobelia (1825)
42	Lapis (1831)
43	Proper Purple (1855)
44	Violet (1277)
45	Magenta (1084)
46	Fiesta (1257)
47	Fondant (1241)
48	Bright Pink (1435)
49	Blush (1833)
50	Shrimp (1132)
51	Candyfloss (1130)

Felt

A	White
B	Cream
C	Opal
D	Black
E	Smoke
F	Silver Grey
G	Brown
H	Bright Red
I	Red Velvet
J	Rust
K	Persimmon
L	Sunburst
M	Coral
N	Georgia Peach
O	Custard
P	Eternal Sunshine
Q	Lemon
R	Peacock
S	Blue Spruce
T	Blueberry
U	Royal Blue
V	Cotton Candy
W	Pink Violet

How To Use This Book

Before you begin, make sure you're familiar with pattern abbreviations, gauge (tension) swatching, and skill levels. You can quickly translate crochet instructions and diagrams using the symbols and abbreviations provided in this section.

Skill Levels

All Pokémon squares and projects in this book have been assigned a level of difficulty based on the crochet stitches and techniques used for creating them. Just pick a pattern that suits your skill level and then move up to the next level as you become more comfortable with your projects.

   Easy

Best choice for confident beginners. These patterns include basic and easy-to-learn crochet stitches, with simple repeats and straightforward assembly. Felt elements either have simple shapes or are not present. These Pokémon squares are a breeze to stitch and easy to catch!

   Takes some effort

These patterns include basic stitches, as well as some easy-to-learn special stitches. Assembly details may include more intricate sewing and cutting, accompanied by a larger amount of felt pieces. While crafting these takes some effort, these designs are so much fun to make!

   Challenge accepted

These Pokémon squares incorporate additional crochet components with various shapes, which means sewing might pose a bit of a challenge. Felt appliqués in these designs may include layered elements with notches and seam allowances. This is just a heads-up for those who love to embrace challenges!

Gauge/Tension

Since crochet gauge varies from person to person, it's important to make test swatches and achieve the gauge of the patterns for accurate sizing. The gauge to aim for for the squares is:

19 dc x 9.5 rnds = 4 x 4in (10 x 10cm).

All of the felt appliqués in this book are designed to fit proportionally onto a 7 x 7in (17.5 x 17.5cm) square, so be sure to test your gauge before starting. Simply make a Basic Square with a 4mm (G/6) crochet hook and measure it (see Basic Shapes). You can use a larger or smaller hook size to obtain the correct gauge if necessary.

Reading Patterns

Crochet patterns in this book are written using US terminology. If you are accustomed to UK terminology, you can convert the terms using the chart below.

US Terms	UK Terms
Single crochet	Double crochet
Half double crochet	Half treble crochet
Double crochet	Treble crochet
Treble crochet	Double treble crochet

"Work in rows" means—Crochet a row of stitches, then turn your work to begin the next row. The patterns might specify which rows are right side (RS) or wrong side (WS) when this is helpful or important.

"Work in the round" means—Begin with a magic ring/foundation ring or work along both sides of the foundation chain. Work with the right side (RS) facing you (unless otherwise indicated), joining each round with a slip stitch in the top of the beginning stitch.

The total stitch count is indicated after the equal sign (=) at the end of each row/round. The beginning chain(s) might be counted as a stitch or not, as noted at the beginning of the rows/rounds. Some instructions apply to multiple rows/rounds. Example: Ch 2 (**counts as dc now and throughout**).

Symbols and Abbreviations

Crochet charts are illustrations with symbols to represent stitches that help with visualizing patterns. The beginning of the work in the charts is marked with a small black arrow, and each row/round is marked with a number. The following symbols and abbreviations will help you translate pattern instructions and diagrams.

ABBREVIATIONS	STITCH NAME	SYMBOL
Beg	Beginning	
BLO	(Work in) back loop(s) only	
Bphdc	Back post half double crochet	
Bpsc	Back post single crochet	
Ch	Chain	
Ch-sp	Chain space	
Dc	Double crochet	
D-ch cord	Double chain crochet cord	
Dc2tog	Double crochet 2 together	
Dc3tog	Double crochet 3 together	
Dc4tog	Double crochet 4 together	
Dc5tog	Double crochet 5 together	
FLO	(Work in) front loop(s) only	
Fpdc	Front post double crochet	
Fphdc	Front post half double crochet	
Fpsc	Front post single crochet	
Fpslst	Front post slip stitch	
Fptr	Front post treble crochet	
Fptr3tog	Front post treble crochet 3 together	
Hdc	Half double crochet	
JAYGO	Join as you go	
Join	Slip stitch into first stitch	
Rnd(s)	Round(s)	

ABBREVIATIONS	STITCH NAME	SYMBOL
RS	Right side	
Sc	Single crochet	× +
Sc2tog	Single crochet 2 together	
Sl st	Slip stitch	•
Sp(s)	Space(s)	
St(s)	Stitch(es)	
Tr	Treble crochet	
Tr2tog	Treble crochet 2 together	
Tr3tog	Treble crochet 3 together	
5-tr PC	5 treble crochet popcorn	
WS	Wrong side	
	Starting point/direction	
	Magic ring	
	Picot	
	2 sc in same stitch	
	3 sc in same stitch	
	Third loop(s) of hdc	
	Standing (beg) st	
	Yarn tail	
	Whipstitch	
	Backstitch	
	Surface sl st	
	Stitch marker	

Basic Shapes

The Basic Shapes can be used for testing your gauge (tension) and tackling your crochet skills. These patterns are also used as the basis for most of the squares in the book.

When you make Pokémon squares from this book, often the center of each square will form a seamless outline of the Pokémon's head, Poké Ball, or berry, which means these shapes are integral parts of the squares and are not attached. However, some designs require the use of the Basic Square as a background and all other crochet elements are sewn onto the square (for example, Froakie, Snivy, Mudkip, Sobble, and Scorbunny). Basic Squares are also great fillers and can be incorporated into your projects alongside Pokémon squares. To make one of the Basic Squares, you will need approximately ½oz (16g) or 52yds (48m) of Stylecraft Special DK yarn.

Basic Square

Work in the round with a 4mm/G/6 hook, or any size needed to obtain gauge.

To begin: Ch 4, sl st in last ch from hook to form a ring

Rnd 1: Ch 3 (counts as dc now and throughout), work in ring—2 dc, [ch 2, 3 dc] 3 times; ch 1, sc in top of beg ch-3 (counts as last corner now and throughout) = 12 sts and 4 ch-2 corners

Rnds 2–7: Ch 3, dc in same sp, *dc in each st to next corner, (2 dc, ch 2, 2 dc) in ch-2 sp**; repeat from * to ** 2 more times; dc in each st to last corner, 2 dc in last ch-sp; ch 1, sc in top of beg ch-3 = 28/44/60/76/92/108 sts and 4 ch-2 corners

Rnd 8: Ch 3, dc in same sp, *dc in each st to next corner, (2 dc, ch 2, 2 dc) in ch-2 sp**; repeat from * to ** 2 more times; dc in each st to last corner, 2 dc in last ch-sp; ch 2, sl st in top of beg ch-3 = 124 sts and 4 ch-2 corners

Fasten off and weave in the ends.

Basic square

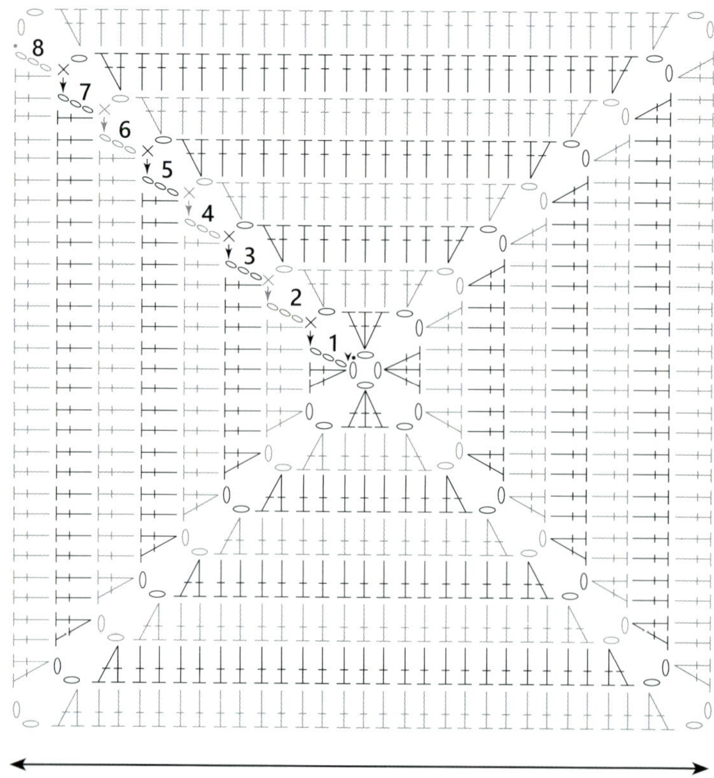

Basic Circle

Make a magic ring and work in the round with a 4mm/G/6 hook, or any size needed to obtain gauge.

Rnd 1: Ch 2 (does not count as a st now and throughout), 12 dc in ring; join = 12 sts

Rnd 2: Ch 2, 2 dc in each st around; join = 24 sts

Rnd 3: Ch 2, dc in same st as join, 2 dc in next st, [dc in next st, 2 dc in next st] 11 times; join = 36 sts

Rnd 4: Ch 2, 2 dc in same st as join, dc in next 2 sts, [2 dc in next st, dc in next 2 sts] 11 times; join = 48 sts

Basic circle

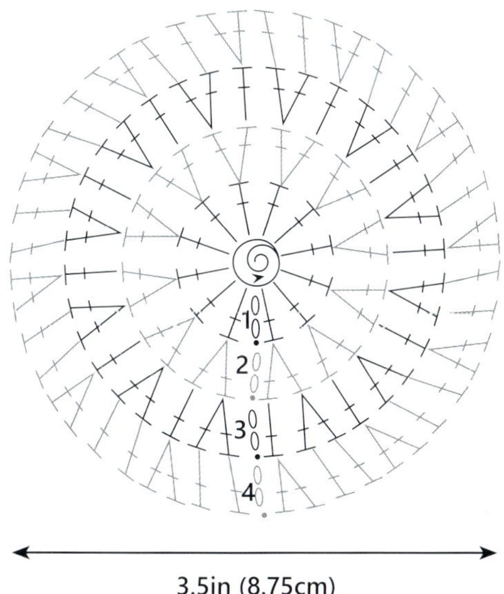

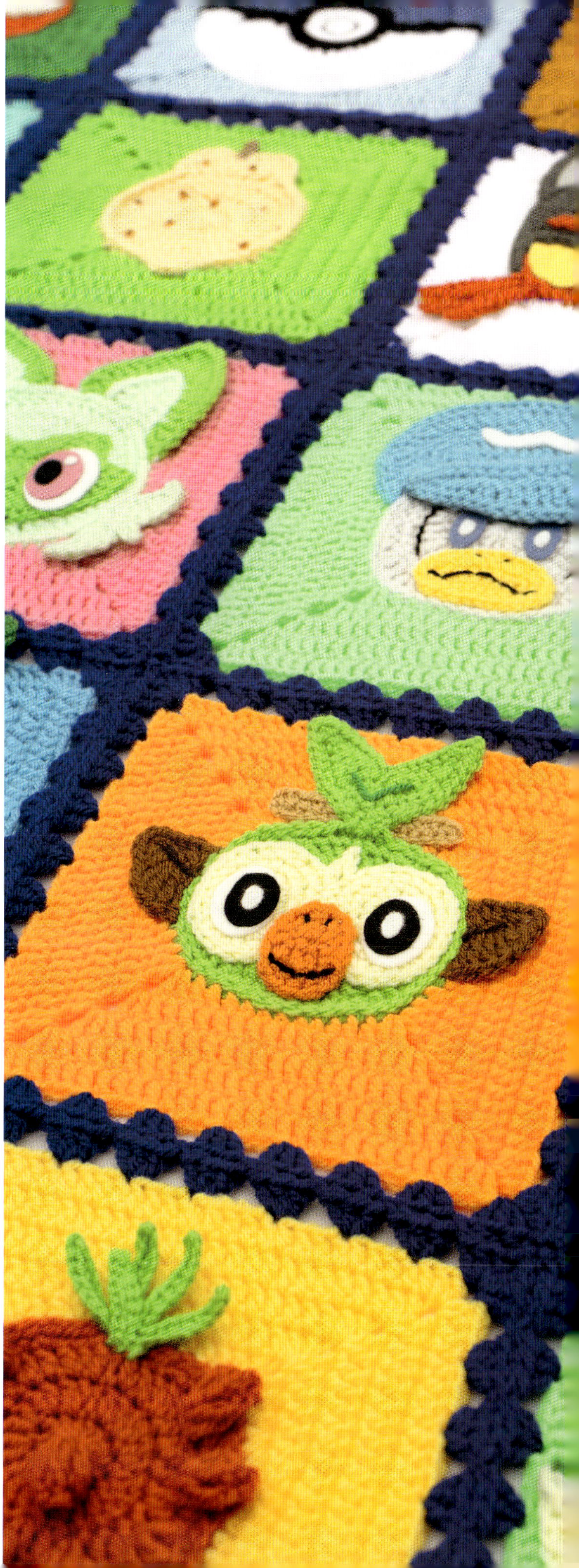

The Squares

This section includes 36 crochet squares with amazing Pokémon, Poké Ball, and berry designs on them. Make them all to complete a cozy throw blanket or finish just a few for a smaller project. Be sure to check out the Pokémon grouping considerations when choosing your squares (see Projects).

You can also download full-size printable versions of the templates from: www.bookmarkedhub.com.

Type Key
Electric
Water
Fire
Poison
Grass

Pikachu

When it is angered, this Pokémon immediately discharges the energy stored in the pouches in its cheeks.

Key

Difficulty level

Type

Square (4mm/G/6 hook)

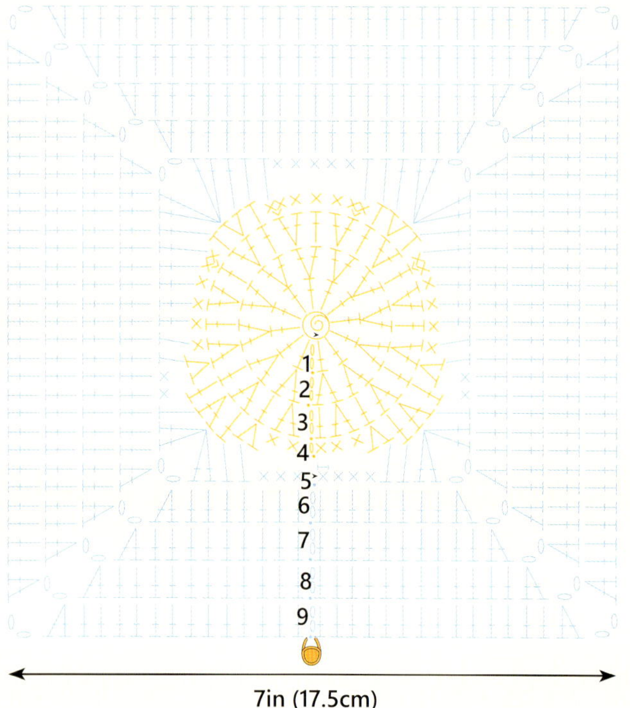

Cheek
(3.5mm/E/4 hook)

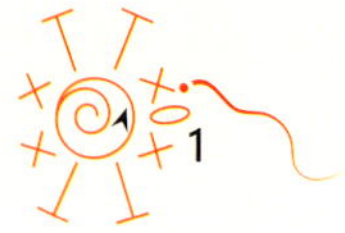

Felt templates

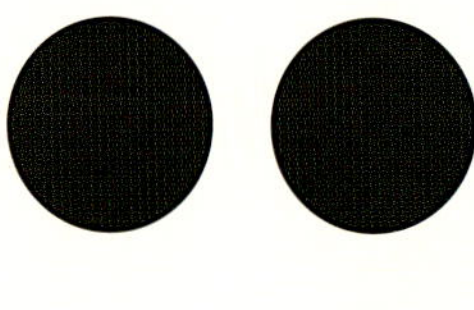

Square

Make a magic ring using **Color 23** and work in the round with a 4mm hook.

Follow Rnds 1–3 of Basic Circle (see Basic Shapes).

Rnd 4: Ch 1 (does not count as a st), sc in same st as join, sc in next 2 sts, *2 hdc in next st, dc in next st, 2 dc in next st, dc in next st, 2 hdc in next st**, sc in next 4 sts; [2 sc in next st, hdc in next st, 2 hdc in next st, hdc in next st, 2 sc in next st, sc in next 3 sts] 2 times; sc in next st, repeat from * to **, sc in last 2 sts; join and fasten off without breaking off **Color 23**, hold it on WS (see Finishing/Surface Crochet) = 48 sts

Rnd 5: Join **Color 37** with a standing sc in first st, sc in next 3 sts, hdc in next 2 sts, (2 dc, ch 2, 2 dc) in next st; hdc in next st, sc in next 2 sts, hdc in next 2 sts, dc in next 6 sts, (2 dc, ch 2, 2 dc) in next st; dc in next st, hdc in next 2 sts, sc in next 5 sts, hdc in next 2 sts, dc in next st, (2 dc, ch 2, 2 dc) in next st; dc in next 6 sts, hdc in next 2 sts, sc in next 2 sts, hdc in next st, (2 dc, ch 2, 2 dc) in next st, hdc in next 2 sts, sc in last 3 sts; join = 60 sts and 4 ch-2 sps

Rnds 6–9: Ch 2 (does not count as a st now and throughout), dc in same st as join, [dc in each st to next ch-2 sp, (2 dc, ch 2, 2 dc) in ch-2 sp] 4 times, dc in each st to end; join = 76/92/108/124 sts and 4 ch-2 sps

Place marker in final join to indicate the bottom of the square. Fasten off **Color 37** and weave in the ends.

Cheek (make 2)

Make a magic ring using **Color 7** and work in the round with a 3.5mm hook.

Rnd 1: Ch 1 (does not count as a st); work in ring—sc, 2 hdc, 2 sc, 2 hdc, sc; join = 8 sts

Fasten off, leaving a long tail for sewing.

Ears (make 1 left and 1 right)

Begin by working in rows with **Color 23** and a 3.5mm hook

Row 1 (Same for both ears): (RS) Ch 11, sc in second ch from hook, sc in next ch, *hdc in next 2 chs, dc in next 3 chs, hdc in next 2 chs**, 3 sc in last ch; work across the opposite side of the foundation ch—repeat from * to **, sc in last 2 chs; fasten off **Color 23**, leaving a long tail for sewing = 21 sts

Row 2 (Right ear): (RS) Work in BLO—Join **Color 3** with a sl st in eighth st of Row 1, sl st in next 2 sts; ch 5, sl st in second ch from hook, sc in next ch, hdc in next ch, dc in next ch; skip sc, sl st in next st; fasten off **Color 3** and weave in the ends = 8 sts

Row 2 (Left ear): (RS) Work in BLO—Join **Color 3** with a sl st in tenth st of Row 1; ch 5, sl st in second ch from hook, sc in next ch, hdc in next ch, dc in next ch; skip sc, sl st in next 3 sts; fasten off **Color 3** and weave in the ends = 8 sts

Assembly

Hold the square with the stitch marker at the bottom. Outline the head with **Color 23** by working surface sl sts between Rnds 4 and 5 with a 4mm hook, holding yarn on WS; finish off seamlessly and weave in the end (see Finishing/Surface Crochet). Position the ears as shown. Using **Color 23**, whipstitch across the bottom edge onto the square, then backstitch across the side edges, leaving the black tips unstitched. Finish off and weave in the ends; remove the marker from the square.

From Felts A and D, cut out the indicated pieces using the templates and assemble the layers to complete the eyes (see Working With Felt). Position the eyes referring to the image; use pins to mark the main points. Glue the eyes onto the head and let them dry.

Position the cheeks as shown. Using **Color 7**, backstitch around each cheek onto the head. Finish off and weave in the ends.

Thread the needle with a 4-ply black yarn and stitch the mouth and nose as indicated. Use straight pins to mark the main points prior to stitching. Finish off and weave in the ends.

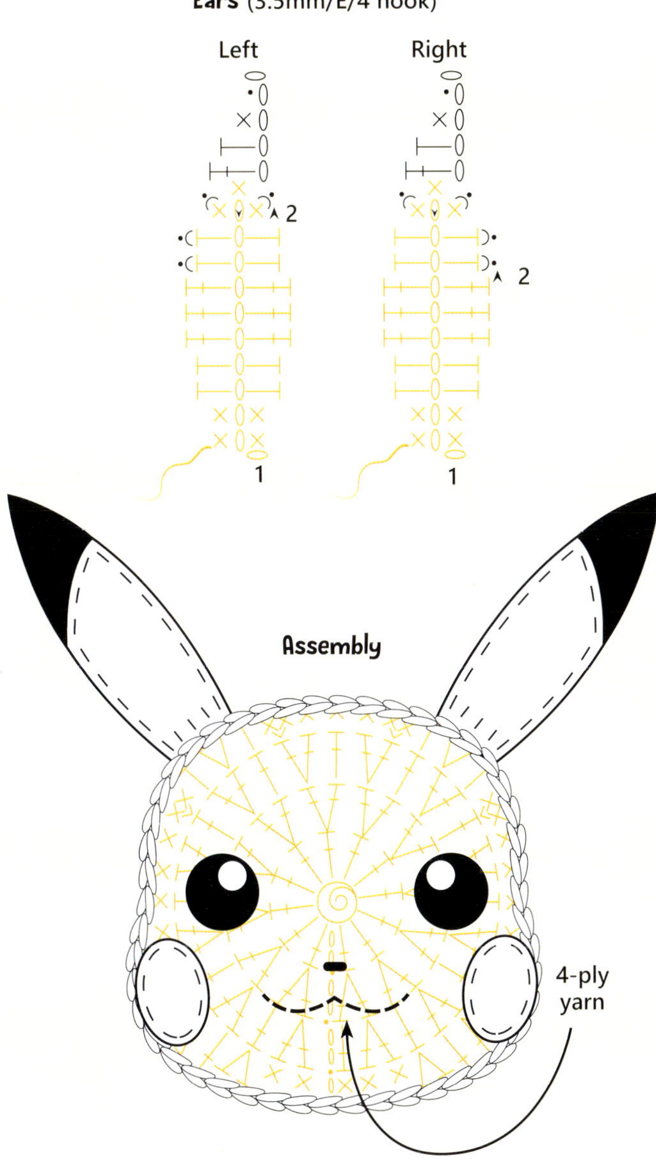

Poké Ball

A Poké Ball is used to catch and store Pokémon of all sizes. It provides a comfortable environment for Pokémon to rest and relax.

Key

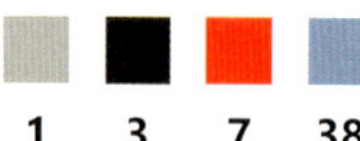

1 3 7 38

Difficulty level

Square (4mm/G/6 hook)

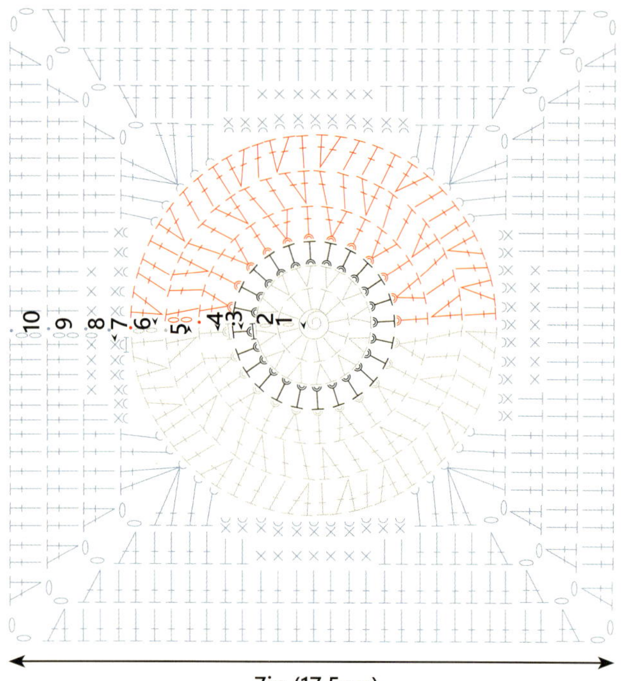

7in (17.5cm)

Square

Make a magic ring using **Color 1** and work in the round with a 4mm hook.

Rnd 1: Ch 1 (does not count as a st now and throughout), 12 hdc in ring; join = 12 sts

Rnd 2: Ch 1, 2 hdc in each st around; join and fasten off **Color 1** = 24 sts

Rnd 3: Work in third loop of every st around—Join **Color 3** with a standing hdc in first st, hdc in each st around; join and fasten off without breaking off **Color 3**, hold it on WS (see Finishing/Surface Crochet) = 24 sts

Rnd 4: (RS) Work in third loop of every st around—Join **Color 1** with a standing dc in first st, 2 dc in next st, [dc in next st, 2 dc in next st] 5 times; change to **Color 7**, [dc in next st, 2 dc in next st] 6 times; join and turn = 36 sts

Rnd 5: (WS) With **Color 7**—Ch 2 (does not count as a st now and throughout), skip join, [dc in next 2 sts, 2 dc in next st] 6 times; change to **Color 1**, [dc in next 2 sts, 2 dc in next st] 6 times; join and turn = 48 sts

Rnd 6: (RS) With **Color 1**—Ch 2, skip join, *[dc in next st, 2 dc in next st] 2 times, [dc in next 3 sts, 2 dc in next st] 2 times**, repeat from * to ** 1 more time; change to **Color 7** and break off **Color 1**, repeat from * to ** 2 times; join and fasten off **Color 7** = 64 sts

Rnd 7: Work in BLO—Join **Color 38** with a standing sc in first st, sc in next 5 sts, hdc in next st, dc in next st; *(2 dc, ch 2, 2 dc) in next st, dc in next st, hdc in next st, sc in next 11 sts, hdc in next st, dc in next st**; repeat from * to ** 2 more times; (2 dc, ch 2, 2 dc) in next st, dc in next st, hdc in next st, sc in last 5 sts; join = 76 sts and 4 ch-2 sps

Rnd 8: Ch 1, sc in same st as join, sc in next 3 sts, hdc in next 2 sts, dc in next 4 sts; *(2 dc, ch 2, 2 dc) in next ch-2 sp, dc in next 4 sts, hdc in next 2 sts, sc in next 7 sts, hdc in next 2 sts, dc in next 4 sts**; repeat from * to ** 2 more times; (2 dc, ch 2, 2 dc) in next ch-2 sp, dc in next 4 sts, hdc in next 2 sts, sc in last 3 sts; join = 92 sts and 4 ch-2 sps

Rnds 9–10: Ch 2, dc in same st as join, [dc in each st to next ch-2 sp, (2 dc, ch 2, 2 dc) in ch-2 sp] 4 times, dc in each st to end; join = 108/124 sts and 4 ch-2 sps

Fasten off and weave in the ends.

Outline the black circle with **Color 3** by working surface sl sts between Rnds 3 and 4 with a 4mm hook, holding yarn on WS; finish off seamlessly and weave in the end (see Finishing/ Surface Crochet).

Shaping

Work around the ball edge (Rnd 6 of the square) with a 4mm hook.

Rnd 1: (RS) Work in FLO—Join **Color 1** with a standing tr in first white st, tr in next 2 sts, 2 tr in next st, [tr in next 3 sts, 2 tr in next st] 7 times; change to **Color 7** and break off **Color 1**, leaving a long tail for sewing; [tr in next 3 sts, 2 tr in next st] 8 times; join and fasten off **Color 7**, leaving a long tail for sewing = 80 sts

Backstitch the top and bottom edges onto the square using the corresponding color tails. Finish off and weave in the ends.

Finishing

Stitch a locking bar on each side of the ball using 2 strands of **Color 3** and a 5mm hook—Work surface sl sts between the top and bottom shells on each side (see Finishing/Surface Crochet). Fasten off and weave in the ends carefully without tightening the sides of the locking bars.

Thread the needle with a 4-ply black yarn and backstitch between Rnds 1 and 2 to complete the release button. Finish off and weave in the end.

Shaping (4mm/G/6 hook)

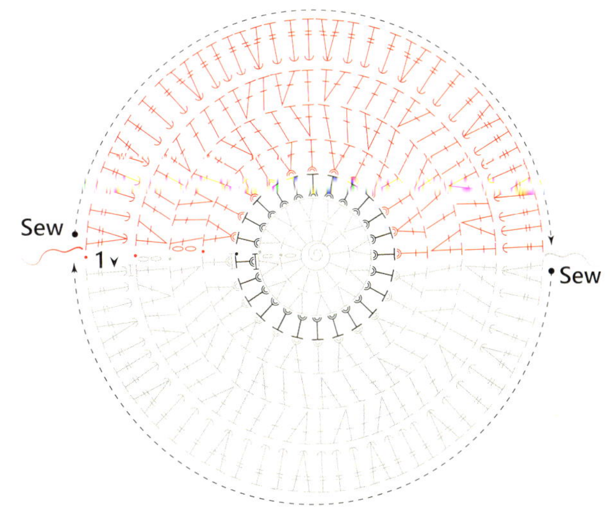

Assembly

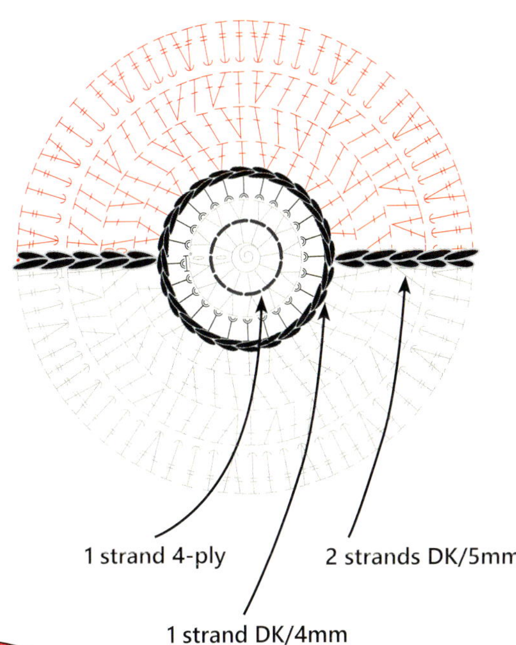

Piplup

A poor walker, this Pokémon often falls down. However, its strong pride makes it puff up its chest without a care.

Key

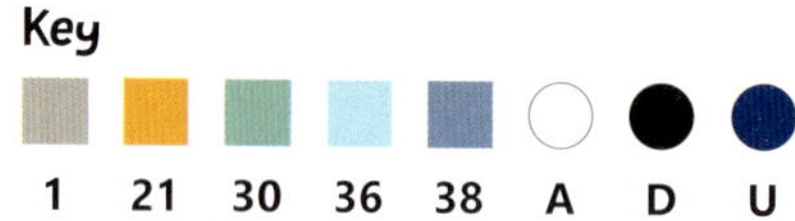

Difficulty level

Type

Square (4mm/G/6 hook)

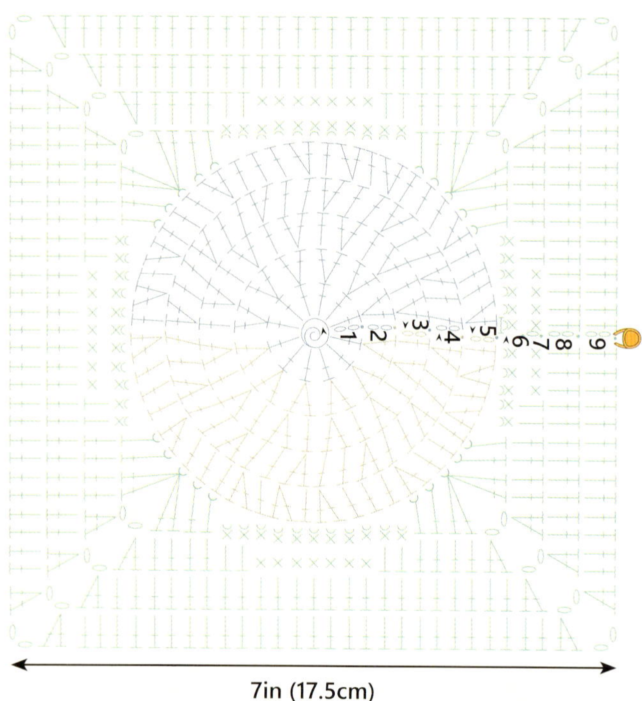

Outer eyes (4mm/G/6 hook)

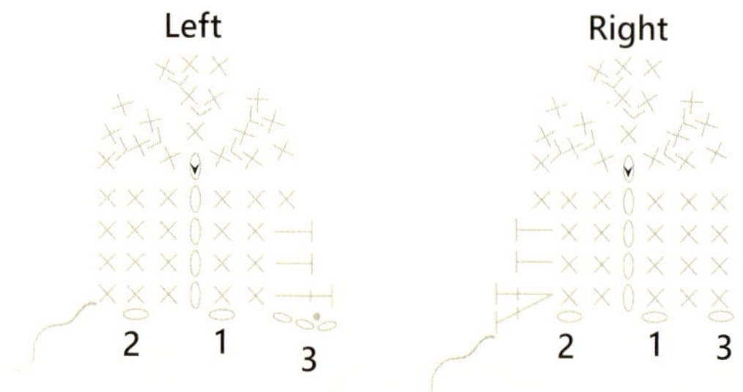

Square

Make a magic ring using **Color 38** and work in the round with a 4mm hook. When changing colors, keep yarn on WS without breaking it unless indicated.

Rnd 1: Ch 2 (does not count as a st now and throughout), 12 dc in ring; join = 12 sts

Rnd 2: (RS) Ch 2, 2 dc in first st, 2 dc in next 5 sts; change to **Color 1**, 2 dc in next 6 sts; join and turn = 24 sts

Rnd 3: (WS) With **Color 1**—Ch 2, skip join, *[dc in next st, 2 dc in next st] 6 times**; pick up **Color 38** and repeat from * to **; join and turn = 36 sts

Rnd 4: (RS) With **Color 38**—Ch 2, skip join, *[dc in next 2 sts, 2 dc in next st] 6 times**; pick up **Color 1** and repeat from * to **; join and turn = 48 sts

Rnd 5: (WS) With **Color 1**—Ch 2, skip join, *[dc in next st, 2 dc in next st] 2 times, [dc in next 3 sts, 2 dc in next st] 2 times**, repeat from * to **; pick up **Color 38** and repeat from * to ** 2 times; join and turn; fasten off both colors = 64 sts

Rnd 6: (RS) Work in BLO—Join **Color 30** with a standing sc in first st, sc in next 5 sts; [hdc in next st, dc in next st, (2 dc, ch 2, 2 dc) in next st, dc in next st, hdc in next st, sc in next 11 sts] 3 times; hdc in next st, dc in next st, (2 dc, ch 2, 2 dc) in next st, dc in next st, hdc in next st, sc in last 5 sts; join = 76 sts and 4 ch-2 sps

Rnd 7: Ch 1, sc in first st, sc in next 3 sts, [hdc in next 2 sts, dc in next 4 sts, (2 dc, ch 2, 2 dc) in next ch-2 sp, dc in next 4 sts, hdc in next 2 sts, sc in next 7 sts] 3 times; hdc in next 2 sts, dc in next 4 sts, (2 dc, ch 2, 2 dc) in next ch-2 sp, dc in next 4 sts, hdc in next 2 sts, sc in last 3 sts; join = 92 sts and 4 ch-2 sps

Rnds 8–9: Ch 2, dc in same st as join, [dc in each st to next ch-2 sp, (2 dc, ch 2, 2 dc) in ch-2 sp] 4 times, dc in each st to end; join = 108/124 sts and 4 ch-2 sps

Place marker in final join to indicate the right edge of the square. Fasten off and weave in the ends.

Beak

Make a magic ring using **Color 21** and work in the round with a 3.5mm hook.

Rnd 1: Ch 1 (does not count as a st now and throughout); 6 sc in ring; join = 6 sts

Rnd 2: Ch 1, 2 sc in same st as join, 2 sc in next 5 sts; join = 12 sts

Rnd 3: Ch 1, sc in same st as join, 2 sc in next st, [sc in next st, 2 sc in next st] 5 times; join and fasten off, leaving a long tail = 18 sts

Outer Eye (make 1 left and 1 right)

Work in rows with **Color 1** and a 4mm hook.

Row 1 (Same for both eyes): Ch 6, sc in second ch from hook, sc in next 3 chs, 3 sc in last ch; work across the opposite side of the foundation ch—sc in next 4 chs; turn = 11 sts

Row 2 (Same for both eyes): Ch 1 (does not count as a st now and throughout), sc in first st, sc in next 3 sts, 2 sc in next 3 sts, sc in last 4 sts; turn = 14 sts

Row 3 (Right eye): (RS) Ch 1, sc in first st, sc in next 4 sts, [2 sc in next st, sc in next st] 3 times, hdc in next 2 sts, 2 dc in last st; fasten off, leaving a long tail = 18 sts

Row 3 (Left eye): (RS) Ch 3, sl st in second ch from hook (counts as dc), dc in first st, hdc in next 2 sts, sc in next st, [sc in next st, 2 sc in next st] 3 times, sc in last 4 sts; fasten off, leaving a long tail = 18 sts

Patch

Work in rows with **Color 36** and a 4mm hook.

Row 1: (WS) Ch 6, sc in second ch from hook, sc in next 3 chs, 3 sc in last ch; work across the opposite side of the foundation ch—sc in next 4 chs; turn = 11 sts

Row 2: (RS) Ch 3, sl st in second ch from hook (counts as dc), 2 dc in first st, hdc in next 2 sts, sc in next st, 2 sc in next 3 sts, sc in next st, hdc in next 2 sts, 2 dc in last st; ch 1, sl st in top of previous dc, ch 2, sl st in same last st (counts as dc); work across the raw edge of Row 1—ch 3 (counts as dc), dc2tog; fasten off, leaving a long tail for sewing = 20 sts

Assembly

Sew the patch and outer eyes onto the head. Fasten off and weave in the ends; remove the marker from the square.

Sew the beak onto the head and stitch the mouth with 4-ply black yarn. Finish off and weave in the ends.

Cut out the indicated pieces from Felts A, D, and U using the templates and assemble the eyes (see Working With Felt). Position the eyes referring to the image; use pins to mark the main points. Glue eyes to the head and let them dry.

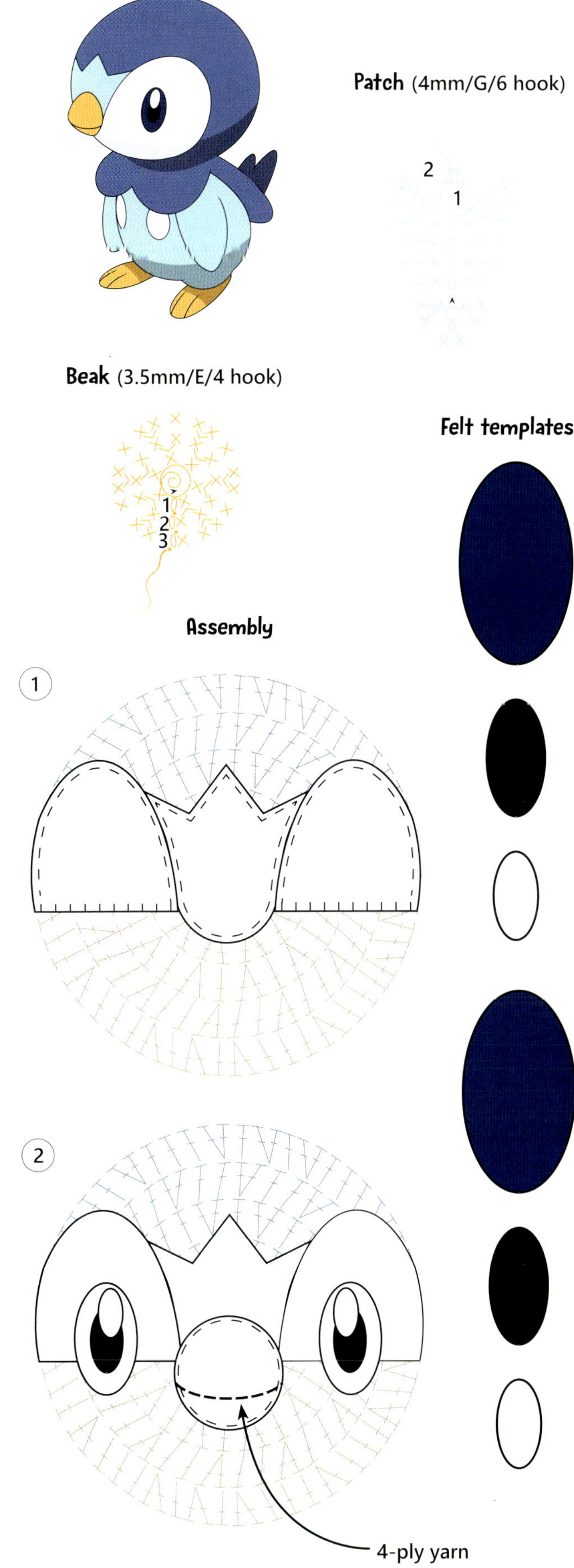

Fuecoco

This Pokémon lies on warm rocks and uses the heat absorbed by its square-shaped scales to create fire energy.

Key

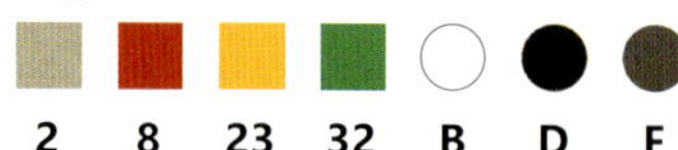

2 8 23 32 B D F

Difficulty level

Type

Square (4mm/G/6 hook)

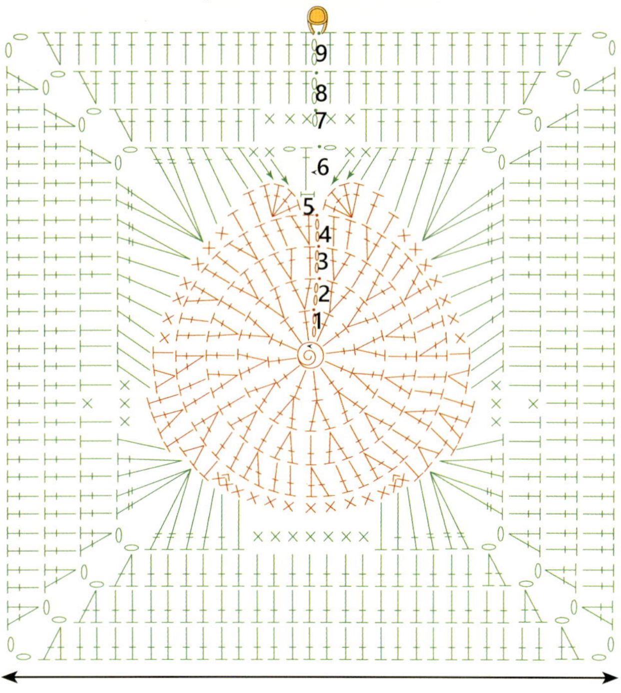

7in (17.5cm)

Felt templates

Square

Make a magic ring using **Color 8** and work in the round with a 4mm hook.

Follow Rnds 1–4 of Basic Circle (see Basic Shapes).

Rnd 5: Skip st with join and next st, 4 dc in third st, dc in next st, hdc in next st, sc in next 7 sts, *hdc in next st, 2 hdc in next st, dc in next st, 2 dc in next st, dc in next st, 2 hdc in next st, hdc in next st**, 2 sc in next st, sc in next 9 sts, 2 sc in next st, repeat from * to **, sc in next 7 sts, hdc in next st, dc in next st, 4 dc in next st, skip last st, sl st in join; fasten off without breaking off **Color 8**, hold it on WS (see Finishing/Surface Crochet) = 60 sts

Rnd 6: Join **Color 32** with a standing dc in last sl st, ch 1, skip dc, sc in next 2 sts, hdc in next st, dc in next 2 sts, tr in next st, (2 tr, ch 2, 2 tr) in next st; 2 tr in next st, dc in next 4 sts, hdc in next 3 sts, sc in next 3 sts, hdc in next st, 2 dc in next st, (2 tr, ch 2, 2 tr) in next st; tr in next st, dc in next 2 sts, hdc in next st, sc in next 7 sts, hdc in next st, dc in next 2 sts, tr in next st, (2 tr, ch 2, 2 tr) in next st; 2 dc in next st, hdc in next st, sc in next 3 sts, hdc in next 3 sts, dc in next 4 sts, 2 tr in next st, (2 tr, ch 2, 2 tr) in next st; tr in next st, dc in next 2 sts, hdc in next st, sc in next 2 sts, ch 1, skip last st; join = 74 sts, 2 ch-1 sps and 4 ch-2 sps

Rnd 7: Ch 1 (does not count as a st), sc in same st as join, sc in next ch-1 sp, sc in next st, hdc in next st, dc in next 6 sts, (2 dc, ch 2, 2 dc) in next ch-2 sp; dc in next 6 sts, hdc in next 6 sts, sc in next st, hdc in next 3 sts, *dc in each st to next ch-2 sp, (2 dc, ch 2, 2 dc) in next ch-2 sp**; repeat from * to **, dc in next 3 sts, hdc in next 3 sts, sc in next st, hdc in next 6 sts, repeat from * to **, dc in next 6 sts, hdc in next st, sc in next st, sc in last ch-1 sp; join = 92 sts and 4 ch-2 sps

Rnds 8–9: Ch 2 (does not count as a st), dc in same

st as join, [dc in each st to next ch-2 sp, (2 dc, ch 2, 2 dc) in ch-2 sp] 4 times, dc in each st to end; join = 108/124 sts and 4 ch-2 sps

Place marker in final join to indicate top of the square. Fasten off, weave in ends.

Face

Make a magic ring using **Color 2** and work in the round with a 3.5mm hook.

Rnd 1: Ch 2 (does not count as a st now and throughout), 12 dc in ring; join = 12 sts

Rnd 2: Ch 2, dc in same st as join, dc in next st, 5 dc in next st, [dc in next 3 sts, 5 dc in next st] 2 times, dc in last st; join = 24 sts

Rnd 3: Ch 1 (does not count as a st now and throughout), sc in same st as join, sc in next 2 sts, hdc in next st, 5 dc in next st, dc in next 5 sts, hdc in next 2 sts, 3 sc in next st, hdc in next 2 sts, dc in next 5 sts, 5 dc in next st, hdc in next st, sc in last 2 sts; join = 34 sts

Rnd 4: Ch 1, sc in same st as join, sc in next 3 sts, hdc in next st, dc in next st, (dc, 4 tr) in next st, 2 tr in next st, tr in next st, dc in next 4 sts, 2 dc in next st, 5 dc in next st, skip 2 sts, sl st in next st, skip 2 sts, 5 dc in next st, 2 dc in next st, dc in next 4 sts, tr in next st, 2 tr in next st, (4 tr, dc) in next st, dc in next st, hdc in next st, sc in last 3 sts; join = 50 sts

Fasten off, leaving a long tail.

Snout Outline

Using **Color 2** and a 3.5mm hook, make a 16 d-ch crochet cord (see Techniques/Finishing). Fasten off, leaving a long tail.

Branches

Work in rows with **Color 23** and a 3.5mm hook.

Big Branch

Row 1: (RS) Ch 16, tr in sixth ch from hook (the skipped chs count as a tr), [tr2tog] 2 times, dc in next 2 chs, hdc in next ch, sc in next ch, sl st in last 2 chs. Fasten off, leaving a long tail = 10 sts

Small Branch

Row 1: (RS) Ch 10, dc in fifth ch from hook (the skipped chs count as a dc), dc in next st, hdc in next 2 sts, sc in next st, sl st in last st = 7 sts

Fasten off, leaving long tail.

Assembly

Hold the square with the stitch marker at the top. Outline the head with **Color 8** by working surface sl sts between Rnds 5 and 6 with a 4mm hook, holding yarn on WS. Finish off seamlessly and weave in end (see Finishing/Surface Crochet). Position the face as shown and backstitch around onto the head using **Color 2**. Finish off, weave in ends, and remove the marker.

Position the snout outline and whipstitch across the bottom edge onto the face. Position the branches and sew them onto the head. Finish off and weave in ends. Cut out indicated pieces from Felts B, D, and F using the templates and glue onto the face (see Working With Felt).

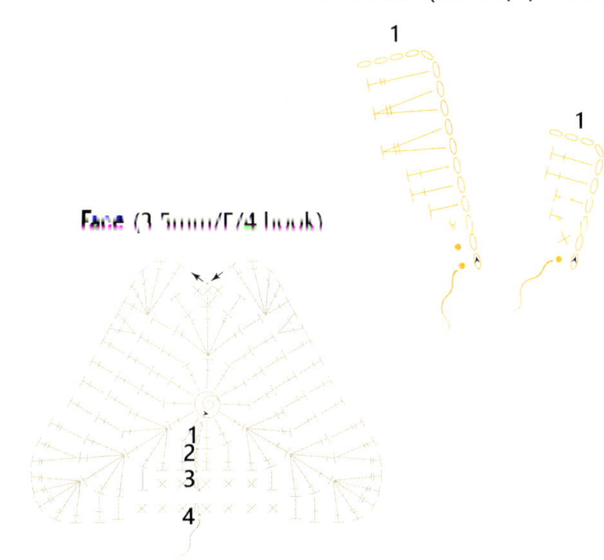

Mudkip

When this Pokémon uses its large tail fin, it picks up speed rapidly in the water. It is strong in spite of its small size.

Key

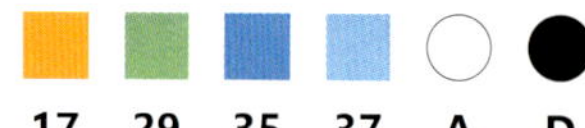

17 29 35 37 A D

Difficulty level

Type

Head (3.5mm/E/4 hook)

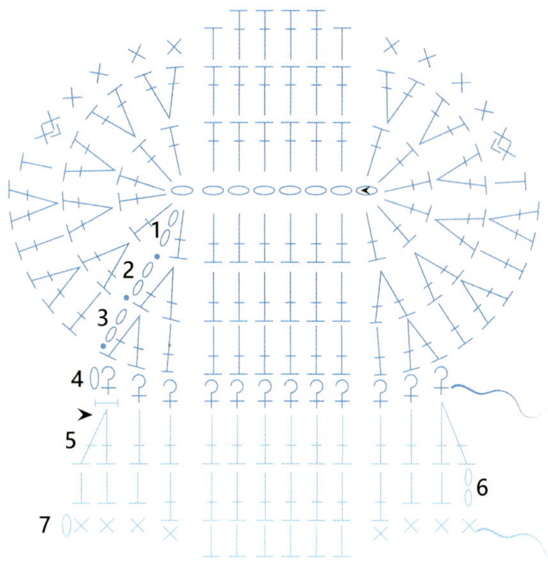

Gill (3mm/D/3 hook)

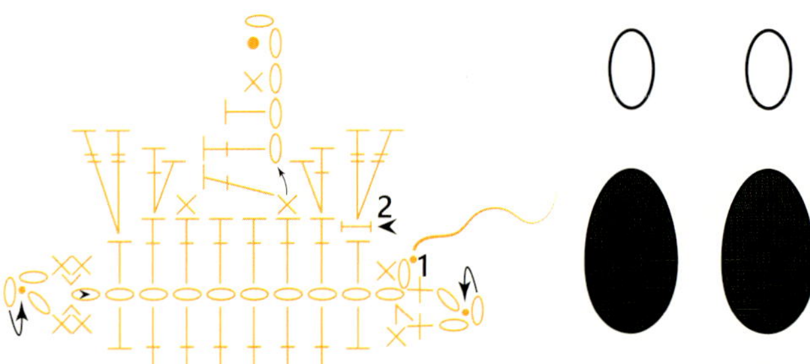

Felt templates

Square

Make one Basic Square using **Color 29** and a 4mm hook (see Basic Shapes).

Head

Begin by working in the round using **Color 35** and a 3.5mm hook.

Rnd 1: Ch 10, dc in third ch from hook (the skipped chs do not count as a st), dc in next 6 chs, 6 dc in last ch; work across the opposite side of the foundation ch—dc in next 6 chs, 5 dc in last ch; join = 24 sts

Rnd 2: Ch 2 (does not count as a st now and throughout), 2 dc in same st as join, dc in next 6 sts, 2 dc in next 6 sts, dc in next 6 sts, 2 dc in next 5 sts; join = 36 sts

Rnd 3: Ch 2, 2 dc in same st as join, dc in next 7 sts, [dc in next st, 2 dc in next st] 3 times, hdc in next st, 2 sc in next st, sc in next 4 sts, hdc in next st, dc in next 4 sts, hdc in next st, sc in next 4 sts, 2 sc in next st, hdc in next st, [2 dc in next st, dc in next st] 2 times; join = 44 sts

Continue to work in rows from now on.

Row 4: (RS) Ch 1 (does not count as a st now and throughout), bpsc in same st as join, bpsc in next 11 sts; leave the remaining sts unworked; fasten off **Color 35**, leaving a long tail for sewing; do not turn = 12 sts

Row 5: (RS) Join **Color 37** with a standing dc in first st of Row 4, dc in same st, dc in next 10 sts, 2 dc in last st; turn = 14 sts

Row 6: (WS) Ch 2 (counts as hdc), skip first st, hdc in next 2 sts, dc in next 8 sts, hdc in last 3 sts; turn = 14 sts

Row 7: (RS) Ch 1, sc in first st, sc in next 3 sts, hdc in next 6 sts, sc in last 4 sts = 14 sts

Fasten off, leaving a long tail for sewing.

Fin

Work in rows using **Color 35** and a 3mm hook.

Row 1: (RS) Ch 17, sc in second ch from hook, sc in next 2 chs, hdc in next 3 chs, dc in next 4 chs, hdc in next 3 chs, sc in last 3 chs = 24 sts

Fasten off, leaving a long tail for sewing.

Gill (make 2)

Begin by working in the round using **Color 17** and a 3mm hook.

Rnd 1: Ch 11, sc in second ch from hook, *hdc in next ch, dc in next 6 chs, hdc in next ch; 2 sc in last ch, (ch 2, sl st in second ch from hook, ch 1)**; work across the opposite side of the foundation ch—2 sc in same ch, repeat from * to **, sc in last foundation ch; join = 24 sts

Fasten off, leaving a long tail for sewing. Now work in rows.

Row 2: (RS) Skip first st of Rnd 1 and join **Color 17** with a standing tr in next hdc, tr in same st, (dc, hdc) in next st, sc in next st, ch 5, sl st in second ch from hook, sc in next ch, hdc in next ch, dc in next ch, dc in post of next sc, skip 2 dc, sc in next st, (hdc, dc) in next st, 2 tr in next st; leave the remaining sts unworked = 15 sts

Fasten off and weave in the ends.

Assembly

Position the head on the square, 1 rnd above the bottom edge and backstitch around using the corresponding color yarn tails. Position the fin as shown; with **Color 35**, whipstitch across the bottom edge and backstitch around the remaining edges onto the square. Finish off and weave in the ends.

Position the gills on each side of the head as shown. Using **Color 17**, backstitch around the base onto the head, leaving the pointy sides unstitched. Finish off and weave in the ends.

From Felts A and D, cut out the indicated pieces using the templates and assemble the layers to complete the eyes (see Working With Felt). Position the eyes referring to the image; use pins to mark the main points. Glue the eyes onto the head and let them dry.

Thread the needle with a 4-ply black yarn and stitch the mouth and nostrils as indicated. Use pins to mark the main points prior to stitching. Finish off and weave in the ends.

Fin (3mm/D/3 hook)

1

Assembly

1

BASIC SQUARE

7in (17.5cm)

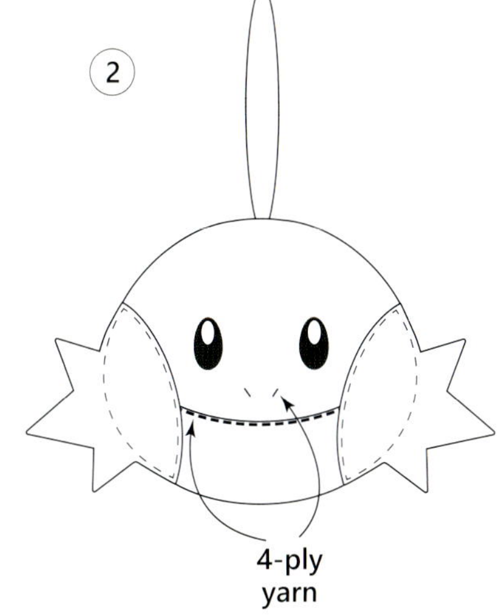

Cyndaquil

This Pokémon usually stays hunched over. If it is angry or surprised, it shoots flames out of its back.

Key

20 24 33

Difficulty level

Type

Square (4mm/G/6 hook)

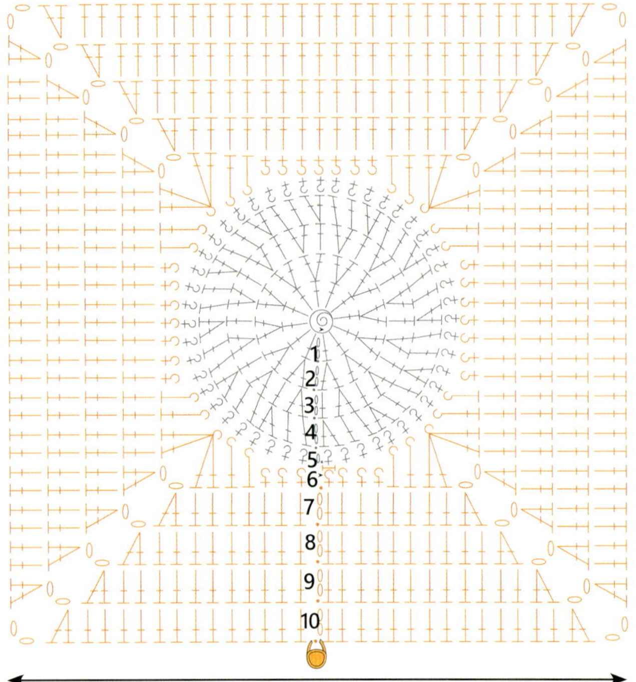

7in (17.5cm)

Square

Make a magic ring using **Color 33** and work in the round with a 4mm hook.

Follow Rnds 1–4 of Basic Circle (see Basic Shapes).

Rnd 5: Ch 1 (does not count as a st), bpsc in each st around; join and fasten off **Color 33** = 48 sts

Rnd 6: Join **Color 20** with a standing fpsc in first st, fpsc in next 3 sts, fphdc in next st, fpdc in next st, (2 fpdc, ch 2, 2 fpdc) in next st; *fpdc in next st, fphdc in next st, fpsc in next 7 sts, fphdc in next st, fpdc in next st, (2 fpdc, ch 2, 2 fpdc) in next st**; repeat from * to ** 2 more times; fpdc in next st, fphdc in next st, fpsc in last 3 sts; join = 60 sts and 4 ch-2 sps

Rnds 7–10: Ch 2 (does not count as a st now and throughout), dc in same st as join, [dc in each st to next ch-2 sp, (2 dc, ch 2, 2 dc) in ch-2 sp] 4 times, dc in each st to end; join = 76/92/108/124 sts and 4 ch-2 sps

Place marker in final join to indicate the bottom of the square. Fasten off and weave in the ends.

Snout

Work in rows with a 4mm hook. Mark 5 bpsc sts across the bottom edge of the head (Rnd 4) and join **Color 33** with a sl st in first marked st.

Row 1: Ch 6, sc in second ch from hook, hdc in next ch, dc in next ch, tr in next 2 chs; skip 3 sts on the head, sl st in last marked st = 5 sts

Fasten off and weave in the ends; remove all markers from the square.

Outer Eye (make 2)

Work in the round using **Color 24** and a 3.5mm hook.

Rnd 1: Ch 13, 2 sc in second ch from hook, *hdc in next 2 chs, dc in next 2 chs, tr in next 2 chs, dc in next 2 chs, hdc in next 2 chs**, (2 sc, ch 2, 2 sc) in last ch; work across the opposite side of the foundation ch—repeat from * to **, 2 sc in last ch, ch 2; join = 28 sts

Fasten off and weave in the ends.

Assembly

Mark 14 sts along the head edge on each side of the snout. Position the outer eyes along the marked edges as shown. With a 4mm hook, join **Color 24** with a standing sl st in ch-2 sp of the first outer eye and continue by working through two layers at the same time to join them—sc in each of next 14 sts of the outer eye and 14 marked sts of the head; sc in ch-2 sp of the outer eye; work around the snout—5 hdc evenly across the side, 4 hdc in bottom corner, 5 hdc evenly across the other side; sc in ch-2 sp of the second outer eye. Continue by working through two layers at the same time to join them, sc in each of next 14 sts of the outer eye and 14 marked sts of the head; sl st in ch-2 sp of outer eye. Fasten off, leaving a long tail for sewing.

Using **Color 24**, backstitch across the inner edges of both outer eyes and across the snout edge, working through the square. Finish off and weave in the end.

Using a 4mm hook and holding **Color 24** on WS, work surface sl st around the hdc edge of the snout. Finish off and weave in the ends.

Thread the needle with a 4-ply black yarn and stitch the nostrils and eyes as indicated. Use pins to mark the main points prior to stitching. Finish off and weave in the ends.

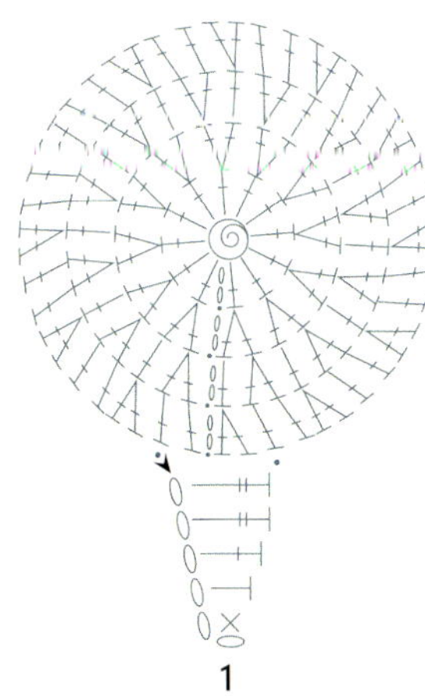

Outer eye (3.5mm/E/4 hook)

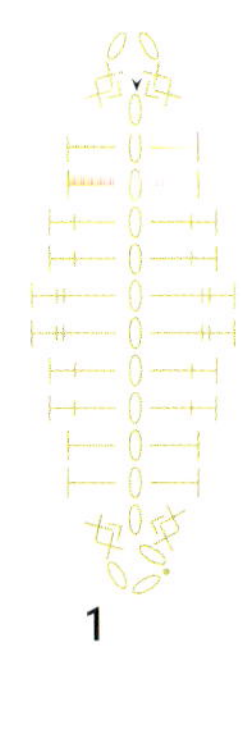

Assembly

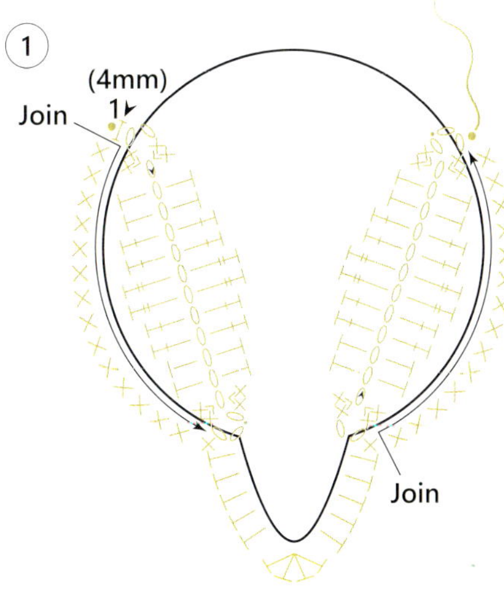

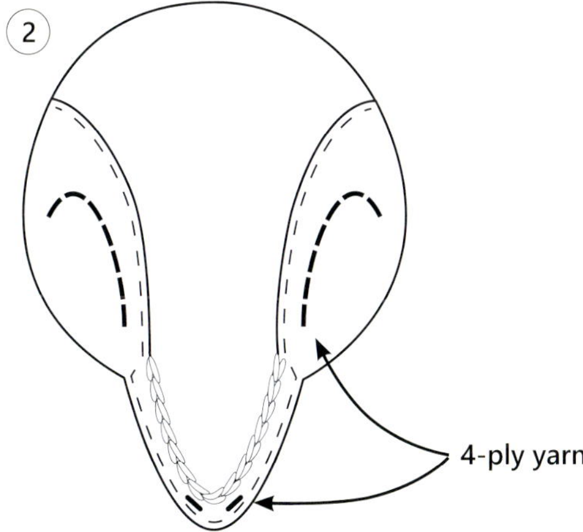

Oshawott

This Pokémon wields the scalchop on its stomach like a knife, blocking the moves of its enemies before swiftly slashing back at them.

Key

1 12 39 47 A D J V

Difficulty level

Type

Square (4mm/G/6 hook)

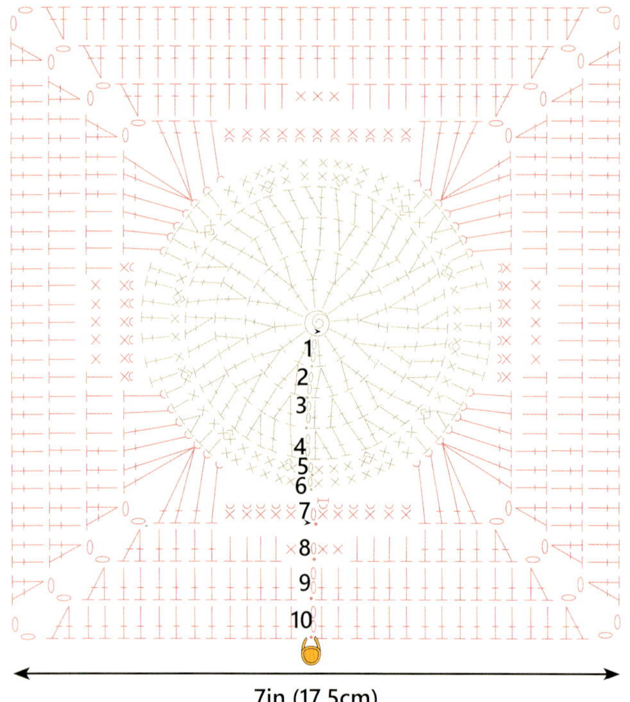

Nose (3.5mm/E/4 hook)

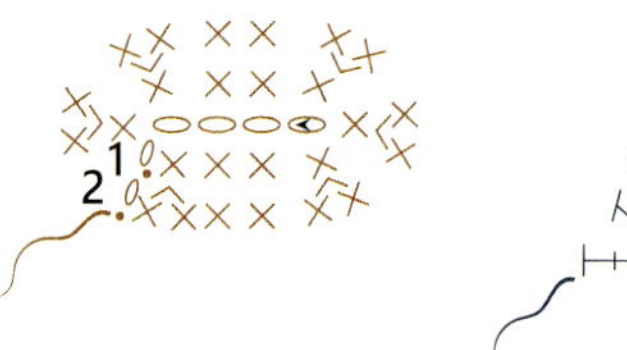

Ear (3.5mm/E/4 hook)

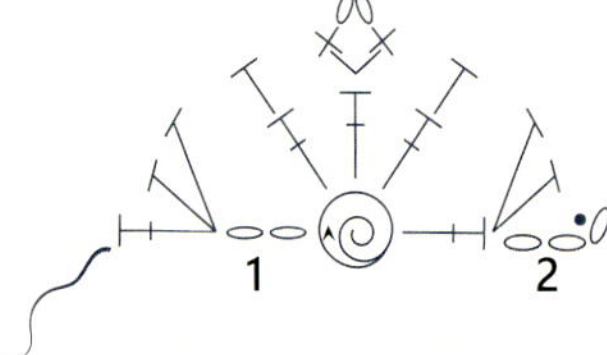

Square

Make a magic ring using **Color 1** and work in the round with a 4mm hook.

Follow Rnds 1–4 of Basic Circle (see Basic Shapes).

Rnd 5: Ch 1 (does not count as a st now and throughout), sc in same st as join, sc in next 2 sts, 2 sc in next st, [sc in next 3 sts, 2 sc in next st] 11 times; join = 60 sts

Rnd 6: Ch 1, sc in same st as join, sc in next 6 sts, *hdc in next 2 sts, 2 hdc in next st, hdc in next 2 sts, dc in next 7 sts, hdc in next 2 sts, 2 hdc in next st, hdc in next 2 sts**; sc in next 13 sts, repeat from * to **, sc in last 6 sts; join and fasten off without breaking off **Color 1**, hold it on WS (see Finishing/Surface Crochet) = 64 sts

Rnd 7: Work in BLO—Join **Color 47** with a standing sc in first st, sc in next 5 sts, *hdc in next st, dc in next st, (2 dc, ch 2, 2 dc) in next st, dc in next 2 sts, hdc in next 2 sts, sc in next 7 sts, hdc in next 2 sts, dc in next 2 sts, (2 dc, ch 2, 2 dc) in next st, dc in next st, hdc in next st**; sc in next 11 sts, repeat from * to **, sc in last 5 sts; join = 76 sts and 4 ch-2 sps

Rnd 8: Ch 1, sc in same st as join, sc in next st, *hdc in next 4 sts, dc in next 4 sts, (2 dc, ch 2, 2 dc) in next ch-2 sp, dc in next 3 sts, hdc in next 4 sts, sc in next 5 sts, hdc in next 4 sts, dc in next 3 sts, (2 dc, ch 2, 2 dc) in next ch-2 sp, dc in next 4 sts, hdc in next 4 sts**; sc in next 3 sts, repeat from * to **, sc in last st; join = 92 sts and 4 ch-2 sps

Rnd 9: Ch 2 (does not count as a st now and throughout), dc in same st as join, *dc in each st to next ch-2 sp, (2 dc, ch 2, 2 dc) in ch-2 sp; dc in next 5 sts, hdc in next 13 sts, dc in next 5 sts, (2 dc, ch 2, 2 dc) in next ch-2 sp**; repeat from * to **; dc in each st to end; join = 108 and 4 ch-2 sps

Rnd 10: Ch 2, dc in same st as join, [dc in each st to next ch-2 sp, (2 dc, ch 2, 2 dc) in ch-2 sp] 4 times, dc in each st to end; join = 124 sts and 4 ch-2 sps

Place marker in final join to indicate the bottom of the square. Fasten off and weave in the ends.

Nose

Work in the round with **Color 12** and a 3.5mm hook.

Rnd 1: Ch 5, sc in second ch from hook, sc in next 2 chs, 3 sc in last ch; work across the opposite side of the foundation ch—sc in next 2 chs, 2 sc in last ch; join = 10 sts

Rnd 2: Ch 1 (does not count as a st), 2 sc in first st, sc in next 2 sts, 2 sc in next 3 sts, sc in next 2 sts, 2 sc in last 2 sts; join = 16 sts

Fasten off, leaving a long tail for sewing.

Ear (make 2)

Make a magic ring using **Color 39** and work in rows with a 3.5mm hook.

Row 1: (WS) Ch 2 (counts as dc), 4 dc in ring; turn without joining = 5 sts

Row 2: (RS) Ch 3, sl st in second ch from hook (counts as dc), 2 hdc in first st, hdc in next st, (sc, ch 2, sc) in next st, hdc in next st, (2 hdc, dc) in last st = 10 sts and 1 ch-2 sp

Fasten off, leaving a long tail for sewing.

Assembly

Outline the head with **Color 1** by working surface sl sts between Rnds 6 and 7 with a 4mm hook, holding yarn on WS. Finish off seamlessly and weave in the end (see Finishing/Surface Crochet). Holding the square with the stitch marker at the bottom, position the ears as shown. Using **Color 39**, whipstitch across the bottom edge onto the square, then backstitch across the center of each ear, leaving the side edges unstitched. Position the nose in the center of the head and backstitch around with **Color 12**. Finish off and weave in the ends; remove the marker from the square.

Cut out the indicated pieces from Felts A, D, J, and V using the templates, and assemble the layers to complete the mouth and eyes (see Working With Felt). Referring to the image, position all complete pieces and use pins to mark the main points. Glue each piece onto the head and leave them to dry.

Use pins to indicate freckles referring to the image. Sew black beads (Mill Hill size 8 [1814]), removing pins as you go. Instead of beads, you could use 3 strands of black DMC floss (310) to stitch French knots for the freckles.

Felt templates

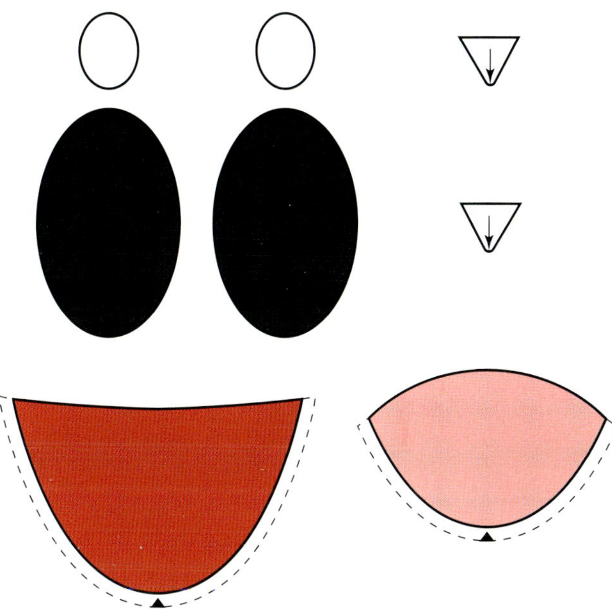

Assembly

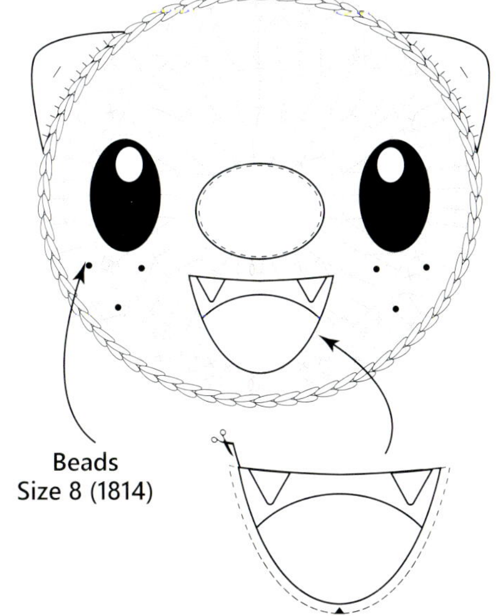

Oran Berry

An Oran Berry has a wondrous mix of flavors. If consumed by a Pokémon, it restores its energy.

Key

6 37 42

Difficulty level

Square (4mm/G/6 hook)

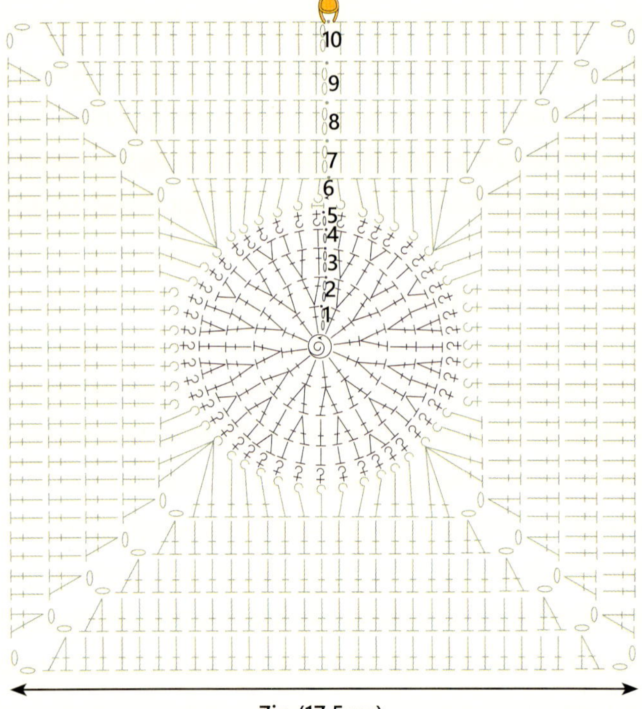

Square

Make a magic ring using **Color 42** and work in the round with a 4mm hook.

Follow Rnds 1–3 of Basic Circle (see Basic Shapes).

Rnd 4: Ch 1 (does not count as a st now and throughout), hdc in same st as join, *[hdc in next 2 sts, 2 hdc in next st] 2 times, [dc in next st, 2 dc in next st] 2 times, dc in next st, [2 hdc in next st, hdc in next 2 sts] 2 times**, hdc in next st, repeat from * to **; join = 48 sts

Rnd 5: Ch 1, bpsc in each st around; join and break off **Color 42** = 48 sts

Rnd 6: Join **Color 6** with a standing fphdc in first st, *fphdc in next 2 sts, fpdc in next 3 sts, (2 fpdc, ch 2, 2 fpdc) in next st, fpdc in next st, fphdc in next st, fpsc in next 7 sts, fphdc in next st, fpdc in next st, (2 fpdc, ch 2, 2 fpdc) in next st, fpdc in next 3 sts, fphdc in next 2 sts**, fphdc in next st, repeat from * to **; join = 60 sts and 4 ch-2 sps

Rnds 7–10: Ch 2 (does not count as a st), dc in same st as join, [dc in each st to next ch-2 sp, (2 dc, ch 2, 2 dc) in ch-2 sp] 4 times, dc in each st to end; join = 76/92/108/124 sts and 4 ch-2 sps

Place marker in final join to indicate the top of the square. Fasten off and weave in the ends.

Stem

Make a magic ring using **Color 37** and work in spiral rounds with a 3.5mm hook.

Rnd 1: Ch 1 (does not count as a st), 8 sc in ring; do not join now and throughout = 8 sts

Rnds 2–3: Sc in each st around = 8 sts

Rnd 4: Bpsc in next st, 2 bphdc in next 3 sts, bpsc in next st, sl st in next st; leave the remaining sts unworked = 9 sts

Fasten off, leaving a long tail for sewing.

Assembly

Holding the square with the stitch marker at the top, position the stem as shown. Using **Color 37**, backstitch around the edge onto the berry, leaving the top of the stem unstitched. Finish off and weave in the end; remove the marker from the square. Use pins to indicate pores referring to the image. Sew black beads (Mill Hill size 8 [1814]), removing pins as you go. As an alternative to beads, you can use 3 strands of black DMC floss (310) to stitch French knots.

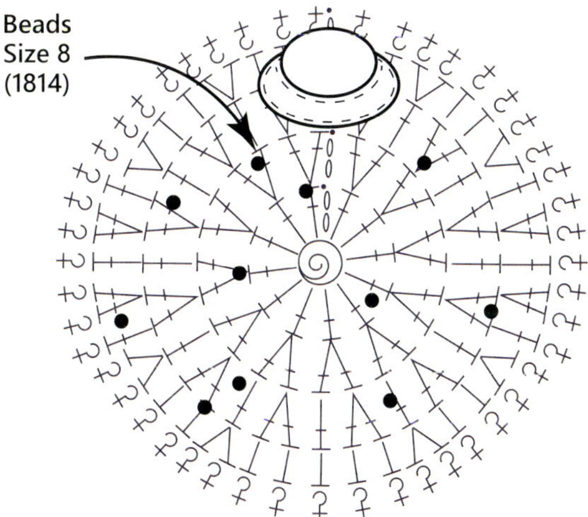

Quaxly

This Pokémon migrated to Paldea from distant lands long ago. The gel secreted by its feathers repels water and grime.

Key

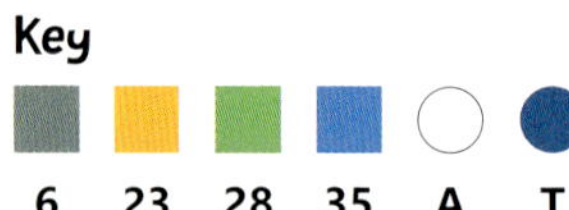

6 23 28 35 A T

Difficulty level

Type

Square (4mm/G/6 hook)

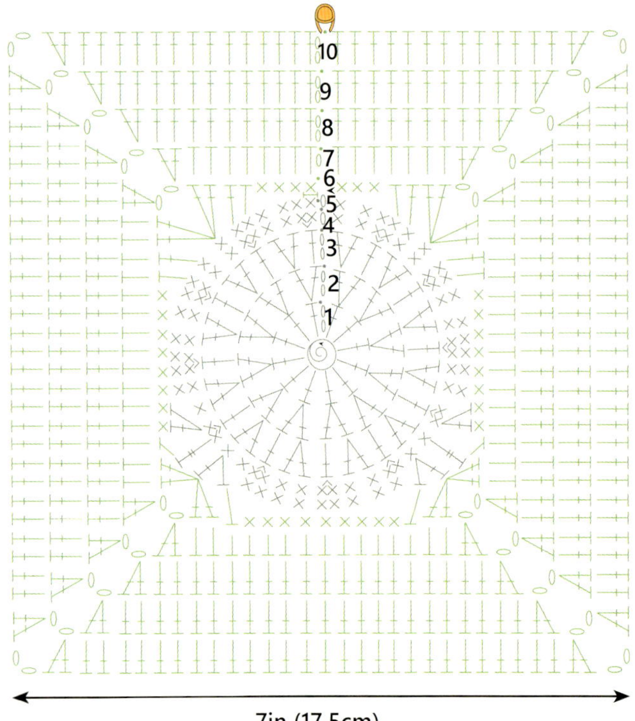

Beak (3.5mm/E/4 hook)

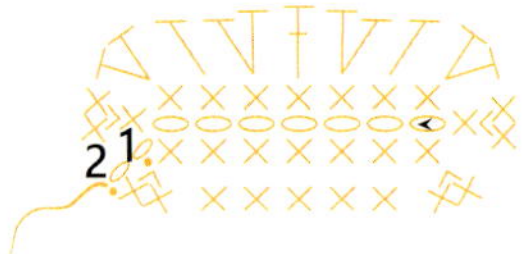

Square

Make a magic ring using **Color 6** and work in the round with a 4mm hook.

Follow Rnds 1–3 of Basic Circle (see Basic Shapes).

Rnd 4: Ch 1 (does not count as a st now and throughout), 2 sc in same st as join, sc in next 2 sts, [2 sc in next st, sc in next 2 sts] 11 times; join = 48 sts

Rnd 5: Ch 1, sc in same st as join, sc in next 14 sts, *skip st, (hdc, dc) in next st, tr in next st, (dc, hdc) in next st, skip st**, sc in next 9 sts, repeat from * to **, sc in next 14 sts; join and fasten off without breaking off **Color 6**, hold it on WS (see Finishing/Surface Crochet) = 48 sts

Rnd 6: Join **Color 28** with a standing sc in first st, sc in next 3 sts, hdc in next st, dc in next st, (2 dc, ch 2, 2 dc) in next st, dc in next st, hdc in next st; *sc in next 8 sts, hdc in next st, (2 dc, ch 2, 2 dc) in next st, hdc in next st**; sc in next st, repeat from * to **, sc in next 8 sts, hdc in next st, dc in next st, (2 dc, ch 2, 2 dc) in next st, dc in next st, hdc in next st, sc in last 3 sts; join = 60 sts and 4 ch-2 sps

Rnd 7: Ch 1, hdc in same st as join, [hdc in each st to next ch-2 sp, (2 dc, ch 2, 2 dc) in ch-2 sp] 4 times, hdc in each st to end; join = 76 sts and 4 ch-2 sps

Rnds 8–10: Ch 2 (does not count as a st), dc in same st as join, [dc in each st to next ch-2 sp, (2 dc, ch 2, 2 dc) in ch-2 sp] 4 times, dc in each st to end; join = 92/108/124 sts and 4 ch-2 sps

Place marker in final join to indicate the top of the square. Fasten off and weave in the ends.

Felt templates

Beak

Work in the round using **Color 23** and a 3.5mm hook.

Rnd 1: Ch 8, sc in next 5 chs, 3 sc in last ch; work across the opposite side of the foundation ch—sc in next 5 chs, 2 sc in last ch, join = 16 sts

Rnd 2: Ch 1 (does not count as a st), 2 sc in same st as join, sc in next 5 sts, 2 sc in next 2 sts, 2 hdc in next st, hdc in next st, 2 hdc in next st, dc in next st, 2 hdc in next st, hdc in next st, 2 hdc in next st, 2 sc in last st; join = 24 sts

Fasten off, leaving a long tail for sewing.

Hat

Begin by working in the round using **Color 35** and a 3.5mm hook.

Rnd 1: Ch 14, dc in third ch from hook (the skipped chs do not count as a st), dc in next 10 chs, 6 dc in last ch; work across the opposite side of the foundation ch—dc in next 10 chs, 5 dc in last ch, join = 32 sts

Rnd 2: Ch 1 (does not count as a st now and throughout), 2 sc in same st as join; *hdc in next 2 sts, dc in next 6 sts, hdc in next 2 sts**; 2 sc in next 6 sts, repeat from * to **, 2 sc in last 5 sts; join = 44 sts

Rnd 3: Ch 1, sc in same st as join, sc in next 3 sts; *hdc in next st, dc in next 4 sts, hdc in next st**; sc in next 16 sts, repeat from * to **, sc in last 12 sts; join = 44 sts

Rnd 4: Ch 1, 2 hdc in same st as join, hdc in next 12 sts, [2 hdc in next st, hdc in next st] 6 times, hdc in next 9 sts, [2 hdc in next st, hdc in next st] 5 times; place marker in last st made and join; fasten off and weave in the end = 55 sts

Continue to work in rows from now on.

(continued overleaf)

Hat (3.5mm/E/4 hook)

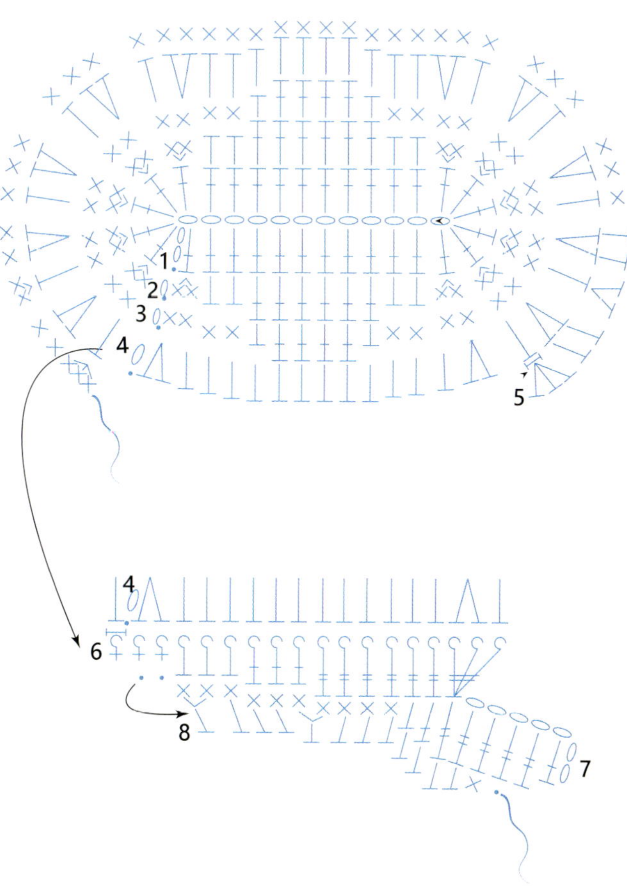

Mouth and nostrils

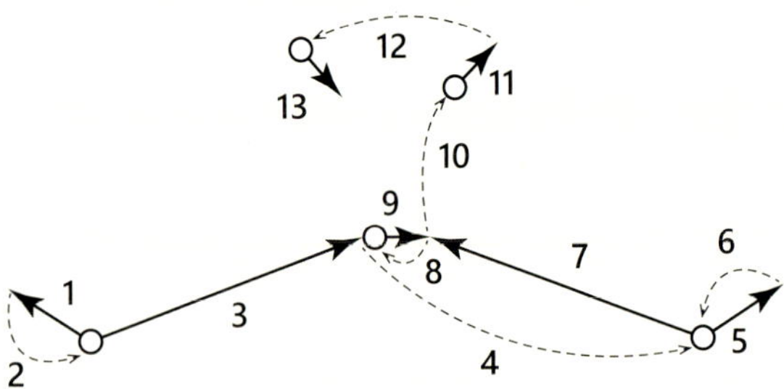

Assembly

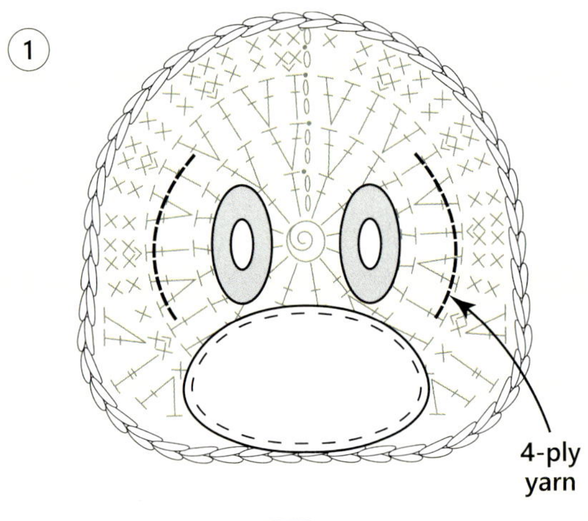

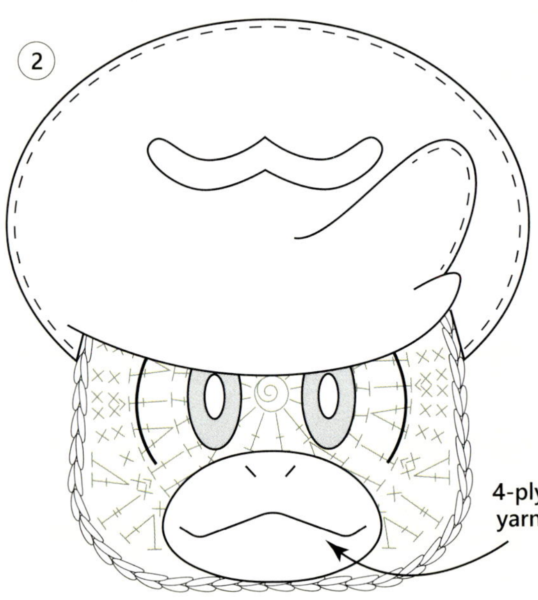

Row 5: (RS) Skip 16 sts and join **Color 35** with a standing hdc in next st, 2 hdc in same st, hdc in next 2 sts, 2 hdc in next st, hdc in next 2 sts, sc in next 30 sts, 2 sc in next st, sc in next 2 sts, 3 sc in last st with marker (do not remove the marker yet); fasten off, leaving a long tail for sewing = 46 sts

Row 6: (RS) Join **Color 35** with a standing fpsc in the post of st with marker and work across the next 17 sts of Rnd 4—fpsc in next 2 sts, fphdc in next 3 sts, fpdc in next 3 sts, fptr in next 6 sts, fptr3tog, ch 7; turn = 16 sts and ch-7

Row 7: (WS) Dc in third ch from hook (the skipped chs count as a dc), tr in next 4 chs, tr in next st, dc in next st, hdc in next st, [sc in next 3 sts, sc2tog] 2 times, sl st in next 2 sts; turn, leaving the last st unworked = 19 sts

Row 8: (RS) Skip 2 sts, hdc in next 12 sts, sc in next st, sl st in next st, leave the remaining sts unworked; fasten off, leaving a long tail for sewing; flip the brim up = 14 sts

Assembly

Hold the square with the stitch marker at the top. Outline the head with **Color 6** by working surface sl sts between Rnds 5 and 6 with a 4mm hook, holding yarn on WS. Finish off seamlessly and weave in the end (see Finishing/ Surface Crochet).

Position the beak as shown in the image. Using **Color 23**, backstitch around the beak onto the head. Finish off and weave in the ends. Remove the marker from the square.

Cut out the indicated pieces from Felts A and T, using the templates and assemble the layers to complete the eyes (see Working With Felt). Position the eyes referring to the image; use pins to mark the main points. Glue the eyes onto the head and leave to dry.

Thread the needle with 4-ply black yarn and backstitch the outer eyes as indicated. Use pins to mark the main points prior to stitching. Finish off and weave in the ends.

Also using 4-ply black yarn and the needle, stitch the mouth and nostrils as indicated in the diagram. Use pins to mark the main points prior to stitching. Finish off and weave in the end.

Position the hat, partially covering the eyes. Using **Color 35**, backstitch around the outer edge of the hat onto the square and backstitch the folded brim onto the hat. Leave the bottom edges unstitched. Finish off and weave in the ends.

Position and glue the white mark onto the hat as shown. Leave the glue to dry.

Master Ball

The Master Ball is one of the rarest balls in the Pokémon world and can catch any wild Pokémon without fail.

Key

1 3 43 45 48 A

Difficulty level

Square

Make the square by following the instructions for the Poké Ball (including shaping and finishing), but using **Color 43** for the upper shell, and **Color 45** for the background.

Pink Accent (make 2)

Work in the round using **Color 48** and a 3.5mm hook.

Rnd 1: Ch 15, sc in second ch from hook, *hdc in next 2 chs, dc in next 8 chs, hdc in next 2 chs**, 3 sc in last ch; work across the opposite side of the foundation ch—repeat from * to **, 2 sc in last ch; join = 30 sts

Fasten off, leaving a long tail for sewing.

Assembly

Position the pink accents as shown. Using **Color 48**, backstitch around the edges onto the ball. Finish off and weave in the ends.

Cut out the M template from Felt A (see Working With Felt). Position the M symbol, referring to the image, and use pins to mark the main points; glue and leave to dry.

Pink accent (3.5mm/E/4 hook)

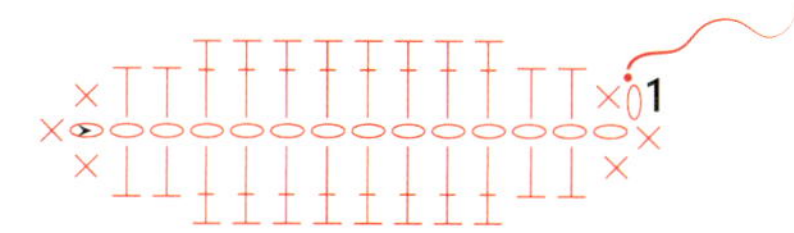

Assembly

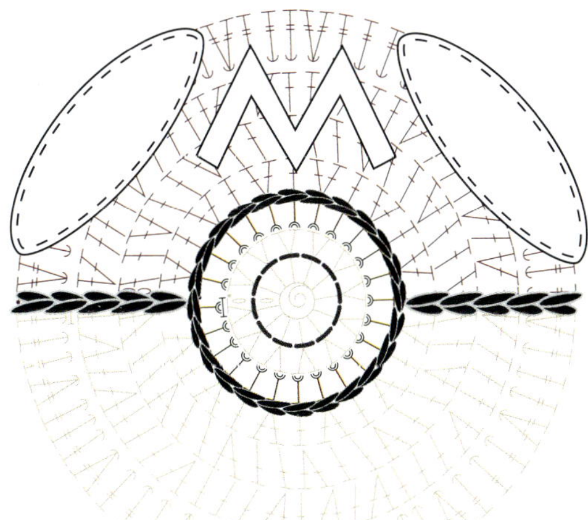

Felt template

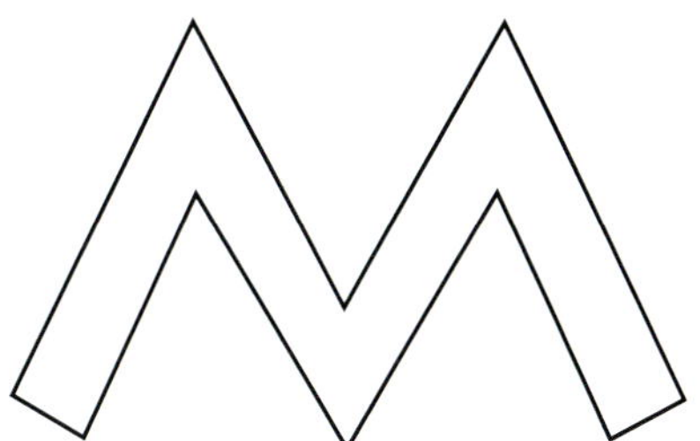

Chespin

When Chespin tenses up just before landing a headbutt, the spikes on its head sharpen to points, piercing the enemy's body on contact.

Key

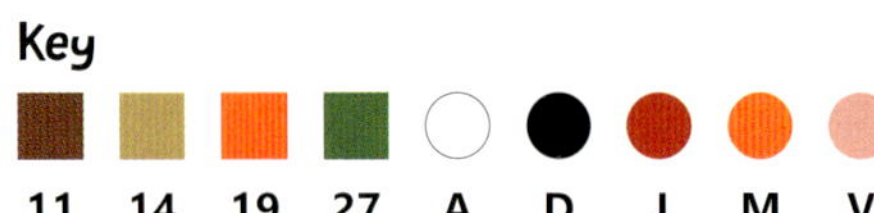

Difficulty level

Type

Square (4mm/G/6 hook)

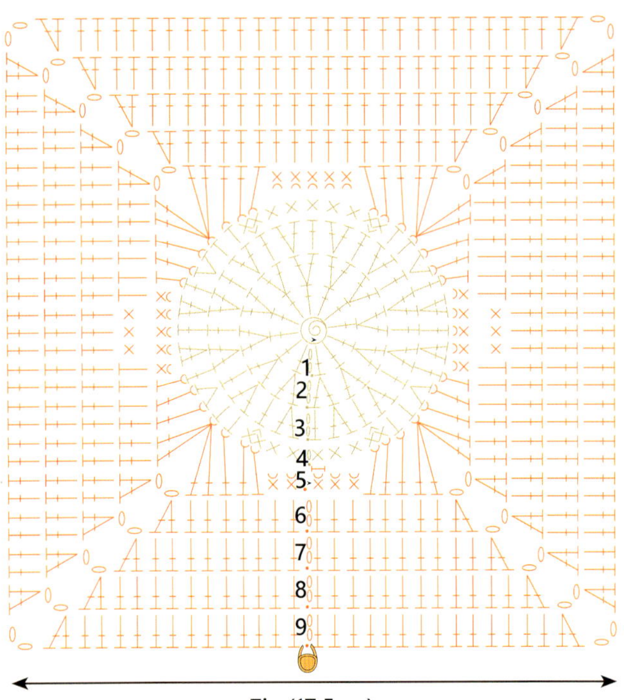

7in (17.5cm)

Square

Make a magic ring using **Color 14** and work in the round with a 4mm hook.

Follow Rnds 1–3 of Basic Circle (see Basic Shapes).

Rnd 4: Ch 1 (does not count as a st), sc in same st as join, sc in next 2 sts, *2 sc in next st, hdc in next 2 sts, 2 hdc in next st, [dc in next st, 2 dc in next st] 2 times, dc in next st, 2 hdc in next st, hdc in next 2 sts, 2 sc in next st**, sc in next 5 sts; repeat from * to **, sc in last 2 sts; join and fasten off without breaking off **Color 14**, hold it on WS (see Finishing/Surface Crochet) = 48 sts

Rnd 5: Work in BLO—Join **Color 19** with a standing sc in first st, sc in next 2 sts, hdc in next st, dc in next 2 sts, *(2 dc, ch 2, 2 dc) in next st, dc in next 2 sts, hdc in next st, sc in next 5 sts, hdc in next st, dc in next 2 sts**; repeat from * to ** 2 more times; (2 dc, ch 2, 2 dc) in next st, dc in next 2 sts, hdc in next st, sc in next 2 sts; join = 60 sts and 4 ch-2 sps

Rnd 6: Ch 2 (does not count as a st now and throughout), dc in same st as join, *dc in each st to next ch-2 sp, (2 dc, ch 2, 2 dc) in ch-2 sp, dc in next 3 sts, hdc in next 3 sts, sc in next 3 sts, hdc in next 3 sts, dc in next 3 sts, (2 dc, ch 2, 2 dc) in next ch-2 sp**; repeat from * to **, dc in each st to end; join = 76 sts and 4 ch-2 sps

Rnds 7–9: Ch 2, dc in same st as join, [dc in each st to next ch-2 sp, (2 dc, ch 2, 2 dc) in ch-2 sp] 4 times, dc in each st to end; join = 92/108/124 sts and 4 ch-2 sps

Place marker in final join to indicate the bottom of the square. Fasten off and weave in the ends.

Head Cover

Work around the head edges (Rnd 4 of the square) with **Color 27** and a 4mm hook.

Rnd 1: (RS) Work in FLO—Sl st in sixth st of Rnd 4, sl st in next 2 sts, sc in next 3 sts, hdc in next 2 sts, 2 dc in next st, dc in next 2 sts, [2 tr in next st, tr in next 3 sts] 4 times, 2 tr in next st, dc in next 2 sts, 2 dc in next st, hdc in next 2 sts, sc in next 3 sts, sl st in next 3 sts; leave the remaining sts unworked = 46 sts

Fasten off, leaving a long tail for sewing and use it to backstitch the edge of the head cover onto the square. Finish off and weave in the ends.

Top Leaf Bunch

Work in rows with **Color 27** and a 3.5mm hook.

Rows 1–3: (RS) Ch 12, sl st in second ch from hook, sc in next ch, hdc in next 2 chs, dc in next 3 chs, hdc in next 2 chs, sc in next ch, sl st in last ch; do not turn = 11 sts

To finish, work across the bottom edge of the leaves—sc into center row, sl st in first row; fasten off, leaving a long tail for sewing.

Large Leaf (make 2)

Work in rows with **Color 27** and a 3.5mm hook.

Row 1: (RS) Ch 14, sl st in second ch from hook, sc in next ch, hdc in next ch, dc in next ch, tr in next 5 chs, dc in next 2 chs, hdc in next ch, sc in last ch = 13 sts

Fasten off, leaving a long tail for sewing.

Small Leaf (make 2)

Work in rows with **Color 27** and a 3mm hook.

Row 1: (RS) Ch 7, sl st in second ch from hook, sc in next ch, hdc in next 2 chs, sc in next ch, sl st in last ch = 6 sts

Fasten off, leaving a long tail for sewing.

Large Patch

Make a magic ring using **Color 11** and work in rows with a 3.5mm hook.

Row 1: (RS) Ch 1 (does not count as a st now and throughout), 3 sc in ring; turn = 3 sts

Row 2: (WS) Ch 1, 2 sc in first st, 3 sc in next st, 2 sc in last st; turn = 7 sts

Row 3: (RS) Ch 1, 2 sc in first st, sc in next 2 sts, (sc, ch 2, sc) in next st, sc in next 2 sts, 2 sc in last st = 10 sts and 1 ch-2 sp

Fasten off, leaving a long tail for sewing.

Small Patch (make 2)

Make a magic ring using **Color 11** and work in rows with a 2.5mm hook.

Row 1: Ch 1 (does not count as a st now and throughout), 3 sc in ring; turn = 3 sts

Row 2: Ch 1, 2 sc in first st, (sc, ch 2, sc) in next st, (hdc, dc) in last st = 6 sts and 1 ch-2 sp

(continued overleaf)

Large leaf (3.5mm/E/4 hook)

1

Large patch (3.5mm/E/4 hook)

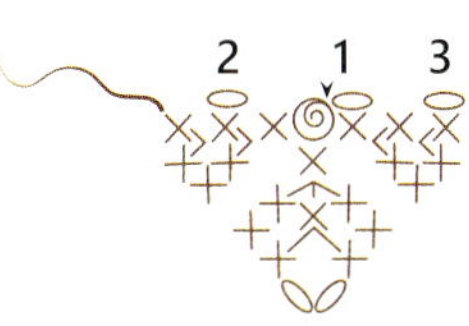

Small patch (2.5mm/B/1 hook)

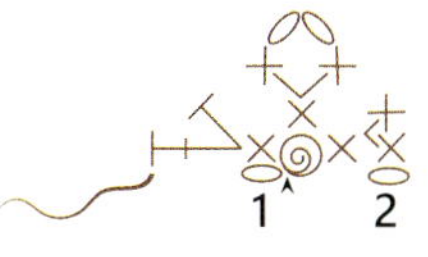

Small leaf (3mm/D/3 hook)

Top leaf bunch (3.5mm/E/4 hook)

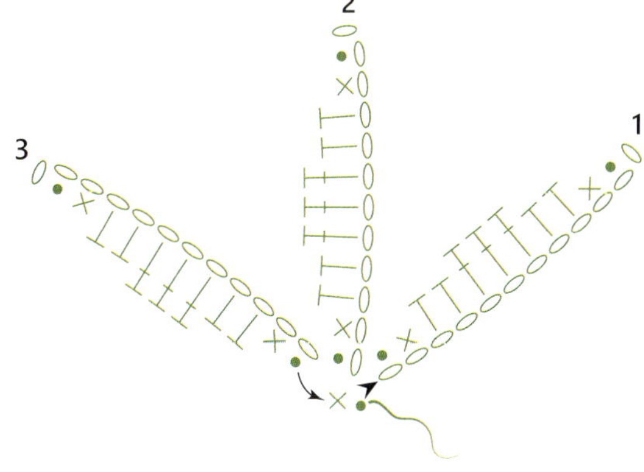

Head cover (4mm/G/6 hook)

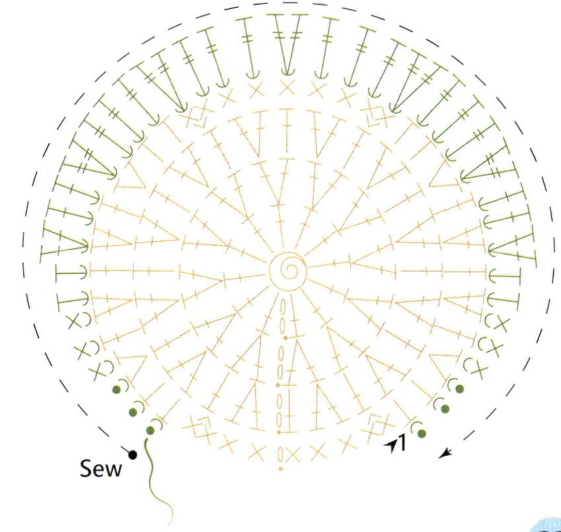

Felt templates

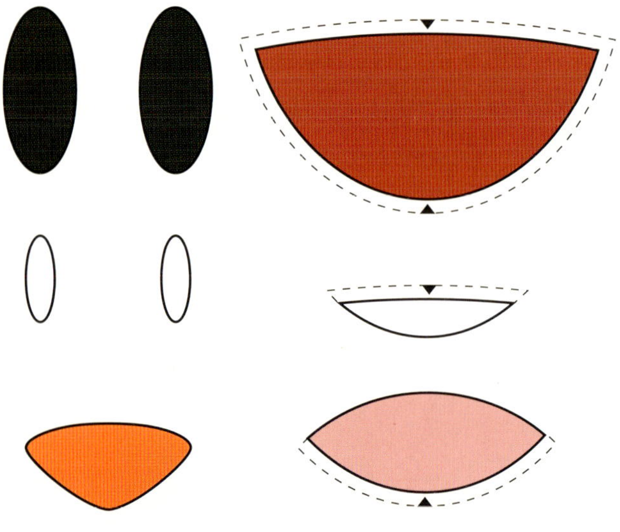

Assembly

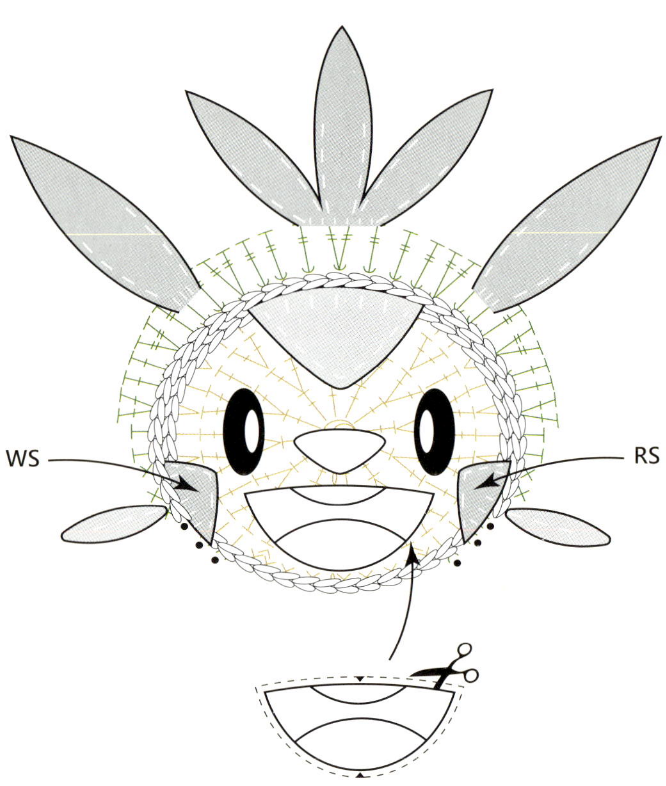

Fasten off, leaving a long tail for sewing. Use the RS piece on the right and the WS piece on the left of the face (see Assembly).

Assembly

Hold the square with the stitch marker at the bottom. Outline the head with **Color 14** by working surface sl sts between Rnds 4 and 5 with a 4mm hook, holding yarn on WS. Finish off seamlessly and weave in the ends (see Finishing/Surface Crochet).

Holding **Color 27** on WS, outline the inner edge of the head cover by working surface sl sts with a 4mm hook next to the head outline. Finish off and weave in the ends.

Position the leaf bunch and large leaves on the top of the head cover. Using **Color 27**, whipstitch across the bottom edges onto the square, then backstitch across the side edges partially, leaving the tips unstitched. Fasten off and weave in the ends; remove the marker from the square.

Position the small leaves as shown. Using **Color 27**, backstitch across the center of the leaves onto the square, leaving the side edges unstitched. Finish off and weave in the ends.

Position the large and small patches as shown. Using **Color 11**, whipstitch across the raw edges onto the head and backstitch around the remaining edges. Finish off and weave in the ends.

Cut out the indicated pieces from Felts A, D, J, M, and V, using the templates and assemble the layers to complete the eyes and mouth (see Working With Felt). Position all the pieces referring to the image, and use pins to mark the main points. Glue the eyes, nose, and mouth onto the head and let them dry.

Pecha Berry

A Pecha Berry has a sweet and delicous flavor. It can be used to heal Pokémon that have been poisoned.

Key

27 29 47 51 C

Difficulty level

Square

Make the square as for Chimchar, but using **Color 47** for the center, and **Color 29** for the background. Place marker in final join to indicate the bottom of the square.

Shaping

Hold the square with the stitch marker at the bottom. Begin by working around the berry edge (Rnd 4 of the square) using **Color 47** and a 4mm hook.

Rnd 1: (RS) Skip first st and work in FLO—Leaving a long tail at the beg for sewing, join **Color 47** with a sl st in second st, sc in next st, 2 hdc in next st, *dc in next st, [2 tr in next st, tr in next 2 sts] 2 times, 2 tr in next st, dc in next st**, hdc in next 2 sts, sc in next 2 sts, sl st in next st; break off **Color 47**; with **Color 51**—sl st in next 4 sts, ch 3 (counts as dc) and place marker in last ch made, dc2tog, dc in next st, dc2tog, ch 3 (counts as dc), sl st in next 5 sts; break off **Color 51**, leaving a long tail for sewing; with **Color 47**—sl st in next st, sc in next st, hdc in next 2 sts, repeat from * to **, 2 hdc in next st, sc in next st, sl st in last st; fasten off **Color 47**, leaving a long tail for sewing = 55 sts

(continued overleaf)

Square (4mm/G/6 hook)

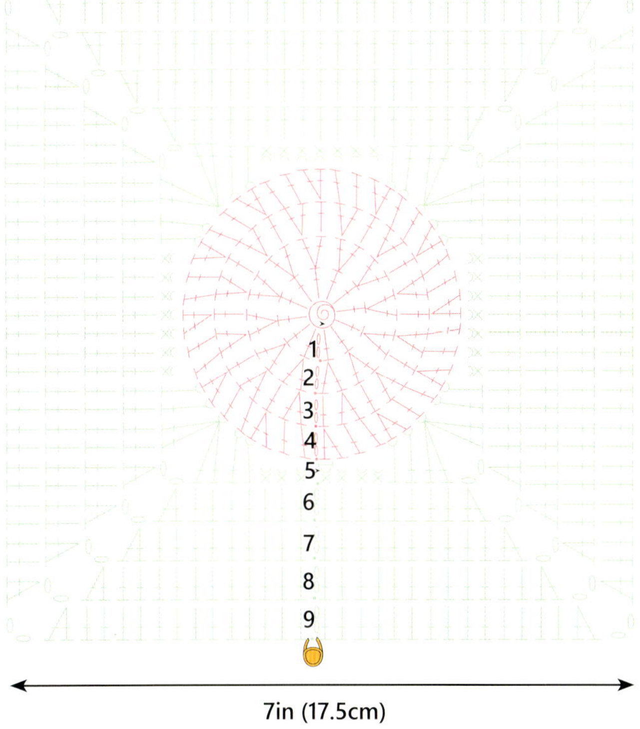

Leaves (3.5mm/E/4 hook)

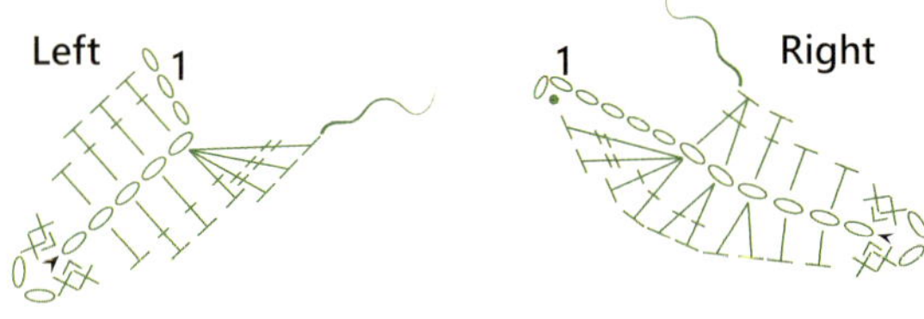

Outline (3.5mm/E/4 hook)

Shaping (4mm/G/6 hook)

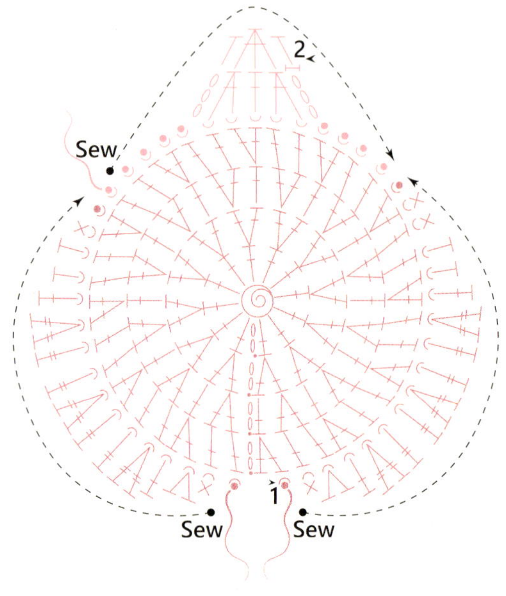

Tip base (3.5mm/E/4 hook)

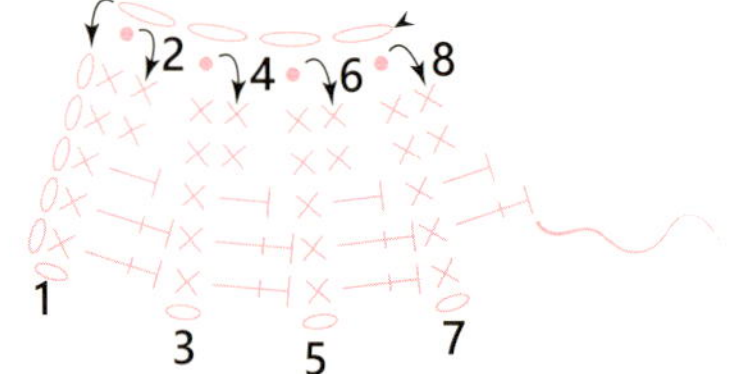

Rnd 2: (RS) Join **Color 51** with a standing hdc in st with marker and remove marker, dc3tog, hdc in next st; fasten off and weave in ends, leaving the remaining sts unworked = 3 sts

Backstitch the top and bottom edges onto the square using the corresponding colors. Finish off and weave in the ends.

Outline

Using **Color 47** and a 3.5mm hook, make a 5 d-ch crochet cord (see Techniques/Finishing). Fasten off, leaving a long tail for sewing.

Left Leaf

Work in rows with **Color 27** and a 3.5mm hook.

Row 1: (RS) Ch 8, dc in fourth ch from hook (skipped chs count as dc), dc in next 2 chs, hdc in next ch, (2 sc, ch 2, 2 sc) in last ch; work across the opposite side of the foundation ch—hdc in next ch, dc in next 2 chs, (dc, 3 tr) in last ch; fasten off, leaving a long tail for sewing = 16 sts and ch-2 sp

Right Leaf

Work in rows with **Color 27** and a 3.5mm hook.

Row 1: (RS) Ch 12, sl st in second ch from hook, skip 4 chs (counts as tr), (2 tr, 2 dc) in next ch, 2 dc in next ch, 2 hdc in next ch, hdc in next 2 chs, (2 sc, ch 2, 2 sc) in last ch; work across the opposite side of the foundation ch—hdc in next 2 chs, dc in next ch, dc2tog; fasten off, leaving a long tail for sewing = 19 sts and ch-2 sp

Tip Base

Work in rows with **Color 51** and a 3.5mm hook.

Row 1: (RS) Ch 10, sc in second ch from hook, sc in next 4 chs, sl st in next ch; turn, leaving the remaining chs unworked = 6 sts and 3 chs

Row 2: (WS) Skip sl st, sc in next 2 sts, hdc in next st, dc in last 2 sts; turn = 5 sts

Row 3: (RS) Ch 1 (does not count as a st), sc in first st, sc in next 4 sts, sl st in next ch of Row 1; turn = 6 sts

Rows 4–7: Repeat Rows 2–3 twice

Row 8: (WS) Skip sl st, sc in next 2 sts, hdc in next st, dc in next st; leave the last st unworked; fasten off, leaving a long tail for sewing – 4 sts

Assembly

Hold the square with the stitch marker at the bottom. Sew on the tip base using **Color 51,** creating a zigzag edge as shown. Finish off and weave in the end; remove the marker from the square.

Position and sew the leaves as shown using **Color 27**. Using the same yarn, make a French knot between the leaves. Position the outline as shown and whipstitch across its edge onto the berry. Finish off and weave in the ends.

Cut out the indicated pieces from Felt C, using the templates (see Working With Felt). Position the spots and glue them onto the berry.

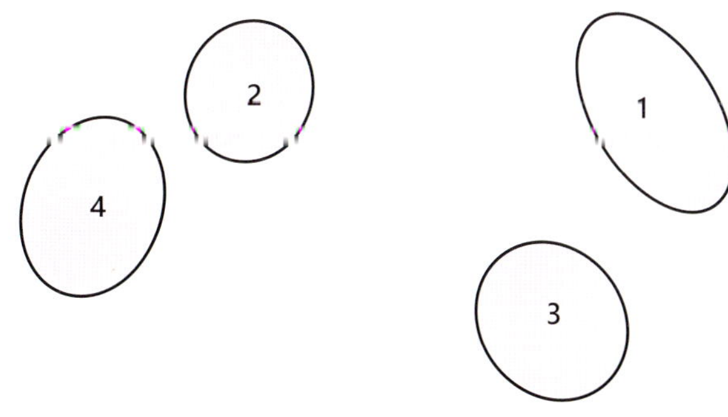

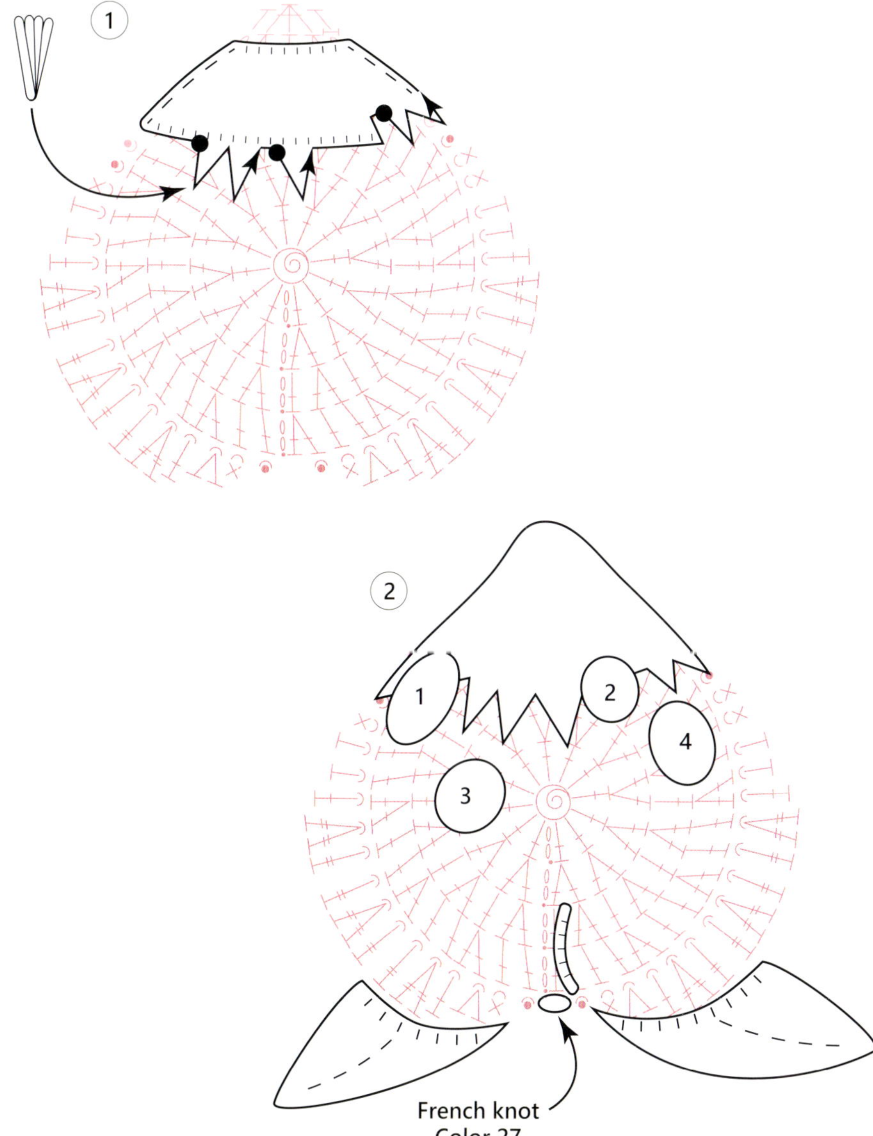

Grookey

As Grookey strikes everything in sight with its stick, it has more and more fun, and its rhythm becomes livelier.

Key

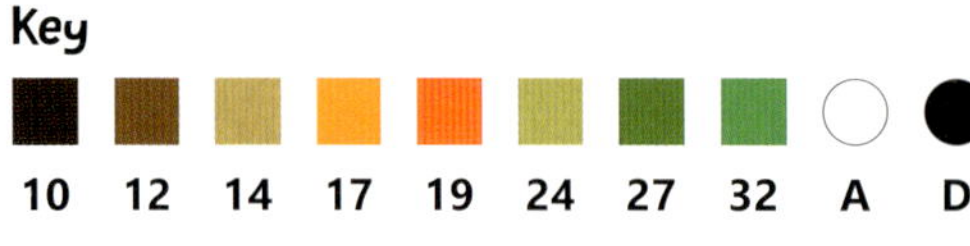

10 12 14 17 19 24 27 32 A D

Difficulty level

Type

Square (4mm/G/6 hook)

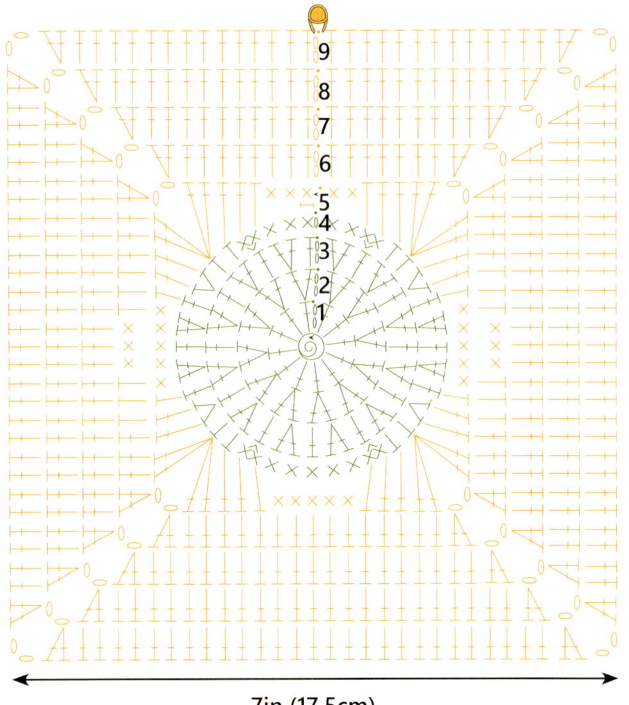

7in (17.5cm)

Ears (3.5mm/E/4 hook)

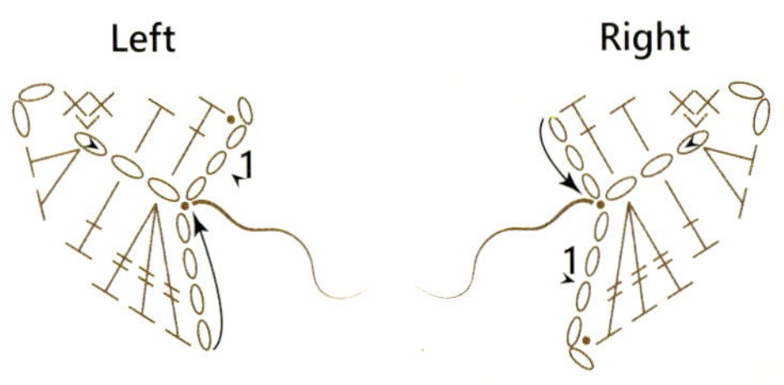

Square

Make the square as for Torchic, but using **Color 27** for the center, and **Color 17** for the background.

Face (make 2 ovals for 1 face)

Work in the round with **Color 24** and a 3.5mm hook.

Rnd 1: Ch 4, sc in second ch from hook, sc in next ch, 3 sc in last ch; work across the opposite side of the foundation ch—sc in next ch, 2 sc in last ch, join = 8 sts

Rnd 2: Ch 1 (does not count as a st now and throughout), 2 sc in same st as join, sc in next st, 2 sc in next 3 sts, sc in next st, 2 sc in last 2 sts; join = 14 sts

Rnd 3: Ch 1, sc in same st as join, 2 sc in next st, sc in next st, [sc in next st, 2 sc in next st] 3 times, sc in next st, [sc in next st, 2 sc in next st] 2 times; join = 20 sts

Rnd 4: Ch 1, 2 sc in same st as join, sc in next 3 sts, [2 sc in next st, sc in next 2 sts] 3 times, sc in next st, [2 sc in next st, sc in next 2 sts] 2 times; join = 26 sts

Fasten off, leaving a long tail for sewing. Position 2 ovals vertically side by side and whipstitch across 5 center sts using one of the yarn tails; finish off and weave in the end. Finish the tip between the ovals using the other yarn tail. Sl st in each st to seam, ch 2, dc in seam st of next oval; fasten off, leaving the remaining tail for sewing.

Snout

Work in the round with **Color 19** and a 4mm hook.

Rnd 1: Ch 5, sc in second ch from hook, sc in next 2 chs, 3 sc in last ch; work across the opposite side of the foundation ch—sc in next 2 chs, 2 sc in last ch, join = 10 sts

Rnd 2: Ch 1 (does not count as a st), 2 sc in same st as join, hdc in next 2 sts, 2 sc in next 3 sts, hdc in next 2 sts, 2 sc in last 2 sts; join = 16 sts

Fasten off, leaving a long tail for sewing.

Leafy Top

Work in rows with **Color 27** and a 3mm hook.

Row 1: (WS) Ch 10, sl st in second ch from hook, sc in next ch, hdc in next ch, dc in next ch, tr in next 2 chs, dc in next ch, hdc in next ch, sc in last ch; turn = 9 sts (First leaf made)

Row 2: (RS) Ch 1 (does not count as a st), sc in first st, sc in next 2 sts, ch 7; turn = 3 sts and ch-7

Row 3: (WS) Sl st in second ch from hook, sc in next ch, hdc in next ch, dc in next ch, tr in next 2 chs, dc in next st, hdc in next st, sc in last st; turn = 9 sts (Second leaf made)

Row 4: (RS) Work around the outer edge of both leaves—Sc to first point, (2 sc, ch 2, 2 sc) in point; sc to next point, placing sl st in inner corner between the leaves; (2 sc, ch 2, 2 sc) in point, sc to bottom edge; do not turn

Row 5: (RS) Work across the bottom edge of both leaves—Sc in st between the leaves, sl st in beg st of Row 4

Fasten off, leaving a long tail for sewing.

Stick

Work in rows with **Color 14** and a 4mm hook.

Row 1: (RS) Ch 15, sc in second ch from hook, sc in each ch across = 14 sts

Fasten off, leaving a long tail for sewing.

Left Ear

Work in rows with **Color 12** and a 3.5mm hook.

Row 1: (RS) Ch 7, sl st in second ch from hook, skip 2 chs (the skipped chs count as dc), dc in next ch, hdc in next ch, (2 sc, ch 2, 2 hdc) in last ch; work across the opposite side of the foundation ch—dc in next ch, 3 tr in last ch, ch 4 (counts as tr), sl st in same ch = 12 sts and ch-2 sp

Fasten off, leaving a long tail for sewing.

(continued overleaf)

Face (3.5mm/E/4 hook)

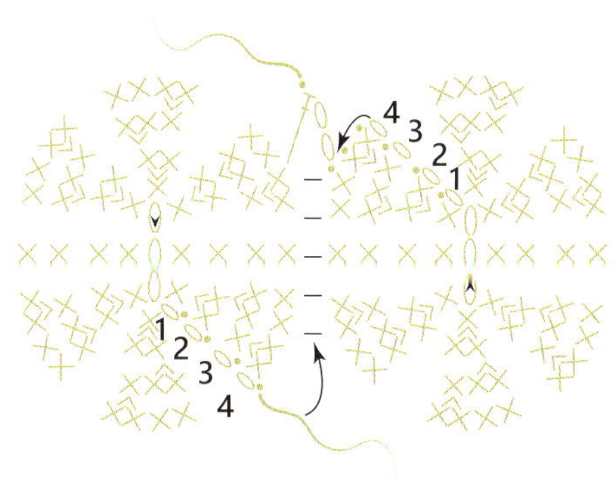

Leafy top (3mm/D/3 hook)

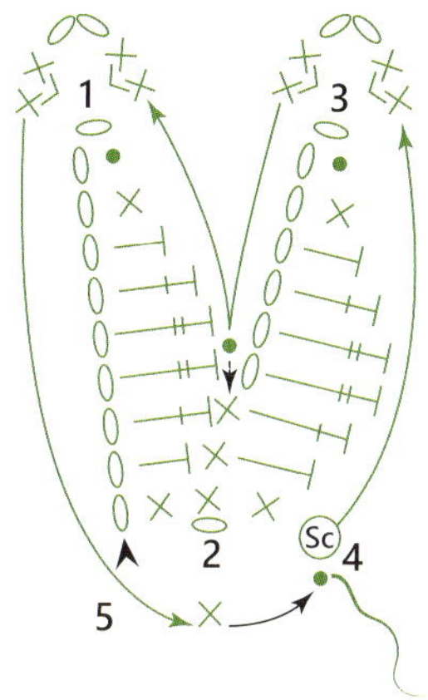

Stick (4mm/G/6 hook)

Snout (4mm/G/6 hook)

Felt templates

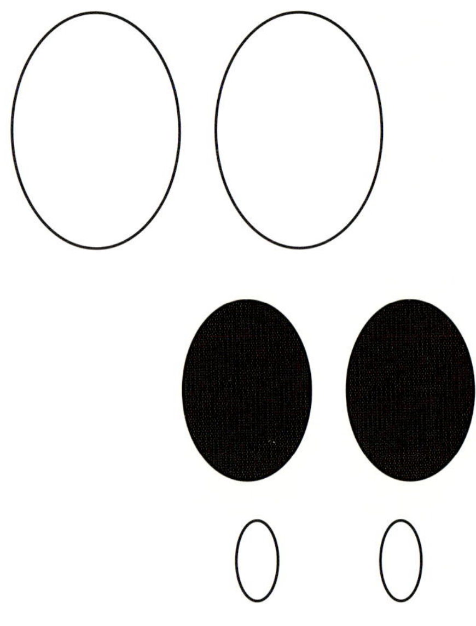

Assembly

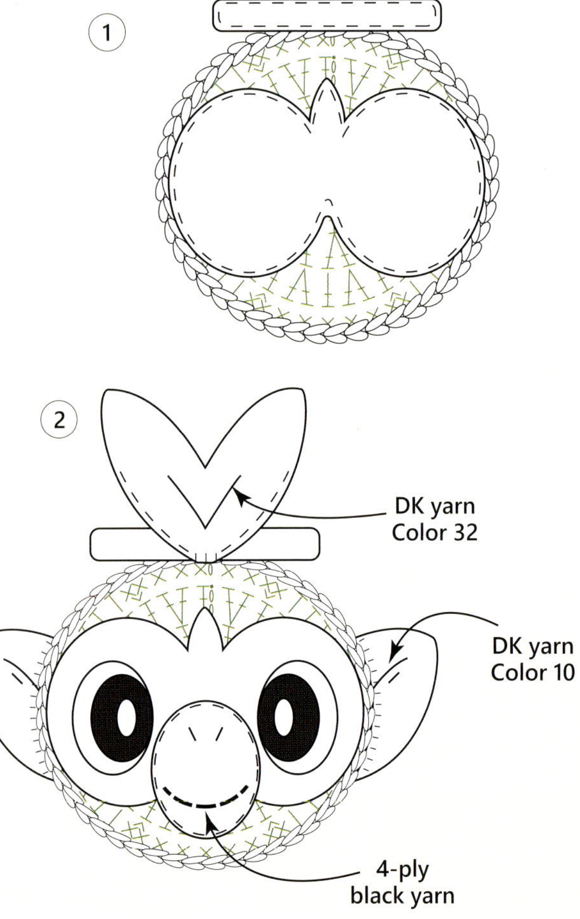

Right Ear

Work in rows with **Color 12** and a 3.5mm hook.

Row 1: (RS) Ch 8, sl st in second ch from hook, skip 3 chs (the skipped chs count as tr), 3 tr in next ch, dc in next ch, (2 hdc, ch 2, 2 sc) in last ch; work across the opposite side of the foundation ch—hdc in next ch, dc in last ch, ch 3 (counts as dc), sl st in same ch = 12 sts and ch-2 sp

Fasten off, leaving a long tail for sewing.

Assembly

Outline the head with **Color 27** by working surface sl sts between Rnds 4 and 5 with a 4mm hook, holding yarn on WS. Finish off seamlessly and weave in the end (see Finishing/ Surface Crochet).

Holding the square with the stitch marker at the top, position the stick and the face as shown. Using a long tail from each piece, backstitch around onto the square. Finish off and weave in the ends; remove the stitch marker from the square.

Position the ears on each side of the head and whipstitch across the inner edges onto the square with **Color 12**. Using the same yarn, stitch the center of the ears to the square, leaving the remaining edges unstitched. Thread the needle with **Color 10** and stitch a line across the center of each ear. Finish off and weave in the ends.

Position the leafy top as shown, covering the stick in the center. Using **Color 27**, whipstitch across the bottom edge and backstitch the sides partially, leaving the remaining edges unstitched. Thread the needle with **Color 32** and stitch a V-shaped center on the leaves. Finish off and weave in the ends.

Position the snout as shown and backstitch around onto the face using **Color 19**. Thread the needle with a 4-ply black yarn and stitch the mouth and nostrils as indicated. Use straight pins to mark the main points prior to stitching. Finish off and weave in the ends.

From Felts A and D, cut out the indicated pieces using the templates and assemble the layers to complete the eyes (see Working With Felt). Position the eyes referring to the image; use pins to mark the main points. Glue the eyes onto the face and leave them to dry.

Great Ball

A Great Ball is an improved version of a regular Poké Ball. It has a higher chance of successfully catching a Pokémon.

Key

1 3 7 37 42

Difficulty level

Square

Make the square by following the instructions for the Poké Ball (including shaping and finishing), but using **Color 42** for the upper shell, and **Color 37** for the background.

Red Flap (make 2)

Work in the round with **Color 7** and a 3.5mm hook.

Rnd 1: Ch 6, sc in second ch from hook, sc in next ch, hdc in next ch, dc in next ch, (dc, ch 2, sl st) in last ch; work across the opposite side of the foundation ch—ch 2, dc in same ch, dc in next ch, hdc in next ch, sc in last 2 chs, ch 1, join = 11 sts, 2 ch-2 sps and 1 ch-1 sp

Rnd 2: Ch 1 (does not count as a st), 3 sc in same st as join, sc in next 3 sts, (sc, hdc, dc) in next st, sc in each of next 2 chs, skip sl st, sc in each of next 2 chs, (dc, hdc, sc) in next st, sc in next 3 sts, 3 sc in next st, sc in last ch-1 sp; join = 23 sts

Fasten off, leaving a long tail for sewing.

Assembly

Position the red flaps on the upper shell of the ball with their narrow sides facing toward the center. Leave 14 sts along the top edge between the flaps. Using the long tail from each flap, backstitch around the edges onto the ball. Finish off and weave in the ends.

Red flap (3.5mm/E/4 hook)

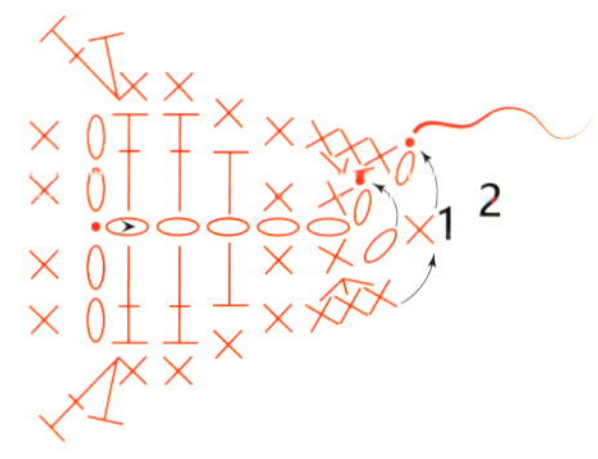

Assembly

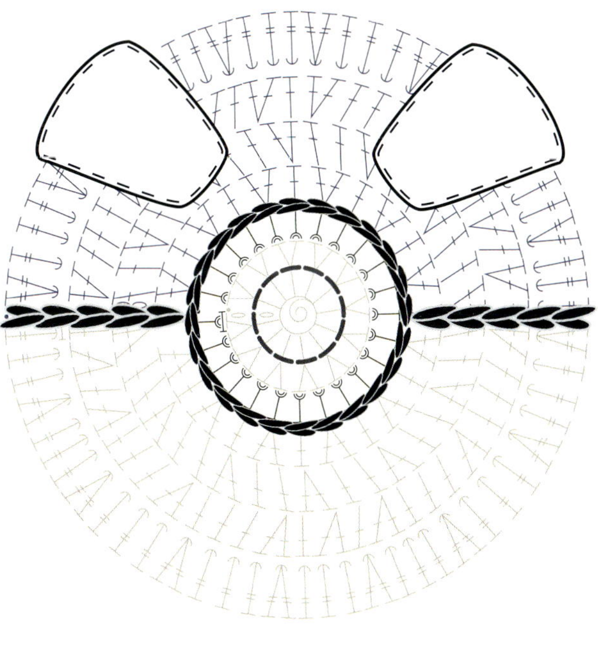

Froakie

This Pokémon uses its extraordinary jumping abilities to confuse its foes, throwing springy bubbles at them from above their heads.

Key

2 23 29 35 39 A D

Difficulty level

Type

Square

Make one Basic Square using **Color 29** and a 4mm hook (see Basic Shapes).

Head

Work in the round using **Color 35** and 3.5mm hook.

Rnd 1: Ch 16, dc in third ch from hook (the skipped chs do not count as a st), dc in next 12 chs, 6 dc in last ch; work across the opposite side of the foundation ch—dc in next 12 chs, 5 dc in last ch; join = 36 sts

Rnd 2: Ch 2 (does not count as a st), dc in same st as join, dc in next 14 sts, 3 dc in next 2 sts, dc in next 16 sts, 3 dc in next 2 sts, dc in last st; join = 44 sts

Rnd 3: Ch 1 (does not count as a st), sc in same st as join, sc in next 15 sts, *skip st, (3 dc, tr) in next st, ch 1, (tr, 3 dc) in next st, skip st**, sc in next 18 sts; repeat from * to **, sc in last 2 sts; join = 52 sts and 2 ch-1 sps

Fasten off, leaving a long tail.

Outer Eyes

Work in rows with **Color 35** and a 3.5mm hook.

Left Eye

Row 1: Ch 8, dc in fourth ch from hook (the skipped chs count as dc), dc in next 3 chs, 6 dc in last ch; work across the opposite side of the foundation ch—dc in next 4 chs, 2 dc in last ch; turn = 17 sts

Row 2: Ch 3 (counts as dc), dc in first st, dc in next 5 sts, 2 dc in next 6 sts, dc in next 3 sts, dc2tog; turn = 23 sts

Row 3: (RS) Ch 1 (does not count as a st), do not skip first st, sc2tog, sc in next 2 sts, [2 sc in next st, sc in next st] 6 times, sc in next 7 sts = 28 sts

Fasten off, leaving a long tail.

Right Eye

Row 1: Ch 9, dc in fourth ch from hook (the skipped chs count as dc), dc in next 4 chs, 6 dc in last ch; work across the opposite side of

Head (3.5mm/E/4 hook)

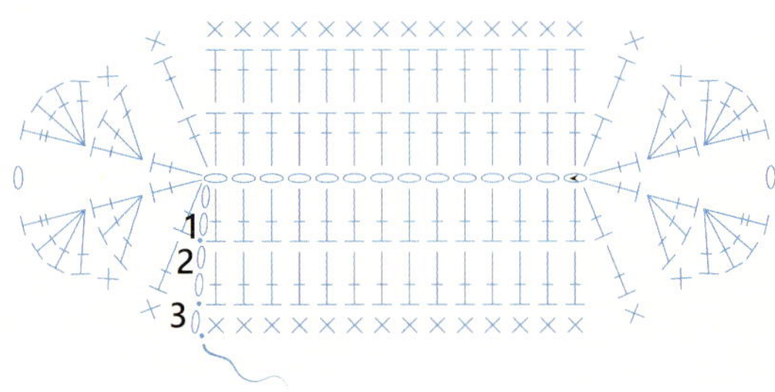

Outer eyes (3.5mm/E/4 hook)

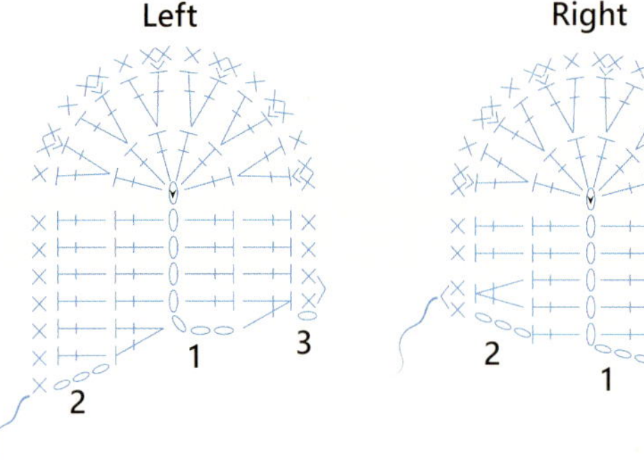

Iris (4mm/G/6 hook)

Nose (3.5mm/E/4 hook)

Nostrils (4mm/G/6 hook)

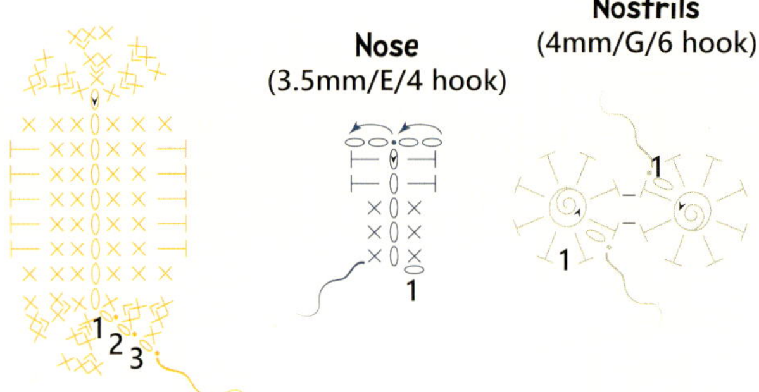

the foundation ch—dc in next 5 chs; turn = 17 sts

Row 2: Ch 3 (counts as dc), skip first st, dc2tog, dc in next 2 sts, 2 dc in next 6 sts, dc in next 5 sts, 2 dc in last st; turn = 23 sts

Row 3: (RS) Ch 1 (does not count as a st), sc in first st, sc in next 6 sts, [sc in next st, 2 sc in next st] 6 times, sc in next 2 sts, sc2tog = 28 sts

Fasten off, leaving a long tail.

Iris (make 2)

Work in the round using **Color 23** and a 4mm hook.

Rnd 1: Ch 10, sc in second ch from hook, sc in next 7 chs, 3 sc in last ch; work across the opposite side of the foundation ch—sc in next 7 chs, 2 sc in last ch; join = 20 sts

Rnd 2: Ch 1 (does not count as a st now and throughout), 2 sc in same st as join, sc in next 7 sts, 2 sc in next 3 sts, sc in next 7 sts, 2 sc in last 2 sts; join = 26 sts

Rnd 3: Ch 1, sc in same st as join, 2 sc in next st, *sc in next st, hdc in next 5 sts, sc in next st**, [sc in next st, 2 sc in next st] 3 times; repeat from * to **, [sc in next st, 2 sc in next st] 2 times; join = 32 sts

Fasten off, leaving a long tail.

Nose

Work in the round using **Color 39** and 3.5mm hook.

Rnd 1: Ch 6, sc in second ch from hook, sc in next 2 chs, hdc in next ch, (hdc, ch 2, sl st) in last ch; work across the opposite side of the foundation ch—ch 2, hdc in same ch, hdc in next ch, sc in last 3 chs = 10 sts and 2 ch-2 sps

Fasten off, leaving a long tail.

Nostril (make 2)

Make a magic ring using **Color 2** and work in the round with a 4mm hook—Ch 1 (does not count as a st), 8 hdc in ring; join and fasten off, leaving a long tail for sewing. Make another nostril in the same manner and sew them together with 2 whipstitches.

Assembly

Position the head on the square, 4 rnds above the bottom edge and backstitch around using **Color 35**. Sew the nose and outer eyes as shown. Finish off and weave in the ends.

Sew the nostrils and irises as shown in the image; finish off and weave in the ends. From Felts A and D, cut out the indicated pieces using the templates and assemble the layers to complete the eyes (see Working With Felt). Position the eyes referring to the image; use pins to mark the main points. Glue the eyes onto the head and leave them to dry. Thread the needle with a 4-ply black yarn and backstitch the mouth as indicated. Use straight pins to mark the main points prior to stitching. Finish off and weave in the ends.

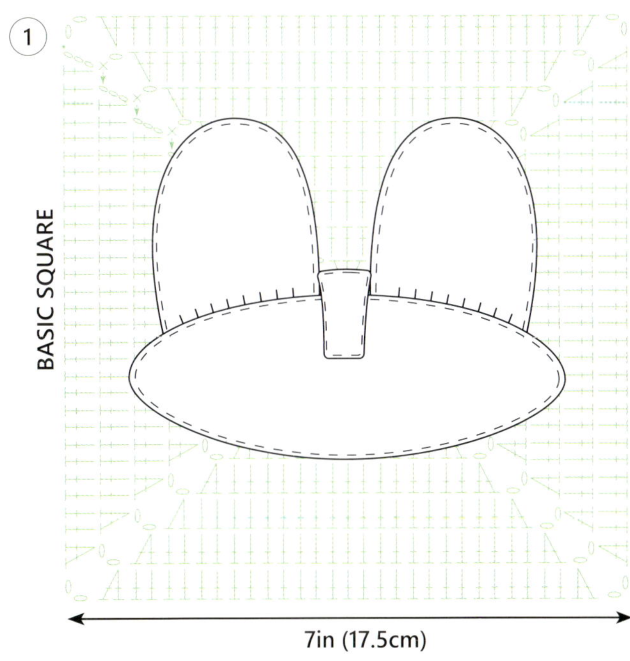

Litten

If you try too hard to get close to this Pokémon it won't open up to you. If you do grow close, giving it too much affection is still a no-no.

Key

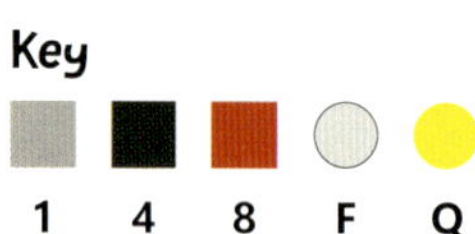

1 4 8 F Q

Difficulty level

Type

Square (4mm/G/6 hook)

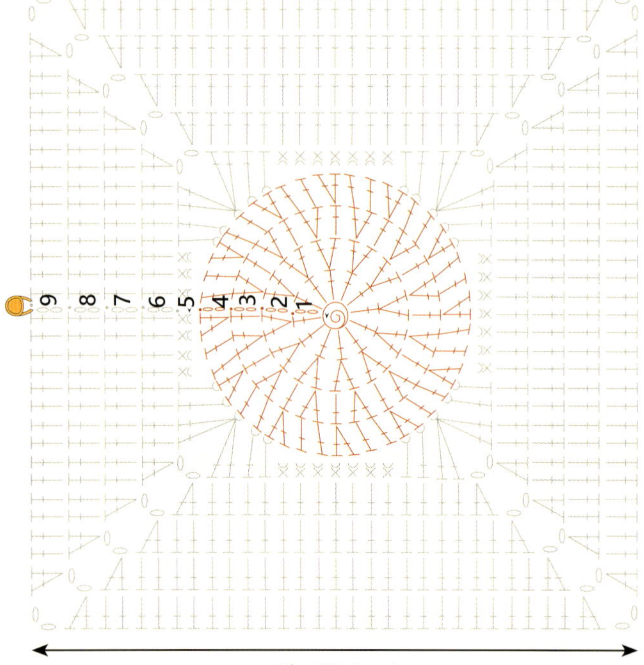

7in (17.5cm)

Square

Make the square as for Chimchar, but using **Color 8** for the center, and **Color 1** for the background. Place marker in final join to indicate the left edge of the square.

Head Shaping

Holding the square with the stitch marker on the left, work across the bottom edge of the head (Rnd 4 of the square) with a 4mm hook.

Row 1: (RS) Work in FLO—leaving a long tail at the beg for sewing, join **Color 8** with a standing dc in first st, dc in same st, hdc in next 3 sts, 2 hdc in next st, sc in next 3 sts, sl st in next 9 sts, sc in next 3 sts, 2 hdc in next st, hdc in next 3 sts, 2 dc in next st; leave the remaining sts unworked; fasten off, leaving a long tail for sewing = 29 sts

Backstitch the side edges onto the square using **Color 8**. Finish off and weave in the ends.

Upper Head

Make a magic ring using **Color 4** and work in rows with a 4mm hook.

Row 1: (WS) Ch 3 (counts as dc now and throughout), 5 dc in ring; turn = 6 sts

Row 2: (RS) Ch 3, dc in first st, 2 dc in next 5 sts; turn = 12 sts

Row 3: (WS) Ch 3, dc in first st, dc in next st, [2 dc in next st, dc in next st] 5 times; turn = 18 sts

Row 4: (RS) Ch 3, dc in first st, dc in next 2 sts, [2 dc in next st, dc in next 2 sts] 5 times; turn = 24 sts

Row 5: (WS) Ch 3, dc in first st, [dc in next 3 sts, 2 dc in next st] 2 times, dc in next 7 sts, [2 dc in next st, dc in next 3 sts] 2 times; turn = 29 sts

Ears (3mm/D/3 hook)

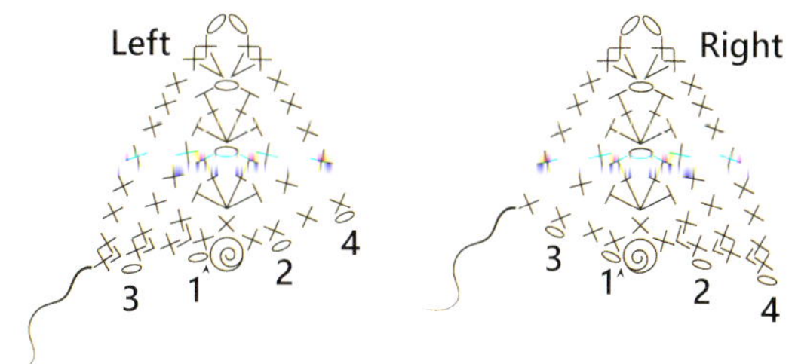

Head shaping (4mm/G/6 hook)

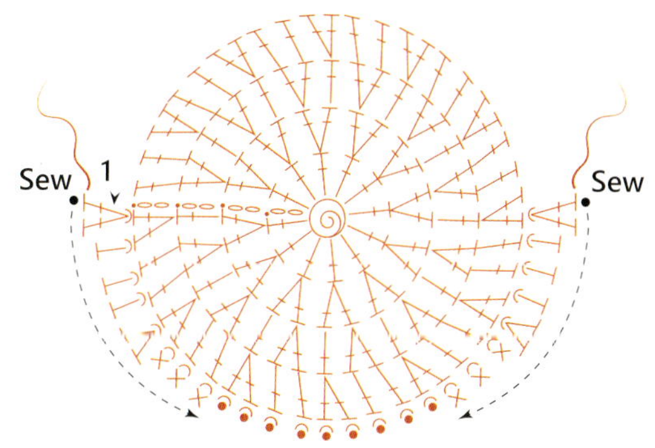

Upper head (4mm/G/6 hook)

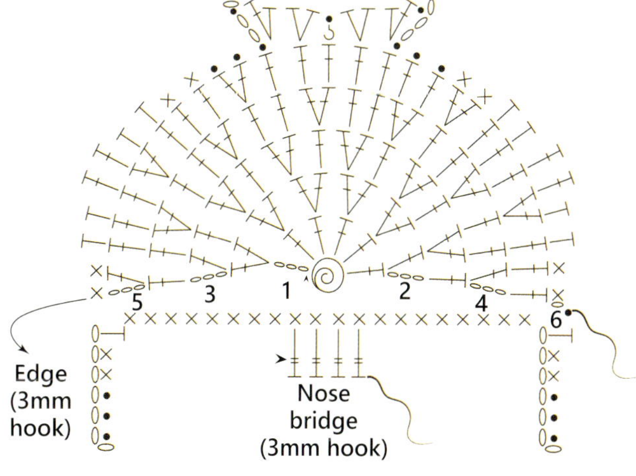

Row 6: (RS) Ch 1 (does not count as a st), sc in first st, sc in next st, *hdc in next 2 sts, dc in next 2 sts, hdc in next 2 sts, sc in next 2 sts**, sl st in next 2 sts; (sl st in next st, ch 3, sl st in second ch from hook), skip ch, (dc, hdc) in same st as sl st below, 2 hdc in next st, fpslst in next st, 2 hdc in next st, (hdc, dc) in next st, (ch 1, sl st in top of the previous dc, ch 2, sl st in same st as dc)—2 center points made; sl st in next 2 sts, sc in next 2 sts, repeat from * to **; do not turn = 24 sts and 2 center points

Change to a 3mm hook and continue to work across the bottom edge:

Edge: (RS) *Ch 7, sl st in second ch from hook, sl st in next 2 chs, sc in next 2 chs, hdc in last ch (side point made)**; skip sc at end of Row 6, 10 sc evenly across the edge to magic ring center, skip the center, 10 sc evenly across the edge, ending before beg sc of Row 6; repeat from * to **; sl st in beg sc of Row 6 = 20 sts and 2 side points

Fasten off, leaving a long tail for sewing. Mark 4 center sts on the bottom edge for the nose bridge and work with a 3mm hook:

Nose Bridge: (RS) Join **Color 4** with a standing tr in st with first marker, tr in next 3 sts ending in st with second marker = 4 sts

Fasten off, leaving a long tail for sewing and remove the markers.

(continued overleaf)

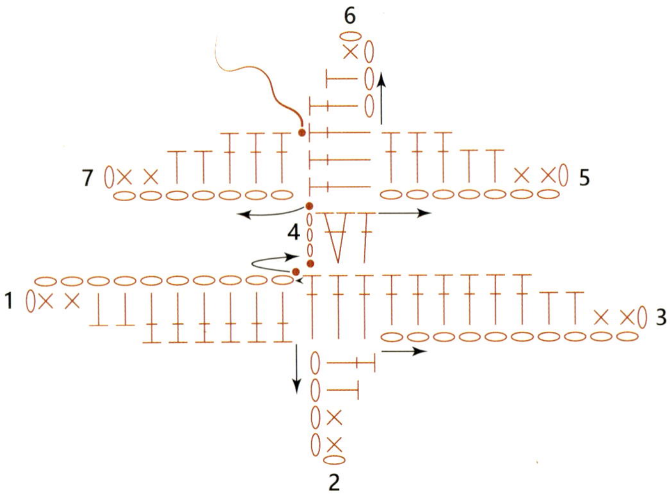

Felt templates

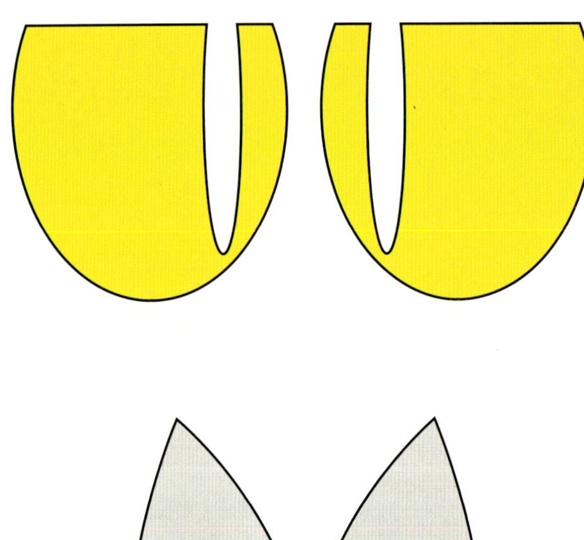

Head Mark

Work in rows with **Color 8** and a 2.5mm hook.

Row 1: (RS) Ch 11, sc in second ch from hook, sc in next ch, hdc in next 2 chs, dc in next 6 chs; do not turn (lower left offshoot made) = 10 sts

Row 2: (RS) Ch 5, sc in second ch from hook, sc in next ch, hdc in next ch, dc in last ch; do not turn (bottom point made) = 4 sts

Row 3: (RS) Ch 11, sc in second ch from hook, sc in next ch, hdc in next 2 chs, dc in next 6 chs, 3 dc evenly across the post of dc in Row 2; join with a sl st in beg ch of Row 1; turn (lower right offshoot made) = 13 sts

Row 4: (WS) Skip join, sl st in dc, ch 3 (counts as dc), 2 dc in next st, dc in next st; turn, leaving the remaining sts unworked (center core made) = 4 sts

Row 5: (RS) Ch 8, sc in second ch from hook, sc in next ch, hdc in next 2 chs, dc in next 3 chs; do not turn (upper right offshoot made) = 7 sts

Row 6: (RS) Ch 4, sc in second ch from hook, hdc in next ch, dc in last ch, 3 dc evenly across the post of dc in Row 5; join with a sl st in top of beg ch-3 of Row 4; turn (top point made) = 6 sts

Row 7: (WS) Ch 8, sc in second ch from hook, sc in next ch, hdc in next 2 chs, dc in next 3 chs; skip 2 dc of Row 6 and join with a sl st in next dc (upper left offshoot made) = 7 sts

Fasten off, leaving a long tail for sewing.

Whiskers (make 2)

Work in rows with **Color 8** and a 4mm hook.

Row 1: (WS) Ch 8, sc in second ch from hook, sc in next 5 chs, 3 sc in last ch; work across the opposite side of the foundation ch—sc in next 6 chs; turn = 15 sts

Row 2: (RS) Skip first st, sl st in next st, sc in next 2 sts, hdc in next 2 sts; dc in next st, ch 3, sl st in second ch from hook, sc in next ch, sl st in same st as previous dc (first point made); ch 4, sl st in second ch from hook, sc in next ch, hdc in last ch, skip sc, sl st in next st (second point made); ch 3, sl st in second ch from hook, sc in next ch, dc in same st as sl st from second point (third point made); hdc in next 2 sts, sc in next 2 sts, sl st in last 2 sts = 11 sts and 3 points

Fasten off, leaving a long tail for sewing.

Left Ear

Make a magic ring using **Color 4** and work in rows with a 3mm hook.

Row 1: (WS) Ch 1 (does not count as a st now and throughout), 3 sc in ring; turn = 3 sts

Row 2: (RS) Ch 1, sc in first st, (hdc, dc, ch 1, dc, hdc) in next st, 2 sc in last st; turn = 7 sts and ch-1 sp

Row 3: (WS) Ch 1, 2 sc in first st, sc in next 3 sts, (hdc, dc, ch 1, dc, hdc) in ch-1 sp, sc in last 3 sts; turn = 12 sts and ch-1 sp

Row 4: (RS) Ch 1, sc in first st, sc in next 4 sts, (2 sc, ch 2, 2 sc) in ch-1 sp, sc in next 6 sts, 2 sc in last st; fasten off, leaving a long tail for sewing = 17 sts and ch-2 sp

Right Ear

Make a magic ring using **Color 4** and work in rows with a 3mm hook.

Row 1: (WS) Ch 1 (does not count as a st now and throughout), 3 sc in ring; turn = 3 sts

Row 2: (RS) Ch 1, 2 sc in first st, (hdc, dc, ch 1, dc, hdc) in next st, sc in last st; turn = 7 sts and ch-1 sp

Row 3: (WS) Ch 1, sc in first st, sc in next 2 sts, (hdc, dc, ch 1, dc, hdc) in ch-1 sp, sc in next 3 sts, 2 sc in last st; turn = 12 sts and ch-1 sp

Row 4: (RS) Ch 1, 2 sc in first st, sc in next 6 sts, (2 sc, ch 2, 2 sc) in ch-1 sp, sc in last 5 sts; fasten off, leaving a long tail for sewing = 17 sts and ch-2 sp

Assembly

Cut out the indicated pieces from Felts F and Q, using the templates (see Working With Felt). Holding the square with the stitch marker on the left, position and glue the eyes as shown. Once the glue has dried, stitch pupils using **Colors 4 and 8** as shown.

Referring to the image, position the upper head, ears, and whiskers. Using the corresponding yarn color, sew each piece onto the square. Stitch the nose using **Color 4** from the nose bridge. Position the head mark on the upper head and backstitch around using **Color 8**. Finish off and weave in the ends; remove the marker from the square.

Thread the needle with 3 strands of DMC floss (535) and stitch the mouth below the nose. Finish off and weave in the ends. Position and glue the felt ear inserts as shown.

Whiskers (4mm/G/6 hook)

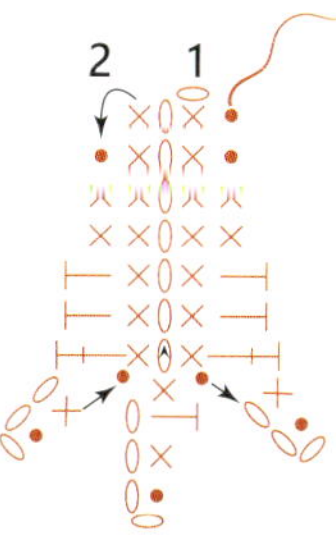

Assembly

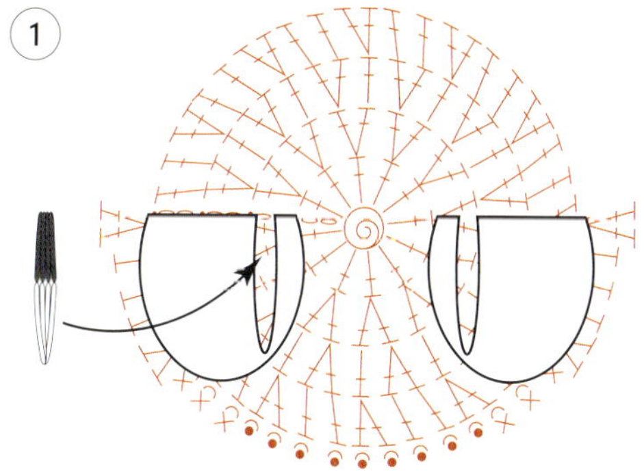

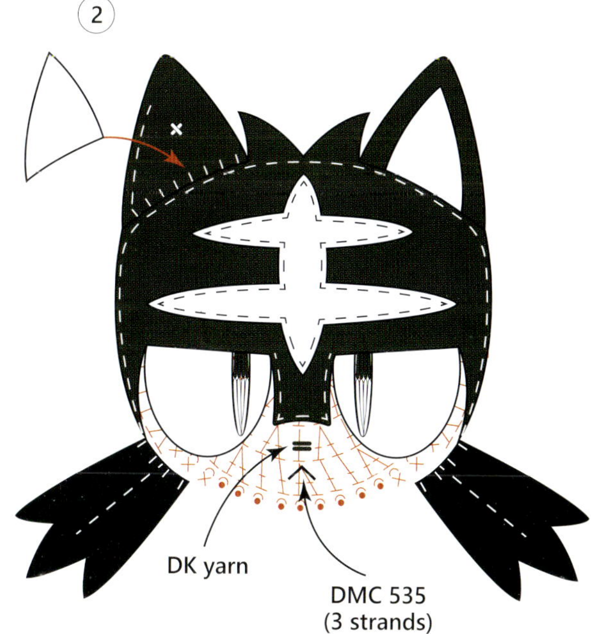

Treecko

The small hooks on the soles of this Pokémon's feet latch onto walls and ceilings, so it will never fall even while hanging upside down.

Key

8 27 50 A D P

Difficulty level

Type

Square

Make the square as for Chimchar, but using **Color 27** for the center and **Color 50** for the background. Place marker in final join to indicate the left edge of the square.

Head Shaping

Holding the square with the stitch marker on the left, work around the head edge (Rnd 4 of the square) using **Color 27** and a 4mm hook.

Rnd 1: (RS) Work in FLO—Join **Color 27** with a standing sl st in first st, sl st in next 2 sts, ch 2 (counts as dc), dc in next 19 sts, ch 2 (counts as dc), sl st in next 6 sts, ch 4 (counts as tr) and place marker-A in last ch made, tr in next 2 sts, dc in next 2 sts, hdc in next 2 sts, sc in next 3 sts and place marker-B in last st made, sc in next 2 sts, hdc in next 2 sts, dc in next 2 sts, tr in next 2 sts, ch 4 (counts as tr), sl st in last 3 sts; join and fasten off, leaving a long tail for sewing = 52 sts

Continue to work outer eyes in rows.

Right Outer Eye

Row 2: (RS) Join **Color 27** with a standing dc in st with marker-A and remove the marker, dc2tog, dc in next 2 sts, hdc in next 2 sts, sc2tog, sc in next st with marker-B; turn, leaving the remaining sts unworked (do not remove marker B) = 8 sts

Row 3: (WS) Ch 3 (counts as dc now and throughout), skip first st, dc2tog, dc in next 3 sts, dc2tog; turn = 6 sts

Row 4: (RS) Ch 3, skip first st, dc2tog, dc in next st, dc2tog; turn = 4 sts

Row 5: (WS) Ch 1 (does not count as a st), do not skip first st, [sc2tog] 2 times; fasten off and weave in the ends = 2 sts

Square (4mm/G/6 hook)

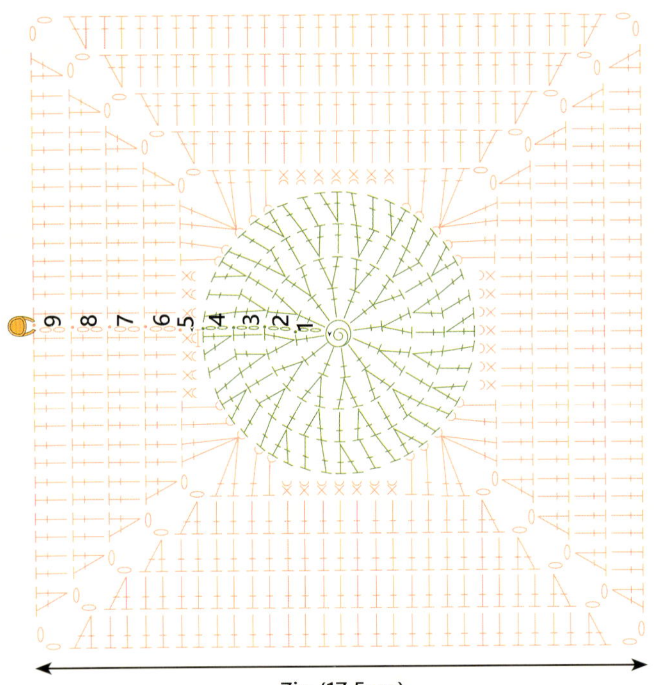

Mouth (3mm/D/3 hook)

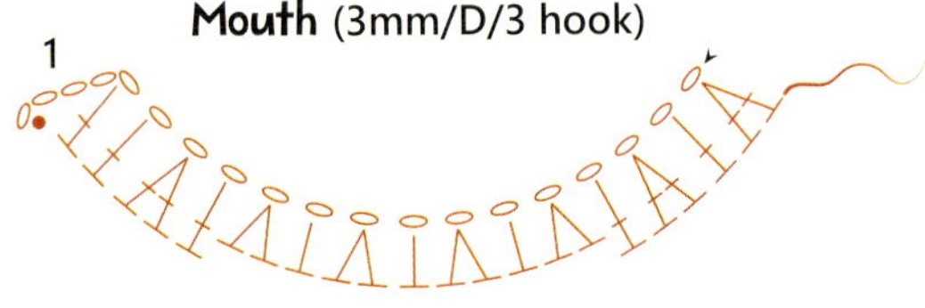

Eyelid (3.5mm/E/4 hook)

Left Outer Eye

Row 2: (RS) Join **Color 27** with a standing sc in st with marker-B and remove the marker, sc2tog, hdc in next 2 sts, dc in next 2 sts, dc2tog, dc in last st; turn = 8 sts

Rows 3–5: As for Right outer eye

Backstitch the top and bottom edges onto the square using **Color 27**. Finish off and weave in the ends.

Mouth

Work in rows with **Color 8** and a 3mm hook.

Row 1: (RS) Ch 19, sl st in second ch from hook, skip 2 chs (counts as dc), dc in next 2 chs, 2 dc in next ch, dc in next ch, 2 hdc in next ch, [hdc in next ch, 2 hdc in next ch] 3 times, [dc in next ch, 2 dc in next ch] 2 times = 23 sts

Fasten off, leaving a long tail for sewing.

Eyelid (make 2)

Using **Color 27** and a 3.5mm hook, make a 9 d-ch crochet cord (see Techniques/Finishing). Fasten off, leaving a long tail for sewing.

Assembly

Hold the square with the stitch marker on the left. Position the mouth as shown. Using **Color 8**, backstitch around, extending the outer corners into a smile with a straight stitch. Finish off and weave in the end; remove the marker from the square.

Cut out the indicated pieces from Felts A, D, and P, using the templates and assemble the layers to complete the eyes (see Working With Felt). Position the eyes referring to the image; use pins to mark the main points. Glue the eyes onto the head and let them dry.

Position the eyelids and whipstitch across the top edges onto the face using **Color 27**. Fasten off and weave in the ends.

Thread the needle with 4-ply black yarn and stitch the nostrils and eyebrows as indicated. Use pins to mark the main points prior to stitching. Finish off and weave in the ends.

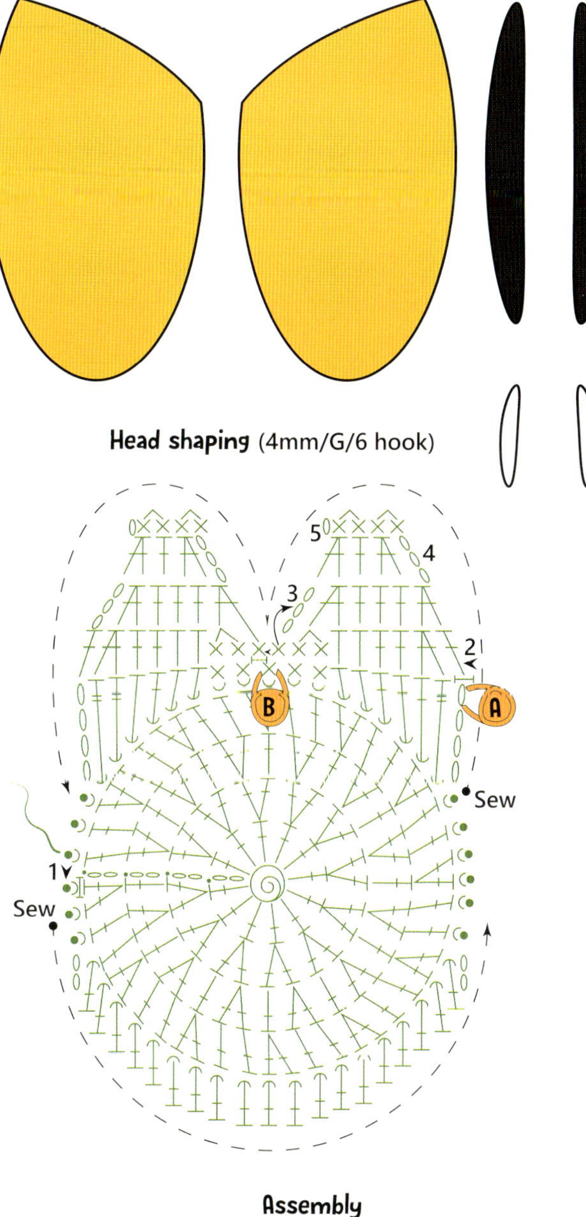

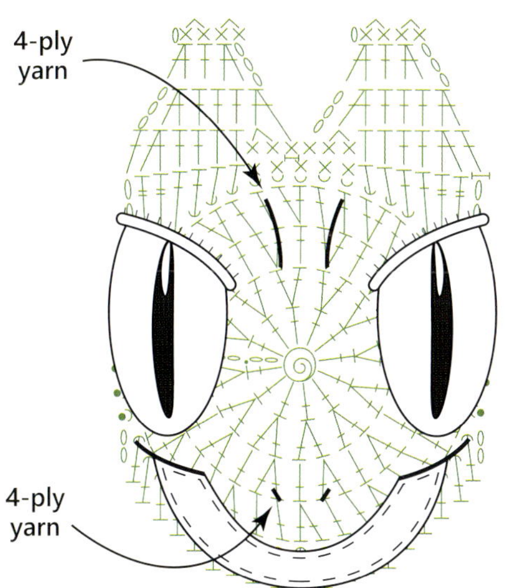

Sitrus Berry

The Sitrus Berry is related to the Oran Berry, but is larger and has a well-rounded flavor. It is to be consumed by Pokémon during battle.

Key

13 15 27

Difficulty level

Square (4mm/G/6 hook)

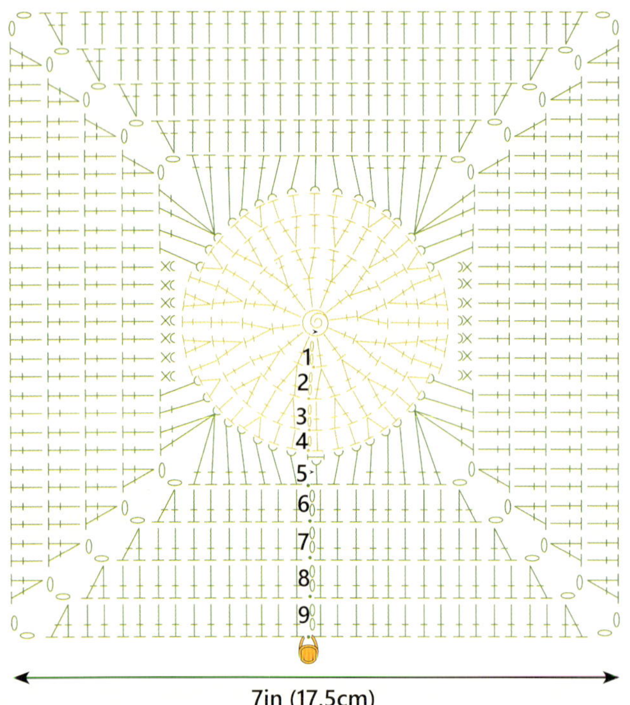

7in (17.5cm)

Square

Make a magic ring using **Color 15** and work in the round with a 4mm hook.

Follow Rnds 1–3 of Basic Circle (see Basic Shapes).

Rnd 4: Ch 1 (does not count as a st), hdc in same st as join, *[hdc in next 2 sts, 2 hdc in next st] 2 times, [dc in next st, 2 dc in next st] 2 times, dc in next st, [2 hdc in next st, hdc in next 2 sts] 2 times**, hdc in next st, repeat from * to **; join and break off **Color 15** = 48 sts

Rnd 5: Work in BLO—join **Color 27** with a standing hdc in first st, *hdc in next 2 sts, dc in next 3 sts, (2 dc, ch 2, 2 dc) in next st, dc in next st, hdc in next st, sc in next 7 sts, hdc in next st, dc in next st, (2 dc, ch 2, 2 dc) in next st, dc in next 3 sts, hdc in next 2 sts**, hdc in next st, repeat from * to **; join = 60 sts and 4 ch-2 sps

Rnds 6–9: Ch 2 (does not count as a st), dc in same st as join, [dc in each st to next ch-2 sp, (2 dc, ch 2, 2 dc) in ch-2 sp] 4 times, dc in each st to end; join = 76 /92 /108 /124 sts and 4 ch-2 sps

Place marker in final join to indicate the bottom of the square. Fasten off and weave in the ends.

Shaping

Hold the square with the stitch marker at the bottom, work around the berry (Rnd 4 of the square) using **Color 15** and a 4mm hook.

Rnd 1: (RS) Work in FLO—skip first st and join **Color 15** with a sl st in next st, sl st in next 19 sts, (hdc, dc) in next st, 2 tr in next 2 sts, dc in next st, 2 tr in next 2 sts, (dc, hdc) in next st, sl st in next 20 sts; ch 2, dc3tog working into the same st as last sl st, the first unworked st and the next st with join; ch 2, sl st in same st with join (bottom point made) = 53 sts and bottom point

Fasten off, leaving a long tail for sewing. Backstitch the top and bottom edges onto the square using **Color 15**. Finish off and weave in the ends. Sew the beads as indicated—Mill Hill size 6 (16606) or use 4 strands of DMC floss (977) to stitch French knots.

Stem

Work in rows with **Color 13** and a 2.5mm hook—Ch 4, sc in second ch from hook, sc in next 2 sts; fasten off, leaving a long tail for sewing. Sew the stem to the center top of the berry using **Color 13**. Finish off and weave in the ends; remove the marker from the square.

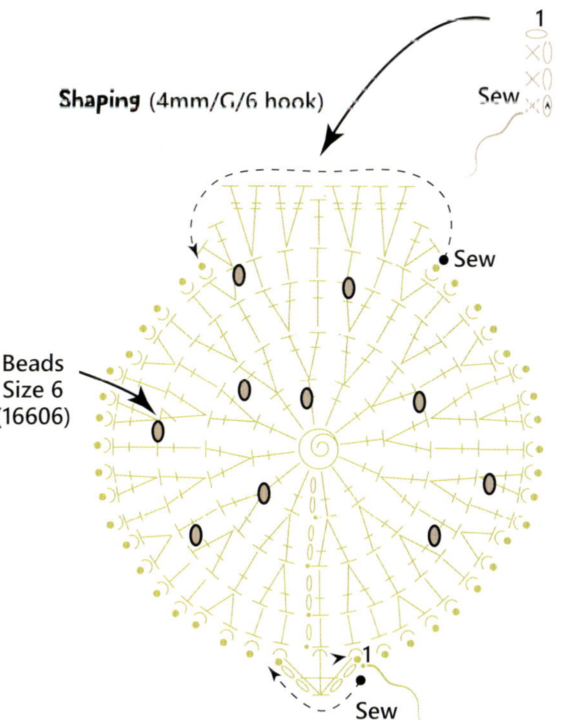

Popplio

This Pokémon can control balloons made of water. It practices diligently so it can learn to make big balloons.

Key

1 36 41 46 47 A D J V

Difficulty level

Type

Square (4mm/G/6 hook)

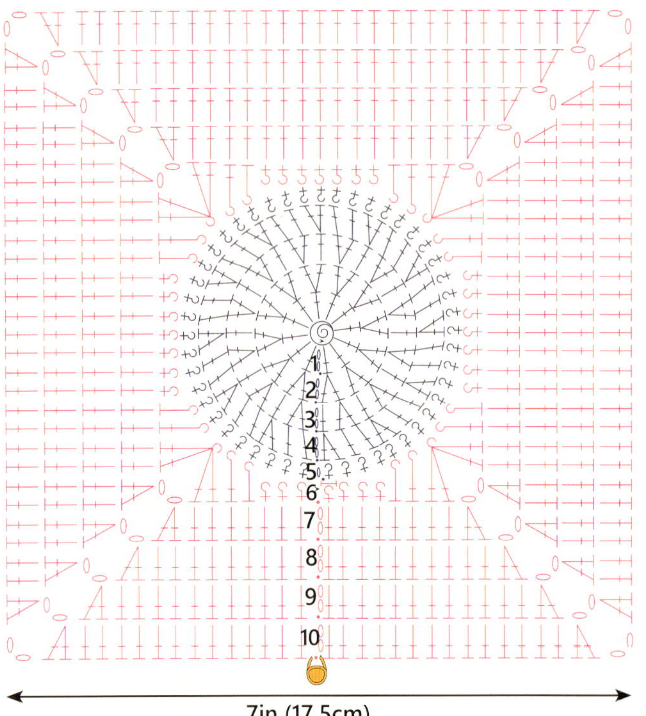

7in (17.5cm)

Ears (3.5mm/E/4 hook)

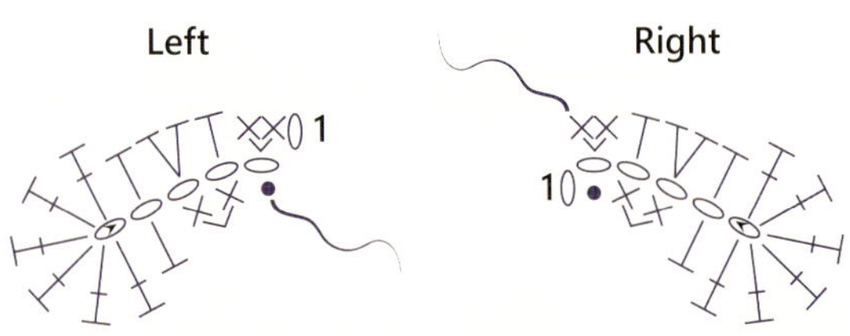

Square

Make the square as for Cyndaquil, but using **Color 41** for the center, and **Color 46** for the background.

Collar

Holding the square with the stitch marker at the bottom, mark 11 center sts across the bottom of the head in Rnd 5. Work in rows with **Color 36** and a 3.5mm hook.

Row 1: (RS) Leaving a long beg tail for sewing, join **Color 36** with a standing fpdc in first st with marker, fpdc in same st, 2 fpdc in each st to last st with marker; turn and remove the markers = 22 sts

Row 2: (WS) Ch 1 (does not count as a st), sc in first st, sc in each st across; turn = 22 sts

Row 3: (RS) Ch 3, tr in first st, ch 4, sl st in next st (counts as first shell); [skip 2 sts, (dc, hdc, 2 sc, hdc, dc) in next st, skip 2 sts, sl st in next st] 3 times; ch 4, tr2tog (counts as last shell) = 5 shells

Fasten off, leaving a long tail.

Left Ear

Work in rows with **Color 41** and a 3.5mm hook.

Row 1: (RS) Ch 6, 2 sc in second ch from hook, hdc in next ch, 2 hdc in next ch, hdc in next ch, 6 dc in last ch; work across the opposite side of the foundation ch—hdc in next ch, sc2tog, sl st in last ch; fasten off, leaving a long tail for sewing = 15 sts

Right Ear

Work in rows with **Color 41** and a 3.5mm hook.

Row 1: (RS) Ch 6, sl st in second ch from hook, sc2tog, hdc in next ch, 6 dc in last ch; work across the opposite side of the foundation ch—hdc in next ch, 2 hdc in next ch, hdc in next ch, 2 sc in last ch; fasten off, leaving a long tail for sewing = 15 sts

Snout

Work in the round with **Color 1** and a 3.5mm hook.

Rnd 1: Ch 6, sc in second ch from hook, sc in next 3 chs, 3 sc in last ch; work across the opposite side of the foundation ch—sc in next 3 chs, 2 sc in last ch, join = 12 sts

Rnd 2: Ch 1 (does not count as a st now and throughout), 2 sc in same st as join, hdc in next 3 sts, 2 sc in next 3 sts, hdc in next 3 sts, 2 sc in last 2 sts; join = 18 sts

Rnd 3: Ch 1, sc in same st as join, 2 sc in next st, hdc in next st, dc in next st, hdc in next st, 2 sc in next st, skip st, (hdc, 2 dc) in next st, (2 dc, hdc) in next st, skip st, 2 sc in next st, hdc in next st, dc in next st, hdc in next st, [sc in next st, 2 sc in next st] 2 times; join = 25 sts

Fasten off, leaving a long tail for sewing.

Nose

Make a magic ring using **Color 47** and work in the round with a 3.5mm hook.

Rnd 1: Ch 1 (does not count as a st now and throughout); 6 sc in ring; join = 6 sts

Rnd 2: Ch 1, 2 sc in same st as join, 2 sc in next 5 sts; join and fasten off, leaving a long tail for sewing = 12 sts

Assembly

Hold the square with the stitch marker at the bottom. Using **Color 36**, whipstitch the left and right edges of the collar onto the square. Position the snout and ears as shown. Using **Color 1**, backstitch around the snout onto the head. Using **Color 41**, whipstitch across the inner edges of the ears onto the head and backstitch across the center, leaving the outer edges unstitched. Finish off and weave in the ends; remove the marker from the square.

Position the nose as shown and backstitch around it onto the head using **Color 47**; finish off and weave in the end.

Cut out the indicated pieces from Felts A, D, J, and V, using the templates and assemble the layers to complete the mouth and eyes (see Working With Felt). Position and glue the eyes and mouth onto the head, using pins to mark the main points. Leave the glue to dry.

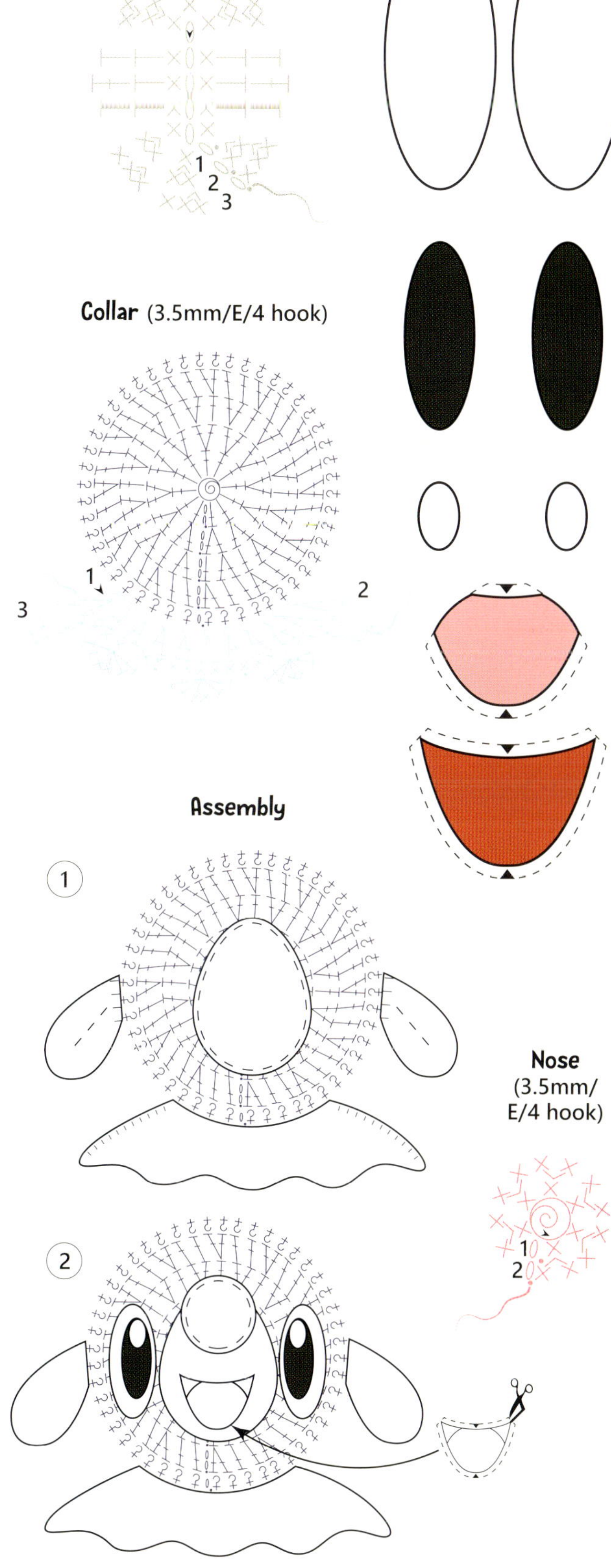

Ultra Ball

An Ultra Ball is an improved version of a Great Ball. This ultra-high performance Poké Ball excels at catching wild Pokémon.

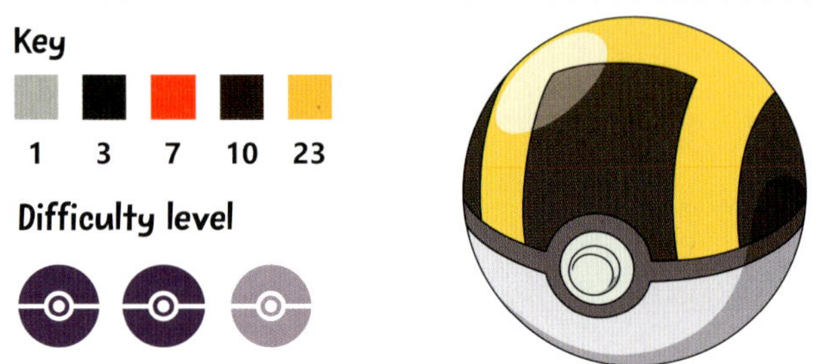

Vertical stripes
(3.5mm/E/4 hook)

Left

Assembly

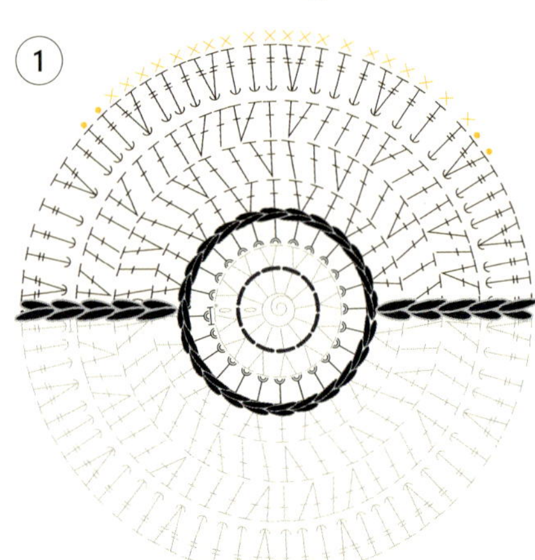

Right

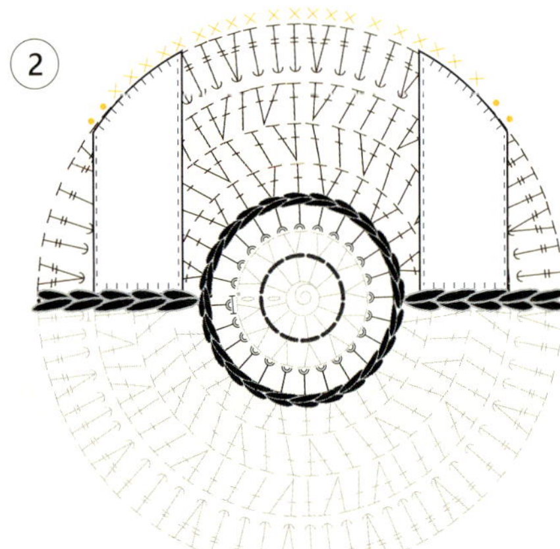

Square

Make the square by following the instructions for the Poké Ball (including shaping and finishing), but using **Color 10** for the upper shell, and **Color 7** for the background.

Left Vertical Stripe

Work in rows with **Color 23** and a 3.5mm hook.

Row 1: (WS) Ch 11, 2 sc in second ch from hook, sc in each ch across; turn = 11 sts

Row 2: (RS) Ch 1 (does not count as a st now and throughout), sc in each st across; turn

Row 3: (WS) Ch 1, 2 sc in first st, sc in each st across; turn = 12 sts

Row 4: (RS) as Row 2; fasten off, leaving a long tail for sewing

Right Vertical Stripe

Work in rows with **Color 23** and a 3.5mm hook.

Row 1: (WS) Ch 11, sc in second ch from hook, sc in next 8 chs, 2 sc in last ch; turn = 11 sts

Row 2: (RS) Ch 1 (does not count as a st now and throughout), sc in each st across; turn

Row 3: (WS) Ch 1, sc in each st to last st, 2 sc in last st; turn = 12 sts

Row 4: (RS) as Row 2; fasten off, leaving a long tail for sewing

Assembly

Finish the top, curved stripe with a 4mm hook—Mark 24 sts across the top edge and join **Color 23** with a sl st in first st, sl st in next st, sc in next 20 sts, sl st in last 2 sts. Fasten off and weave in the ends.

Position the vertical stripes as shown. Using **Color 23**, whipstitch across the top and bottom edges and backstitch across the side edges onto the ball. Finish off and weave in the ends.

Turtwig

The shell on this Pokémon's back is made of soil. If the shell is moist to the touch, Turtwig is very healthy.

Key

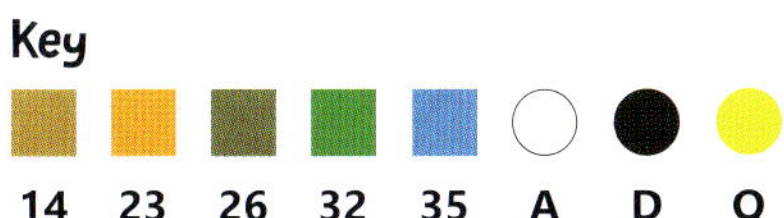

14 23 26 32 35 A D Q

Difficulty level

Type

Square

Make the square as for Chimchar, but using **Color 26** for the center, and **Color 35** for the background. Place marker in final join to indicate the left edge of the square.

Head Shaping

Holding the square with the stitch marker on the left, work around the head edge (Rnd 4 of the square) using **Color 26** and a 4mm hook.

Rnd 1: (RS) Work in FLO—join yarn with a standing sl st in first st, sl st in next 3 sts, ch 3, dc in next 4 sts, hdc in next 9 sts, dc in next 4 sts, ch 3, sl st in each st to end; join and fasten off, leaving a long tail for sewing = 48 sts and 2 ch-3

Row 2: (RS) Skip 4 sts and ch-3, join yarn with a standing dc in next st, dc in next 16 sts; turn, leaving the remaining sts unworked = 17 sts

Row 3: (WS) Ch 1 (does not count as a st now and throughout), hdc in each st across; turn = 17 sts

Row 4: (RS) Ch 1, hdc in each st across; fasten off and weave in the ends = 17 sts

Backstitch the bottom edges onto the square using **Color 26** from Rnd 1. Finish off and weave in the end.

(continued overleaf)

Square (4mm/G/6 hook)

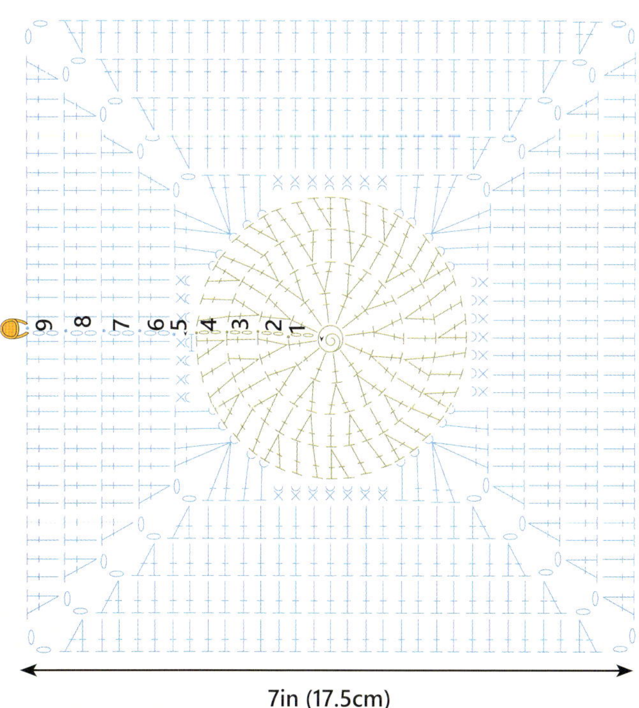

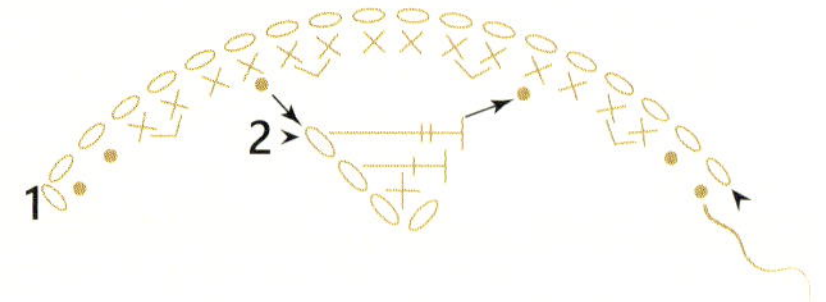

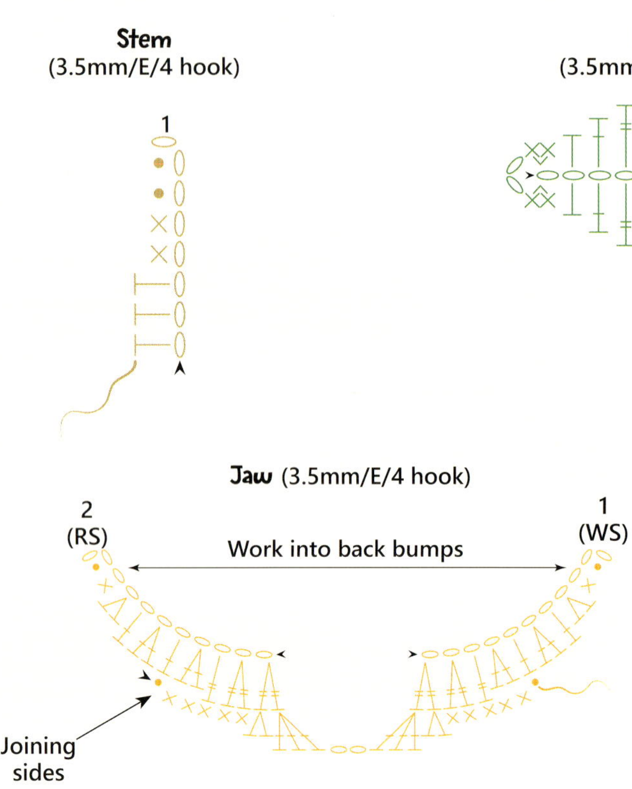

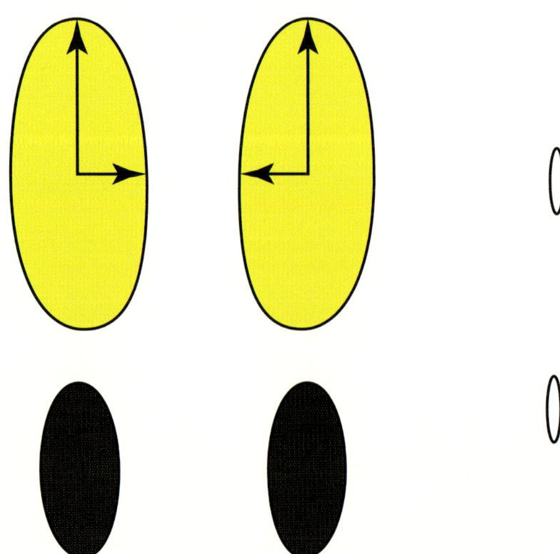

Jaw

Work in rows with **Color 23** and a 3.5mm hook.

Side 1: Ch 11; work into back bumps of the ch—sl st in second ch from hook, sc in next ch, 2 hdc in next ch, [dc in next ch, 2 dc in next ch] 2 times, tr in next ch, 2 tr in next 2 chs; fasten off = 15 sts

Side 2: As Side 1.

Joing sides: (RS) Hold side 1 on the left with WS facing you and side 2 on the right with RS facing you; join **Color 23** with a sl st in eighth st of side 2, sc in next 5 sts, 2 hdc in next st, 3 dc in last st, ch 2, 3 dc in last tr of side 2, 2 hdc in next st, sc in next 5 sts, sl st in next st, leave the remaining sts unworked; fasten off, leaving a long tail for sewing = 22 sts and 1 ch-2 sp

Leaf (make 2)

Work in the round with **Color 32** and a 3.5mm hook.

Row 1: Ch 10, 2 sc in second ch from hook, *hdc in next ch, dc in next ch, tr in next 3 chs, dc in next ch, hdc in next ch**, (2 sc, ch 2, 2 sc) in last ch; work across the opposite side of the foundation ch—repeat from * to **, 2 sc in last ch, ch 2; join = 22 sts and 2 ch-2 sps

Fasten off, leaving a long tail for sewing.

Stem

Work in rows with **Color 14** and a 3.5mm hook.

Row 1: Ch 8, sl st in second ch from hook, sl st in next ch, sc in next 2 chs, hdc in last 3 chs = 7 sts

Fasten off, leaving a long tail for sewing.

Stem Base

Work in rows with **Color 14** and a 3.5mm hook.

Row 1: (RS) Ch 19, sl st in second ch from hook, sl st in next ch, sc2tog, [sc in next 2 chs, sc2tog] 3 times, sl st in last 2 chs; fasten off, leaving a long tail for sewing; do not turn = 14 sts

Row 2: (RS) Join **Color 14** with a sl st in fifth st of Row 1, ch 4, sc in second ch from hook, dc in next ch, tr in next ch, skip 4 sts, sl st in next st; fasten off and weave in the ends = 5 sts

Assembly

Hold the square with the stitch marker on the left. Sew the jaw, stem base, stem, and leaves as shown. Finish off and weave in the ends; remove the marker from the square.

Cut out the indicated pieces from Felts A, D, and Q using the templates and assemble the layers to complete the eyes (see Working With Felt). Position the eyes as indicated, using pins to mark the main points. Glue the eyes onto the head and let them dry.

Thread the needle with 4-ply black yarn and stitch the nostrils as indicated. Finish off and weave in the ends.

Head shaping (4mm/G/6 hook)

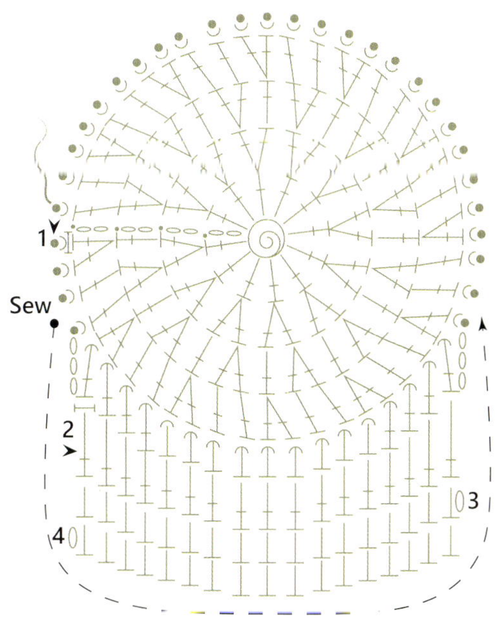

Assembly

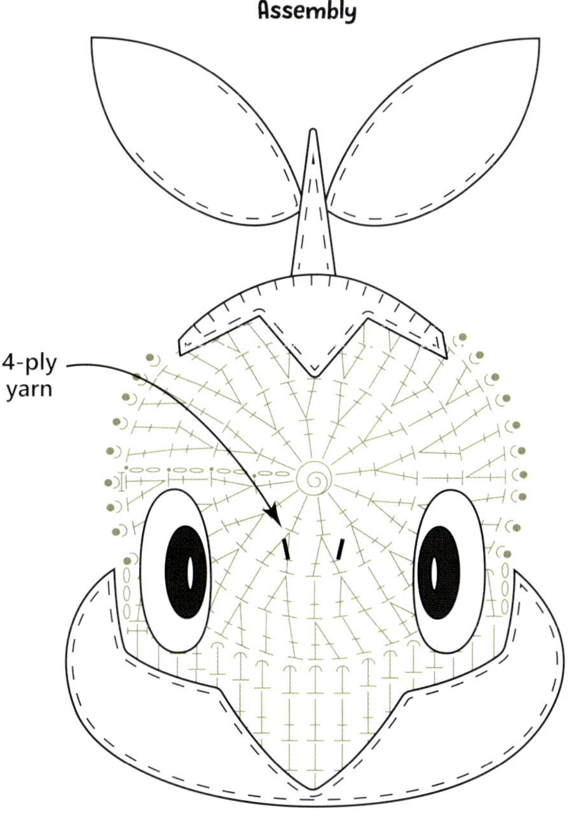

Squirtle

After birth, this Pokémon's back swells and hardens into a shell. It sprays a potent foam from its mouth.

Key

23 37 A D I

Difficulty level

Type

Square (4mm/G/6 hook)

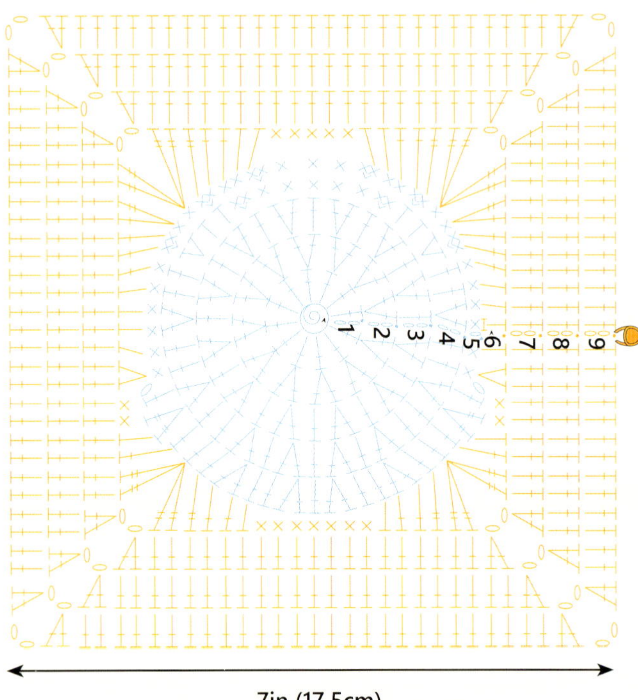

7in (17.5cm)

Square

Make a magic ring using **Color 37** and work in the round with a 4mm hook.

Follow Rnds 1–3 of Basic Circle (see Basic Shapes).

Rnd 4: Ch 2 (does not count as a st now and throughout), 2 dc in same st as join, dc in next 2 sts, 2 hdc in next st, hdc in next 2 sts, 2 sc in next st, sc in next 5 sts, 2 sc in next st, hdc in next 2 sts, 2 hdc in next st, [dc in next 2 sts, 2 dc in next st] 3 times, [dc in next st, 2 dc in next st] 3 times, dc in next 2 sts, 2 dc in next st, dc in last 2 sts; join = 48 sts

Rnd 5: Ch 1 (does not count as a st), sc in same st as join, sc in next 3 sts, *[2 sc in next st, sc in next 2 sts] 3 times**, sc in next st, repeat from * to **, sc in next 4 sts, ch 1, dc in next st, 2 tr in next st, dc in next 3 sts, 2 dc in next st, dc in next 2 sts, 2 dc in next st, dc in next st, 2 dc in next st, dc in next 2 sts, 2 dc in next st, dc in next 3 sts, 2 tr in next st, dc in next st, ch 1, sc in last 2 sts; join and fasten off without breaking off **Color 37**, hold it on WS (see Finishing/Surface Crochet) = 60 sts and 2 chs

Rnd 6: Join **Color 23** with a standing hdc in first st, hdc in next 2 sts, dc in next 3 sts, (dc, tr) in next st, (2 tr, ch 2, 2 tr) in next st; tr in next st, dc in next 2 sts, hdc in next 2 sts, sc in next 5 sts, hdc in next 2 sts, dc in next 2 sts, tr in next st, (2 tr, ch 2, 2 tr) in next st; (tr, dc) in next st, dc in next 3 sts, hdc in next 4 sts, 2 hdc in next st, skip ch, sc in next 2 sts, hdc in next st, dc in next st, (2 tr, ch 2, 2 tr) in next st; tr in next st, dc in next 2 sts, hdc in next st, sc in next 7 sts, hdc in next st, dc in next 2 sts, tr in next st, (2 tr, ch 2, 2 tr) in next st; dc in next st, hdc in next st, sc in next 2 sts, skip ch, 2 hdc in next st, hdc in last st; join = 76 sts and 4 ch-2 sps

Rnds 7–9: Ch 2, dc in same st as join, [dc in each st to next ch-2 sp, (2 dc, ch 2, 2 dc) in ch-2 sp] 4 times, dc in each st to end; join – 92/108/124 sts and 4 ch-2 sps

Place marker in final join to indicate the right edge of the square. Fasten off and weave in the ends.

Assembly

Hold the square with the stitch marker on the right.

Outline the head with **Color 37** by working surface sl sts between Rnds 5 and 6 with a 4mm hook, holding yarn on WS. Finish off seamlessly and weave in the end (see Finishing/Surface Crochet).

Cut out the indicated pieces from felts A, D, and I using the templates and assemble the layers to complete each eye (see Working With Felt). Position the eyes referring to the image; use pins to mark the main points. Glue the eyes onto the head and leave to dry. Thread the needle with a 4-ply white yarn and stitch the eye highlights as indicated. Finish off and weave in the ends.

Thread the needle with a 4-ply black yarn and stitch the mouth, nostrils, and eyebrows as indicated. Use straight pins to mark the main points prior to stitching. Finish off and weave in the ends; remove the marker from the square.

Felt templates

Outer edge

Outer edge

Assembly

Tepig

This Pokémon is more nimble than it looks, and it uses its speed to confound its enemies. It rapidly launches fireballs from both nostrils.

Key

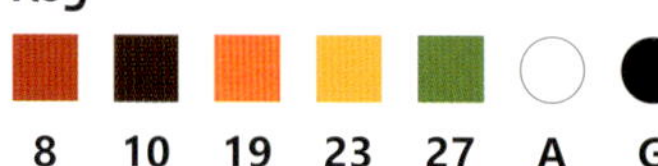

8 10 19 23 27 A G

Difficulty level

Type

Square (4mm/G/6 hook)

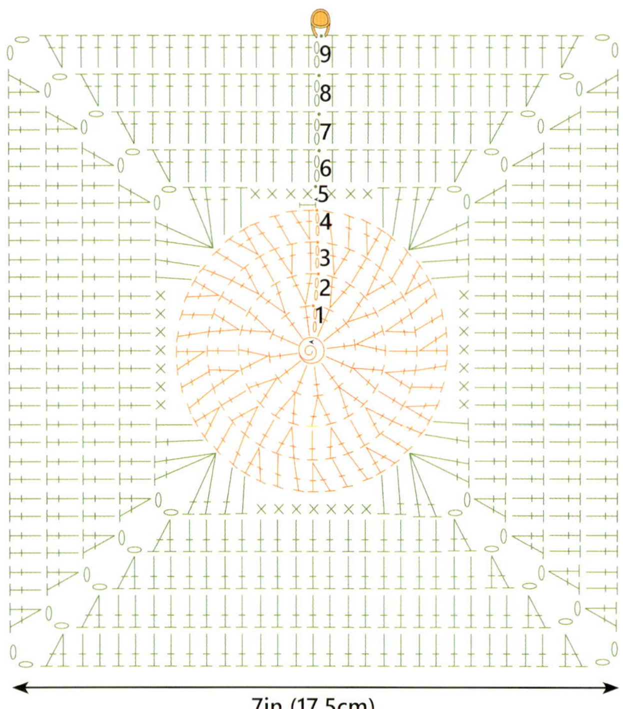

Patch (3.5mm/E/4 hook)

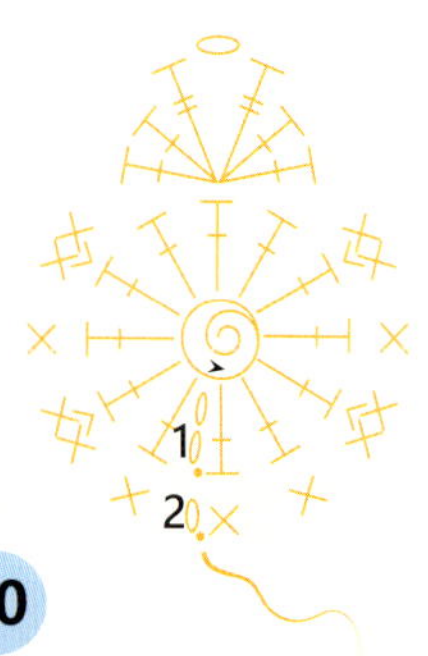

Snout (3.5mm/E/4 hook)

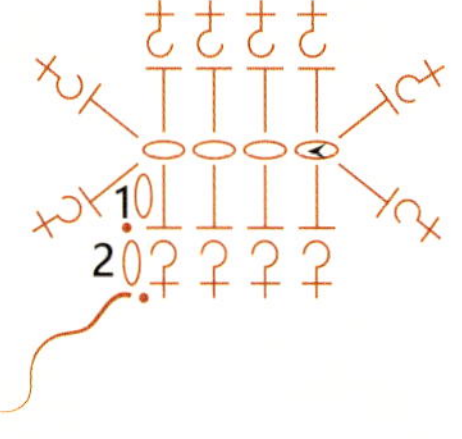

Square

Make a magic ring using **Color 19** and work in the round with a 4mm hook.

Follow Rnds 1–4 of Basic Circle (see Basic Shapes).

Fasten off without breaking off **Color 19**, hold it on WS (see Finishing/Surface Crochet).

Rnd 5: Join **Color 27** with a standing sc in first st, sc in next 3 sts, hdc in next st, dc in next st, (2 dc, ch 2, 2 dc) in next st; [dc in next st, hdc in next st, sc in next 7 sts, hdc in next st, dc in next st, (2 dc, ch 2, 2 dc) in next st] 3 times; dc in next st, hdc in next st, sc in last 3 sts; join = 60 sts and 4 ch-2 sps

Rnds 6–9: Ch 2 (does not count as a st), dc in same st as join, [dc in each st to next ch-2 sp, (2 dc, ch 2, 2 dc) in ch-2 sp] 4 times, dc in each st to end; join = 76/92/108/124 sts and 4 ch-2 sps

Place marker in final join to indicate the top of the square. Fasten off and weave in the ends.

Patch

Make a magic ring using **Color 23** and work in the round with a 3.5mm hook.

Rnd 1: Ch 2 (does not count as a st); 12 dc in ring; join = 12 sts

Rnd 2: Ch 1 (does not count as a st), sc in same st as join, [sc in next st, 2 sc in next st] 2 times, skip st, (2 dc, tr, ch 1, tr, 2 dc) in next st, skip st, [2 sc in next st, sc in next st] 2 times; join = 19 sts and 1 ch-1 sp; join and fasten off, leaving a long tail for sewing.

Snout

Work in the round with **Color 8** and a 3.5mm hook.

Rnd 1: Ch 5, hdc in second ch from hook, hdc in next 2 chs, 4 hdc in last ch; work across the opposite side of the foundation ch—hdc in next 2 chs, 3 hdc in last ch; join = 12 sts

Rnd 2: Ch 1 (does not count as a st), bpsc in each st around; join and fasten off, leaving a long tail for sewing = 12 sts

Upper Head

Make a magic ring using **Color 10** and work in rows with a 3.5mm hook.

Row 1: (RS) Ch 1 (does not count as a st now and throughout), 3 sc in ring; turn without joining = 3 sts

Row 2: (WS) Ch 1, 2 sc in first st, 3 sc in next st, 2 sc in last st; turn =7 sts

Row 3: (RS) Ch 1, sc in first st, 2 sc in next st, sc in next 3 sts, 2 sc in next st, sc in last st; turn = 9 sts

Row 4: (WS) Ch 1, 2 sc in first st, [sc in next 3 sts, 2 sc in next st] 2 times; turn = 12 sts

Row 5: (RS) Ch 3 (counts as dc), skip first st, dc in next st, [dc in next st, 2 dc in next st] 2 times, [2 dc in next st, dc in next st] 2 times, dc in last 2 sts; do not turn = 16 sts

Row 6: (RS) Work evenly across the raw edge of the half-circle—sc, hdc, 2 dc, 3 tr, 2 dc, hdc, sc, sl st in top of beg ch-3 in Row 5; do not turn; fasten off, leaving a long tail for sewing = 11 sts

Row 7: (RS) Join **Color 10** with a sl st in fourth st of Row 6, [ch 14, sc in second ch from hook, hdc in next ch, dc in next ch, tr in next 7 chs, dc in next ch, hdc in next ch, sc in next ch, skip tr, sl st in next st] 2 times = 14 sts in each ear and 3 sl sts

Fasten off, leaving a long tail for sewing.

Assembly

Hold the square with the stitch marker at the top. Outline the head with **Color 19** by working surface sl sts between Rnds 4 and 5 with a 4mm hook, holding yarn on WS. Finish off seamlessly and weave in the end (see Finishing/ Surface Crochet). Position the upper head as shown. Using **Color 10**, backstitch around the edges onto the square, leaving the tips of the ears unstitched. Position the patch as shown and backstitch around the edge onto the upper head with **Color 23**. Finish off and weave in the ends; remove the marker from the square.

Position the snout as shown and whipstitch around the edge onto the head using **Color 8**; finish off and weave in the end. Cut out the indicated pieces from Felts A and G using the templates and assemble the layers to complete the eyes (see Working With Felt). Position the eyes as shown; use pins to mark the main points. Glue the eyes onto the head and leave to dry.

Thread the needle with a 4-ply black yarn and stitch the nostrils and mouth as indicated. Use straight pins to mark the main points prior to stitching. Finish off and weave in the ends.

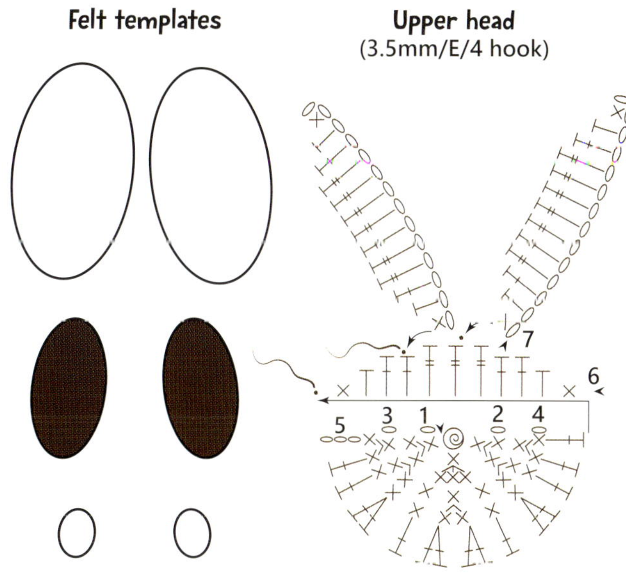

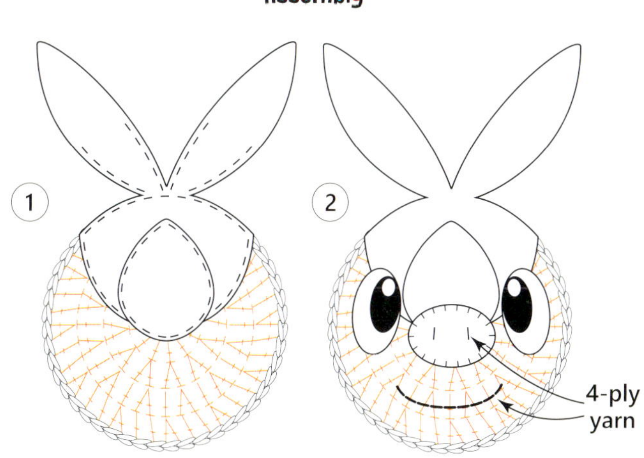

Sprigatito

This Pokémon frequently washes its face to keep it from drying out. Its fluffy fur is similar in composition to plants.

Key

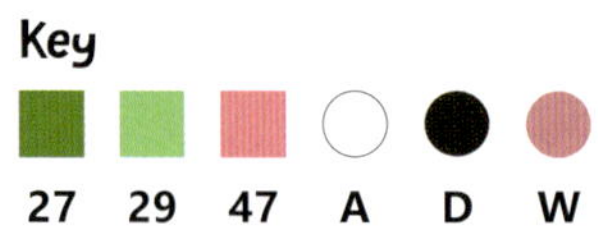

27 29 47 A D W

Difficulty level

Type

Square (4mm/G/6 hook)

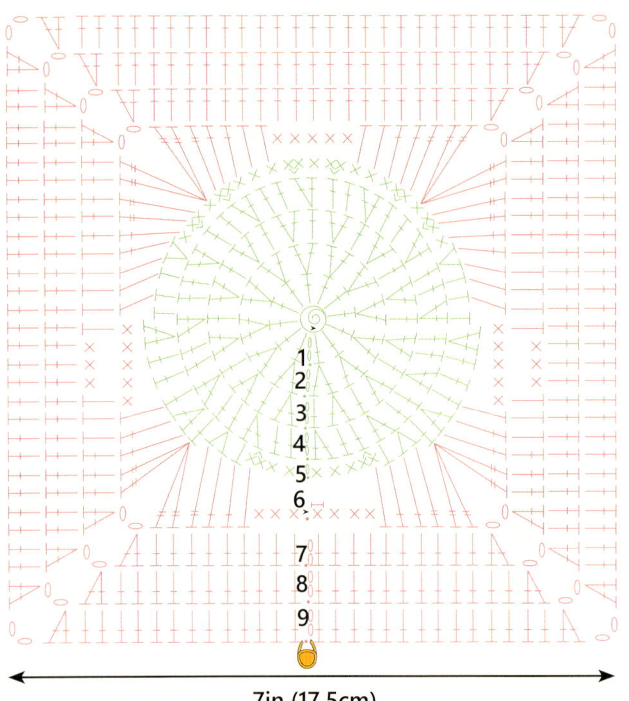

Face mark (3.5mm/E/4 hook)

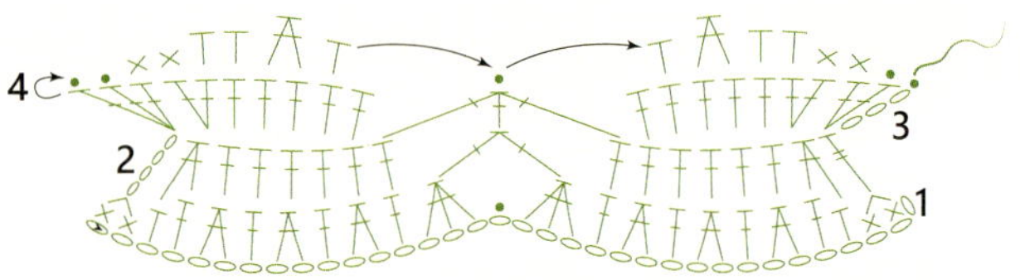

Square

Make a magic ring using **Color 29** and work in the round with a 4mm hook.

Follow Rnds 1–4 of Basic Circle (see Basic Shapes).

Rnd 5: Ch 1 (does not count as a st), sc in same st as join, sc in next 2 sts, 2 sc in next st, hdc in next st, 2 hdc in next st, dc in next st, 2 dc in next st, dc in next 3 sts, 2 dc in next st, hdc in next 3 sts, 2 hdc in next st, [sc in next st, 2 sc in next st] 2 times, sc in next 3 sts, 2 sc in next st, sc in next st, 2 sc in next st, sc in next 3 sts, [2 sc in next st, sc in next st] 2 times, 2 hdc in next st, hdc in next 3 sts, 2 dc in next st, dc in next 3 sts, 2 dc in next st, dc in next st, 2 hdc in next st, hdc in next st, 2 sc in next st, sc in last 2 sts; join and fasten off without breaking off **Color 29**, hold it on WS (see Finishing /Surface Crochet) = 64 sts

Rnd 6: Join **Color 47** with a standing sc in first st, sc in next 3 sts, hdc in next st, dc in next 2 sts, tr in next st, (2 tr, ch 2, 2 tr) in next st; dc in next 2 sts, hdc in next st, sc in next 5 sts, hdc in next 3 sts, dc in next 2 sts, tr in next 2 sts, (2 tr, ch 2, 2 tr) in next st; tr in next st, dc in next 2 sts, hdc in next 2 sts, sc in next 5 sts, hdc in next 2 sts, dc in next 2 sts, tr in next st, (2 tr, ch 2, 2 tr) in next st; tr in next 2 sts, dc in next 2 sts, hdc in next 3 sts, sc in next 5 sts, hdc in next st, dc in next 2 sts, (2 tr, ch 2, 2 tr) in next st; tr in next st, dc in next 2 sts, hdc in next st, sc in last 3 sts; join = 76 sts and 4 ch-2 sps

Rnd 7: Ch 2 (does not count as a st now and throughout), dc in same st as join, *dc in each st to next ch-2 sp, (2 dc, ch 2, 2 dc) in ch-2 sp**; dc in next 3 sts, hdc in next 3 sts, sc in next 3 sts, hdc in next 5 sts, repeat from * to ** 2 times; dc in next 5 sts, hdc in next

5 sts, sc in next 3 sts, hdc in next 3 sts, repeat from * to **; dc in each st to end; join = 92 sts and 4 ch-2 sps

Rnds 8–9: Ch 2, dc in same st as join, [dc in each st to next ch-2 sp, (2 dc, ch 2, 2 dc) in ch-2 sp] 4 times, dc in each st to end; join = 108 /124 sts and 4 ch-2 sps

Place marker in final join to indicate the bottom of the square. Fasten off and weave in the ends.

Face Mark

Work in rows with **Color 27** and a 3.5mm hook.

Row 1: (RS) Ch 34, skip first ch from hook, sc2tog, hdc in next st, dc in next st, [dc2tog, dc in next st] 3 times, dc3tog, sl st in next st, dc3tog, [dc in next st, dc2tog] 3 times, dc in next st, hdc in next st, sc2tog; turn = 21 sts

Row 2: (WS) Ch 4 (counts as tr), skip first st, dc2tog, dc in next 6 sts, dc2tog while skipping sl st in the middle, dc in next 6 sts, dc2tog, tr in last st; turn = 17 sts

Row 3: (RS) Ch 3 (counts as dc), 2 dc in first st, 2 dc in next st, dc in next 5 sts, dc3tog, dc in next 5 sts, 2 dc in next st, 3 dc in last st; turn = 21 sts

Row 4: (WS) Sl st in first and second sts, sc in next 2 sts, hdc in next 2 sts, dc2tog, hdc in next st, skip st, sl st in next st, skip st, hdc in next st, dc2tog, hdc in next 2 sts, sc in next 2 sts, sl st in last 2 sts = 17 sts

Fasten off, leaving a long tail for sewing.

Left Ear

Work in rows with **Color 29** and a 4mm hook.

Row 1: (WS) Ch 4, sc in second ch from hook, sc in next ch, (2 sc, ch 2, 2 sc) in last ch; work across the opposite side of the foundation ch—sc in last 2 chs; turn = 8 sts and ch-2 sp

Row 2: (RS) Ch 3 (counts as dc), skip first st, dc in next st, hdc in next st, sc in next st, (2 sc, ch 2, 2 sc) in ch-2 sp, sc in next st, hdc in next st, dc in next st, 2 dc in last st; fasten off, leaving an extra long tail for surface crochet and sewing; do not turn = 13 sts

Row 3: (RS) Join **Color 27** with a standing dc in top of beg ch-3 in Row 2, dc in same st, dc in next 5 sts, (2 dc, tr, ch 1, tr, 2 dc) in ch-2 sp, dc in next 3 sts, 2 dc in next st, dc in next 2 sts, (dc, 2 tr) in last st; fasten off **Color 27**; do not turn = 23 sts and ch-1 sp

Row 4: (RS) Pick up **Color 29** and wrap around the hook once (1 loop on the hook), hold the yarn on WS; work surface sl sts between Rows 2 and 3; fasten off, leaving a long tail for sewing = 14 sts

Right Ear

Begin by working in rows with **Color 29** and a 4mm hook.

Rows 1–2: As for Left Ear, but start on RS and turn after each row

(continued overleaf)

Ears (4mm/G/6 hook)

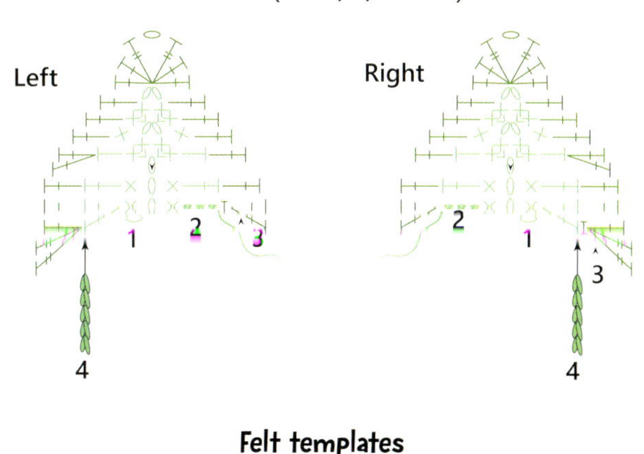

Whiskers (3mm/D/3 hook)

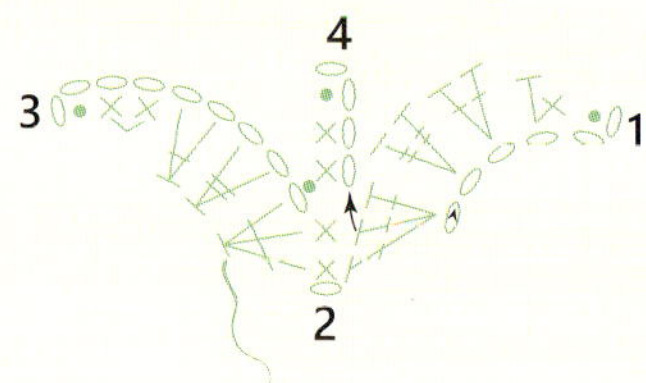

Assembly

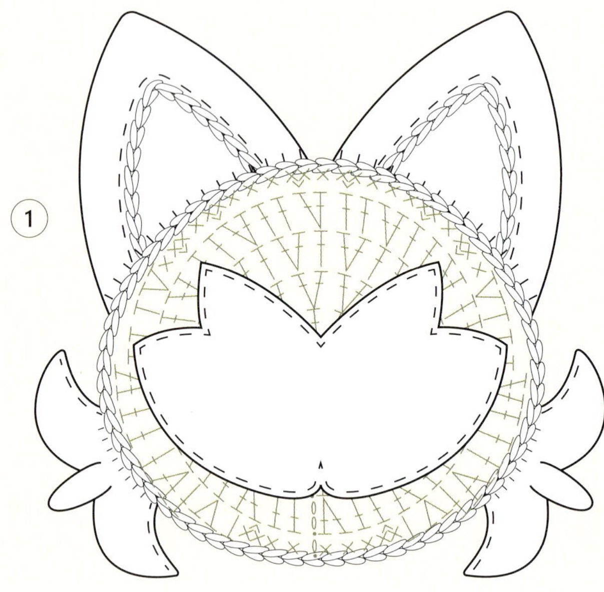

Row 3: (RS) Join **Color 27** with a standing tr in first st, (tr, dc) in same st, dc in next 2 sts, 2 dc in next st, dc in next 3 sts, (2 dc, tr, ch 1, tr, 2 dc) in ch-2 sp, dc in next 5 sts, 2 dc in last st; fasten off **Color 27**; do not turn = 23 sts and ch-1 sp

Row 4: As for Left Ear

Whiskers (make 2)

Work in rows with **Color 29** and a 3mm hook.

Row 1: (RS) Ch 6, sl st in second ch from hook, (sc, hdc) in next ch, 2 dc in next ch, 2 tr in next ch, 3 dc in last ch, turn = 10 sts

Row 2: (WS) Ch 1 (does not count as a st), sc in first st, sc in next st and place marker in same st; turn, leaving the remaining sts unworked = 2 sts

Row 3: (RS) Ch 9, sl st in second ch from hook, sc2tog, dc2tog, tr2tog, dc3tog; fasten off, leaving a long tail for sewing; do not turn = 5 sts

Row 4: (RS) Join **Color 29** with a sl st in st with marker and remove the marker; ch 4, sl st in second ch from hook, sc in next 2 chs, skip sc of Row 2, sl st in next st; fasten off and weave in the ends = 3 sts

Assembly

Hold the square with the stitch marker at the bottom. Outline the head with **Color 29** by working surface sl sts between Rnds 5 and 6 with a 4mm hook, holding yarn on WS. Fasten off seamlessly and weave in the end (see Finishing/Surface Crochet).

Position the ears, face mark, and whiskers as shown. Using **Color 29**, whipstitch the ears across the bottom edge onto the square and backstitch around the row of surface sl sts; leave the outer edges unstitched. Using **Color 27**, backstitch around the face mark onto the head. Using **Color 29**, whipstitch the whiskers across the raw edge onto the square and backstitch across the side edges; leave the remaining edges unstitched. Finish off and weave in ends; remove the marker from the square.

Cut out the indicated pieces from Felts A, D, and W using the templates and assemble the layers to complete the eyes (see Working With Felt). Position the eyes and nose as indicated, using pins to mark the main points. Glue all pieces onto the head and let them dry.

Thread the needle with 4-ply black yarn and stitch the mouth as indicated. Finish off, weave in ends.

Chimchar

This Pokémon is very agile. Before going to sleep, it extinguishes the flame on its tail to prevent fires

Key

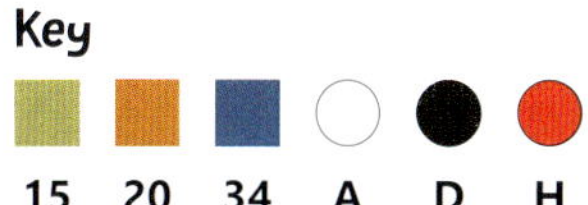

15 20 34 A D H

Difficulty level

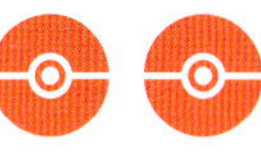

Type

Square

Make a magic ring using **Color 15** and work in the round with a 4mm hook.

Follow Rnds 1–4 of Basic Circle (see Basic Shapes).

Rnd 5: Work in BLO—Join **Color 34** with a standing sc in first st, sc in next 3 sts, hdc in next st, dc in next st, (2 dc, ch 2, 2 dc) in next st, dc in next st, hdc in next st, [sc in next 7 sts, hdc in next st, dc in next st, (2 dc, ch 2, 2 dc) in next st, dc in next st, hdc in next st] 3 times, sc in last 3 sts; join = 60 sts and 4 ch-2 sps

Rnds 6–9: Ch 2 (does not count as a st), dc in same st as join, [dc in each st to next ch-2 sp, (2 dc, ch 2, 2 dc) in ch-2 sp] 4 times, dc in each st to end; join = 76/92/108/124 sts and 4 ch-2 sps

Place marker in final join to indicate the top of the square. Fasten off and weave in the ends.

Head Shaping

Holding the square with the stitch marker at the top edge, work around the head edge (Rnd 4 of the square) with a 4mm hook.

Rnd 1: (RS) Work in FLO—Join **Color 20** with a standing hdc in first st, [hdc in next 3 sts, 2 hdc in next st] 2 times, hdc in next st, sc in next st, sl st in next 2 sts; break off **Color 20**, leaving a long tail for sewing; continue with **Color 15**—sl st in next 4 sts, sc in next st, 2 hdc in next st, hdc in next st, 2 hdc in next st, sl st in next st, hdc in next st, 2 dc in next st, dc in next st, 2 dc in next st, hdc in next st, sl st in next st, 2 hdc in next st, hdc in next st, 2 hdc in next st, sc in next st, sl st in next 4 sts, break off **Color 15**, leaving a long tail for sewing; continue with **Color 20**—sl st in next 2 sts, sc in next st, hdc in next st, [2 hdc in next st, hdc in next 3 sts] 2 times; join = 58 sts

(continued overleaf)

Square (4mm/G/6 hook)

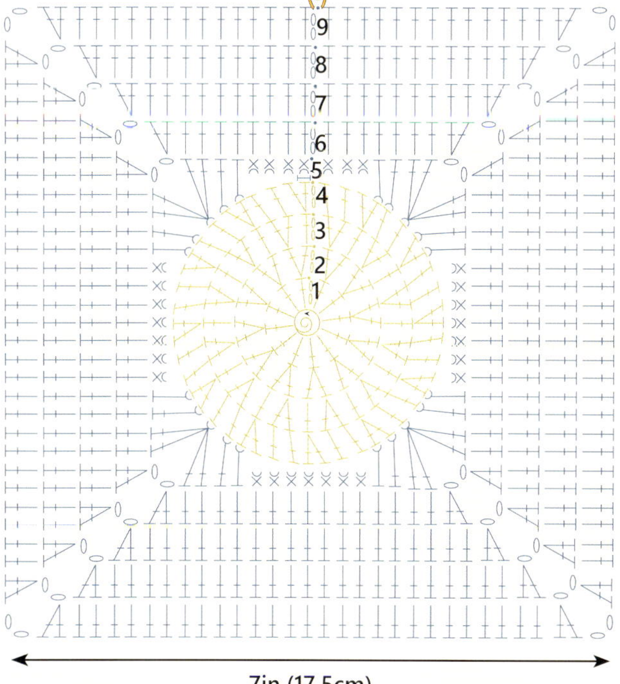

Head shaping (4mm/G/6 hook)

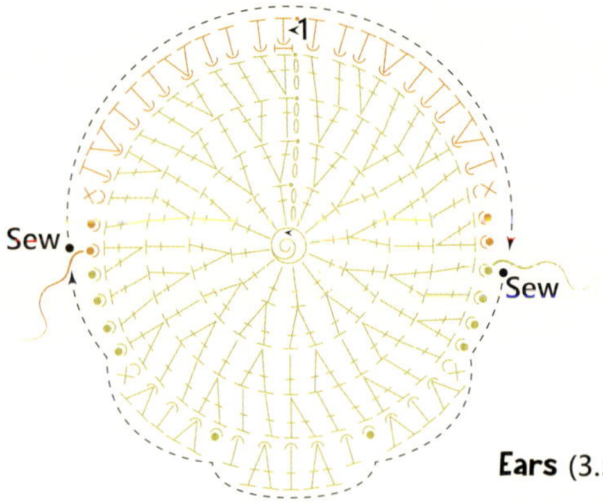

Sew

Sew

Ears (3.5mm/E/4 hook)

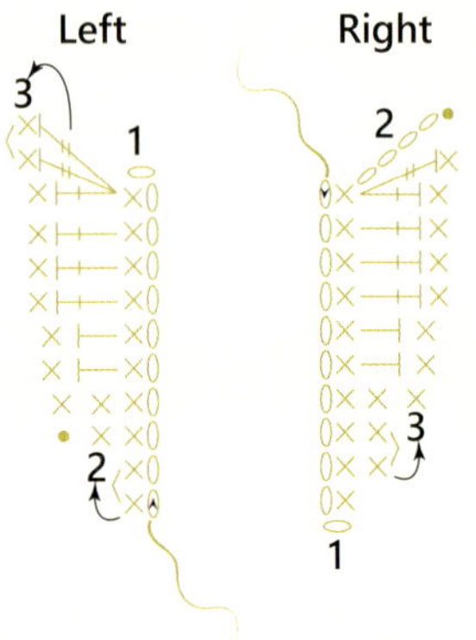

Left

Right

Felt templates

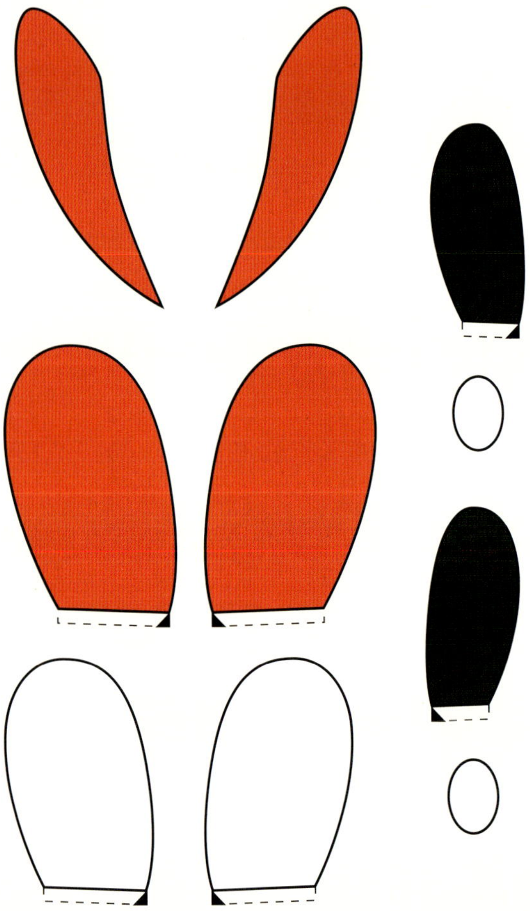

Backstitch the top and bottom edges onto the square using the corresponding color yarn tails. Finish off and weave in the ends.

Left Ear

Work in rows with **Color 15** and a 3.5mm hook.

Row 1: (RS) Ch 11, leaving a long tail at beg for sewing; sc in second ch from hook, sc in next 7 chs, sc2tog; turn = 9 sts

Row 2: (WS) Skip st just made, sc in next 2 sts, hdc in next 2 sts, dc in next 3 sts, (dc, 2 tr) in last st; turn = 10 sts

Row 3: (RS) Do not skip first st, sc2tog, sc in next 7 sts, sl st in last st = 9 sts

Fasten off and weave in the end.

Right Ear

Work in rows with **Color 15** and a 3.5mm hook.

Row 1: (RS) Ch 11, leaving a long tail at beg for sewing; sc in second ch from hook, sc in next 9 chs; turn = 10 sts

Row 2: (WS) Ch 4 (counts as tr), (tr, dc) in first st, dc in next 3 sts, hdc in next 2 sts, sc in next st, sc2tog; turn = 10 sts

Row 3: (RS) Skip st just made, sc in next 8 sts, sl st in last st = 9 sts

Fasten off and weave in the end.

Top Curl

Work in rows with **Color 20** and a 3.5mm hook.

Row 1: (RS) Ch 12, sl st in second ch from hook, sl st in next ch, sc2tog, hdc in next ch, (dc2tog ch 3, sl st in same ch), sc2tog, (hdc, dc) in next ch, dc in last ch, ch 4 (counts as tr), sl st in same ch; do not turn = 10 sts

Row 2: (RS) Work across the opposite side of the foundation ch—ch 1, sc in first ch, sc in next 2 chs, sc2tog, sl st in next ch; fasten off, leaving the remaining chs unworked and weave in the ends; do not turn = 5 sts

Row 3: (RS) Join yarn with a standing tr in first st of Row 2, leaving a long tail at the beg for sewing; dc2tog, ch 2 (counts as dc), sl st in next st; fasten off and weave in the end = 3 sts

Hair

Work in rows with **Color 20** and a 3.5mm hook.

Row 1: (WS) Ch 8, sc in second ch from hook, sc in next 5 chs, (2 sc, ch 2, 2 sc) in last ch; work across the opposite side of the foundation ch—sc in next 6 chs; turn = 16 sts and 1 ch-2 sp

Row 2: (RS) Ch 3 (counts as dc), place marker in top of beg ch for future reference; skip first st, dc in next 4 sts, hdc in next st, sc in next 2 sts, (2 sc, ch 2, 2 sc) in next ch-2 sp, sc in next 2 sts, hdc in next st, dc in last 5 sts; turn = 20 sts and 1 ch-2 sp

Row 3. (WS) Ch 1 (does not count as a st), sc in first st, sc in next 4 sts, ch 4; turn, leaving the remaining sts unworked = 5 sts and ch-4

Row 4: (RS) Sl st in second ch from hook, sc in next ch, hdc in next ch, 2 dc in next st, dc in next 2 sts, dc2tog; turn = 8 sts

Row 5: (WS) Ch 4 (counts as tr), skip first st, tr2tog; turn and fasten off, leaving a long tail for sewing = 2 sts

Row 6: (RS) Join yarn with a standing sc in st with marker (the beg of Rnd 2) and remove the marker, sc in next 4 sts, ch 4; turn, leaving the remaining sts unworked = 5 sts and ch-4

Rows 7–8: As Rows 4–5, ending on RS

Assembly

Holding the square with the stitch marker at the top, position the hair as shown. Using **Color 20**, whipstitch the top edge of the hair onto the head, then backstitch across the bottom edge, leaving the center points unstitched. Position the curl on the top of the head; whipstitch across the bottom edge and backstitch the sides partially, leaving the top point unstitched. Position the ears on each side of the head and whipstitch across the inner edges, leaving the outer edges unstitched. Finish off and weave in the ends; remove the marker from the square.

Cut out the indicated pieces from Felts A, D, and H, using the templates and assemble the layers to complete the eyes (see Working With Felt). Position and glue the eyes and ear inserts onto the head. Let the glue dry. Thread the needle with 4-ply black yarn and stitch the nostrils and eyebrows as indicated. Finish off and weave in the ends.

Hair (3.5mm/E/4 hook)

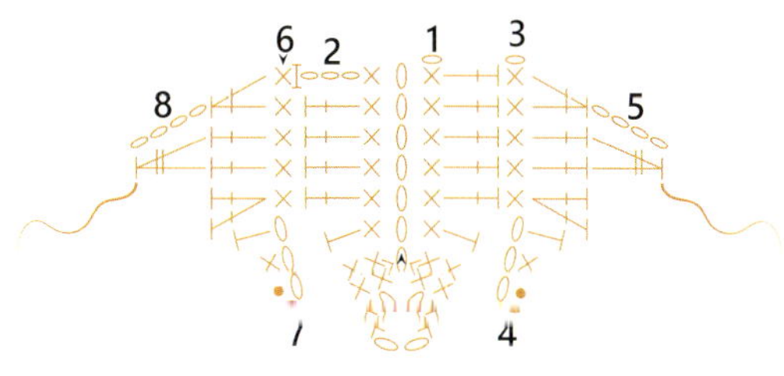

Top curl (3.5mm/E/4 hook)

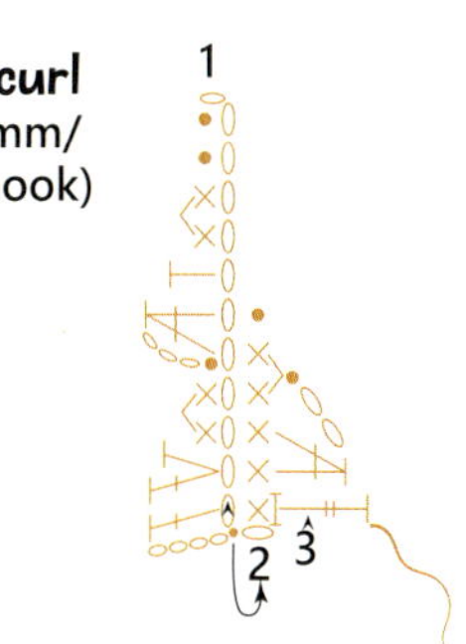

Assembly

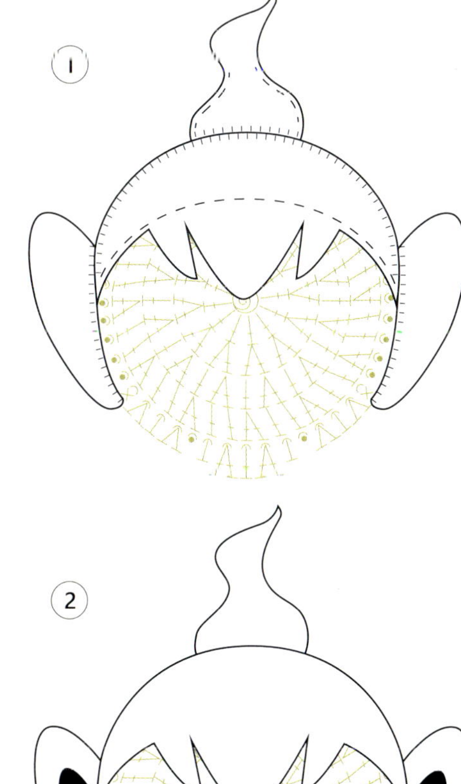

Rowlet

Silently it glides, streaking toward its targets to get close to them. Before they even notice it, it begins to pelt them with vicious kicks.

Key

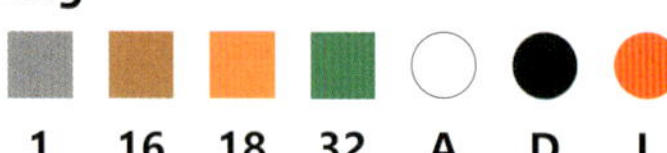

1 16 18 32 A D L

Difficulty level

Type

Square (4mm/G/6 hook)

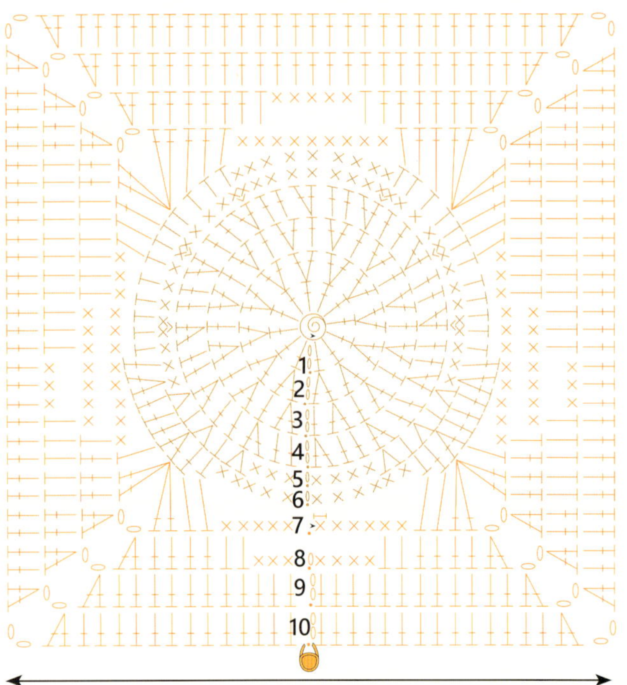

Square

Make a magic ring using **Color 16** and work in the round with a 4mm hook.

Follow Rnds 1–4 of Basic Circle (see Basic Shapes).

Rnd 5: Ch 1 (does not count as a st now and throughout), sc in same st as join, sc in next 3 sts, 2 hdc in next st, [hdc in next st, 2 hdc in next st] 2 times, [sc in next 3 sts, 2 sc in next st] 3 times, sc in next 7 sts, [2 sc in next st, sc in next 3 sts] 3 times, [2 hdc in next st, hdc in next st] 2 times, 2 hdc in next st, sc in last 3 sts; join = 60 sts

Rnd 6: Ch 1, sc in same st as join, sc in next 5 sts, hdc in next st; *dc in next st, 2 dc in next st, dc in next 3 sts, 2 dc in next st, dc in next st**; hdc in next 12 sts, sc in next 9 sts, hdc in next 12 sts; repeat from * to **; hdc in next st, sc in last 5 sts; join and fasten off without breaking off **Color 16**, hold it on WS (see Finishing/Surface Crochet) = 64 sts

Rnd 7: Join **Color 18** with a standing sc in first st, sc in next 5 sts, hdc in next 2 sts, (2 dc, ch 2, 2 dc) in next st; hdc in next st, sc in next 11 sts, hdc in next 2 sts, dc in next st, (2 dc, ch 2, 2 dc) in next st; dc in next 2 sts, hdc in next st, sc in next 9 sts, hdc in next st, dc in next 2 sts, (2 dc, ch 2, 2 dc) in next st; dc in next st, hdc in next 2 sts, sc in next 11 sts, hdc in next st, (2 dc, ch 2, 2 dc) in next st; hdc in next 2 sts, sc in last 5 sts; join = 76 sts and 4 ch-2 sps

Rnd 8: Ch 1, sc in same st as join, sc in next 3 sts, hdc in next 2 sts, *dc in each st to next ch-2 sp, (2 dc, ch 2, 2 dc) in ch-2 sp**; dc in next 3 sts, hdc in next st, sc in next 7 sts, hdc in next 6 sts, repeat from * to **; dc in next 6 sts, hdc in next st, sc in next 5 sts, hdc in next st, repeat from * to **; dc in next 2 sts, hdc in next 6 sts, sc in next 7 sts, repeat from * to **; dc in next 4 sts, hdc in next 2 sts, sc in last 3 sts; join = 92 sts and 4 ch-2 sps

Rnd 9: Ch 2 (does not count as a st now and throughout), dc in same st as join, *dc in each st to next ch-2 sp, (2 dc, ch 2, 2 dc) in ch-2 sp**; dc in next 2 sts, hdc in next 5 sts, sc in next 3 sts, hdc in next 11 sts, repeat from * to ** 2 times; dc in next 2 sts, hdc in next 11 sts, sc in next 3 sts, hdc in next 5 sts, repeat from * to **; dc in each st to end; join = 108 sts and 4 ch-2 sps

Rnd 10: Ch 2, dc in same st as join, [dc in each st to next ch-2 sp, (2 dc, ch 2, 2 dc) in ch-2 sp] 4 times, dc in each st to end; join = 124 sts and 4 ch-2 sps

Place marker in final join to indicate the bottom of the square. Fasten off and weave in the ends.

Face Piece (make 2)

Work in the round with **Color 1** and a 3.5mm hook.

Rnd 1: Ch 5, sc in second ch from hook, sc in next 2 chs, 3 sc in last ch; work across the opposite side of the foundation ch—sc in next 2 chs, 2 sc in last ch; join = 10 sts

Rnd 2: Ch 1 (does not count as a st now and throughout), 3 sc in same st as join, sc in next 2 sts, 3 sc in next st, sc in next st, 2 sc in next st, sc in next 2 sts, 2 sc in next st, sc in last st; join = 16 sts

Rnd 3: Ch 1, sc in same st as join, 3 sc in next st, sc in next 4 sts, 3 sc in next st, sc in next 2 sts, 2 sc in next st, sc in next 4 sts, 2 sc in next st, sc in last st; join = 22 sts

Rnd 4: Ch 1, sc in same st as join, sc in next st, 3 sc in next st, sc in next 6 sts, 3 sc in next st, sc in next 5 sts, 2 sc in next st, sc in next 2 sts, 2 sc in next st, sc in last 3 sts; join = 28 sts

Rnd 5. Ch 1, hdc in same st as join, hdc in next 2 sts, 3 sc in next st, sc in next 8 sts, 3 sc in next st, hdc in next 4 sts, 2 sc in next st, sc in next 8 sts, 2 sc in next st, hdc in last st; join = 34 sts

Fasten off, leaving a long tail for sewing. Place two face pieces side by side with their straight edges touching and whipstitch across 10 sts in the center. Finish off and weave in one of the tails.

Beak

Work in the round using **Color 1** and a 3.5mm hook.

Rnd 1: Ch 6, sc in second ch from hook, sc in next 3 chs, 3 sc in last ch; work across the opposite side of the foundation ch—sc in next 3 chs, 2 sc in last ch; join = 12 sts

Rnd 2: Ch 1 (does not count as a st), sc in same st as join, hdc in next 3 sts, sc in next st, 4 sc in next st, sc in next st, hdc in next 3 sts, sc in next st, 4 sc in last st; join = 18 sts

Fasten off, leaving a long tail for sewing.

Bow

Work in the round using **Color 32** and a 4mm hook.

Rnd 1: Ch 11, sc in second ch from hook, sc in next 8 chs, 3 sc in last ch; work across the opposite side of the foundation ch—sc in next 8 chs, 2 sc in last ch; join = 22 sts

(continued overleaf)

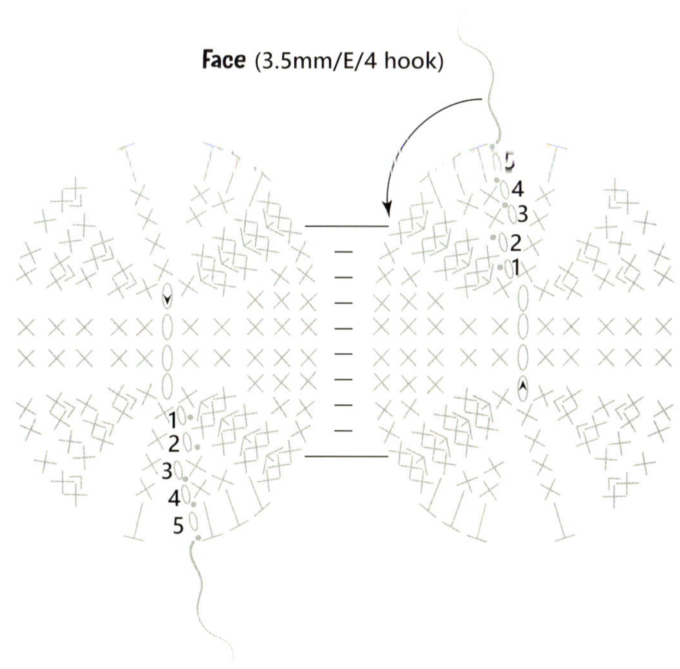

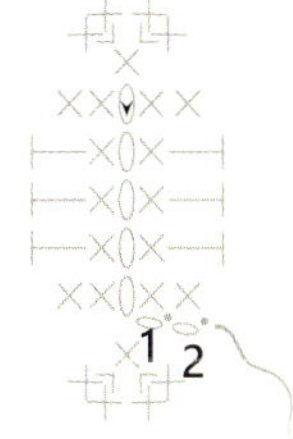

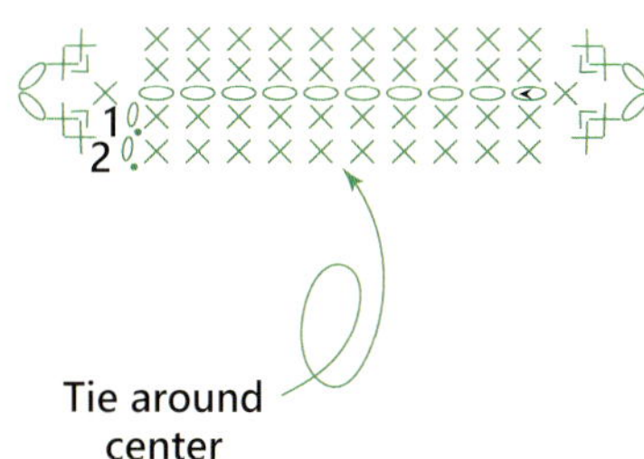

Felt templates

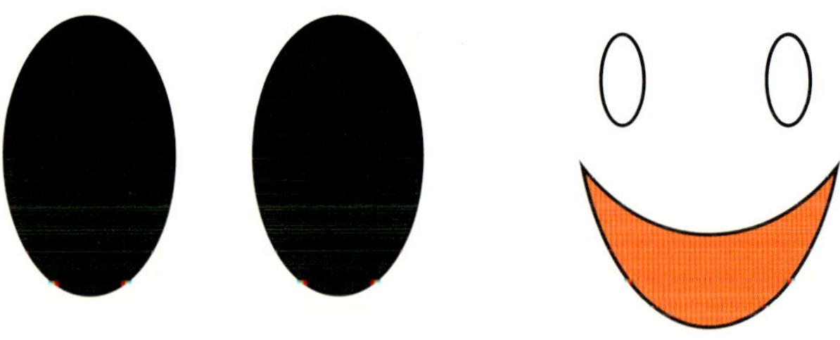

Assembly

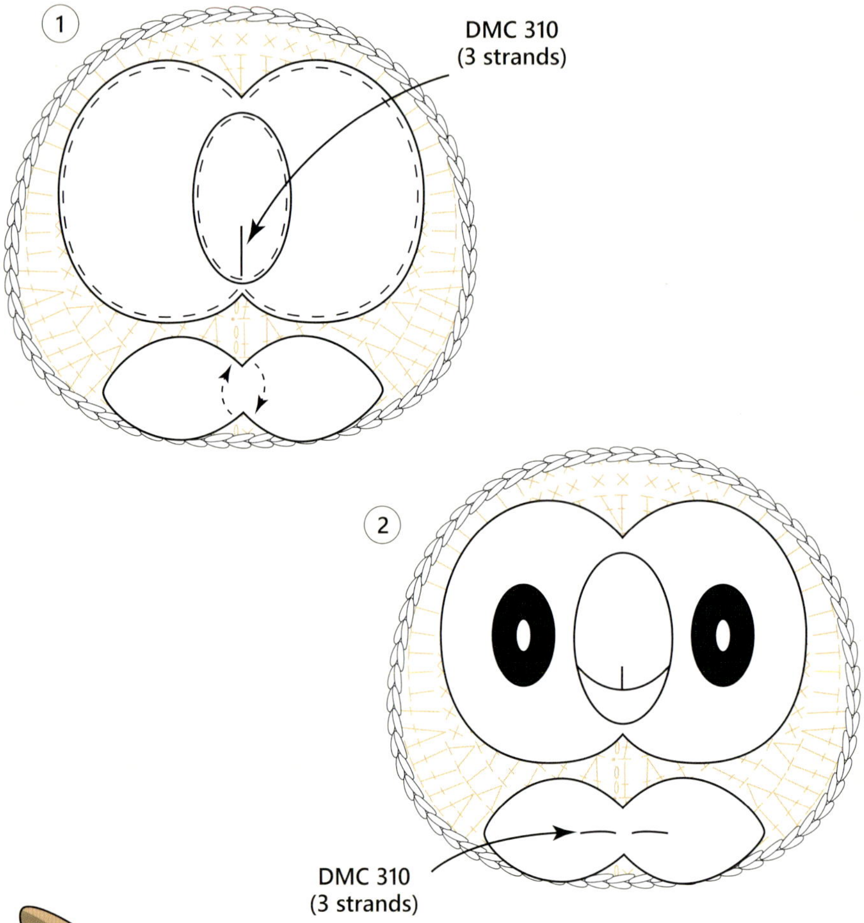

Rnd 2: Ch 1 (does not count as a st), sc in same st as join, sc in next 9 sts, (2 sc, ch 2, 2 sc) in next st, sc in next 10 sts, (2 sc, ch 2, 2 sc) in last st; join =28 sts and 2 ch-2 sps

Fasten off and weave in the ends. With another piece of yarn, tie around the center of the bow to finish and leave a long tail for sewing.

Assembly

Hold the square with the stitch marker at the bottom. Outline the head with **Color 16** by working surface sl sts between Rnds 6 and 7 with a 4mm hook, holding yarn on WS. Finish off seamlessly and weave in the end (see Finishing/Surface Crochet). Sew on the face, beak, and bow as shown; remove the marker from the square. Stitch a line on the beak with 3 strands of DMC floss (310).

Cut out the indicated pieces from Felts A, D, and L, using the templates and assemble the layers to complete the eyes (see Working With Felt). Position the eyes and beak as indicated, using pins to mark the main points. Glue all pieces onto the head and let them dry. Stitch 2 lines on the bow with 3 strands of DMC floss (310).

Fennekin

This Pokémon gets worked up easily. Its body can also overheat, so it uses its ears to dissipate the heat and calm down.

Key

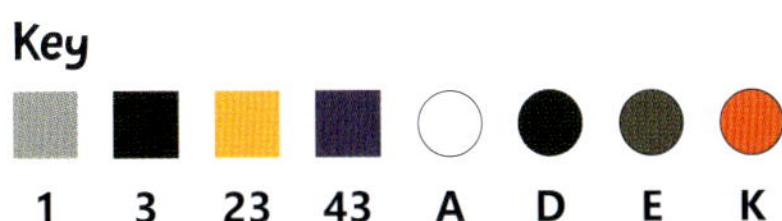

1 3 23 43 A D E K

Difficulty level

Type

Square

Make a magic ring using **Color 23** and work in the round with a 4mm hook.

Rnd 1: Ch 1 (does not count as a st now and throughout), 6 sc in ring; join = 6 sts

Rnd 2: (RS) Ch 1, 2 sc in same st as join, 2 sc in next 2 sts, sc in next st; change to **Color 1**—sc in same st, 2 sc in last 2 sts; join and turn = 12 sts

Rnd 3: (WS) With **Color 1**—Ch 2 (does not count as a st now and throughout), skip join, 2 dc in next 5 sts; pick up **Color 23** and work 2 dc in next 7 sts; join and turn = 24 sts

Rnd 4: (RS) With **Color 23**—Ch 2, skip join, [dc in next st, 2 dc in next st] 6 times, dc in next st; pick up **Color 1** and work [2 dc in next st, dc in next st] 5 times, 2 dc in last st; join and fasten off **Colors 1** and **23** = 36 sts

Rnd 5: Join **Color 43** with a standing sc in first st, sc in next st, hdc in next st, dc in next st; [2 dc in next st, ch 2, 2 dc in next st, dc in next st, hdc in next st, sc in next 3 sts, hdc in next st, dc in next st] 3 times; 2 dc in next st, ch 2, 2 dc in next st, dc in next st, hdc in next st, sc in last st; join = 44 sts and 4 ch-2 sps

Rnds 6–10: Ch 2, dc in same st as join, [dc in each st to next ch-2 sp, (2 dc, ch 2, 2 dc) in ch-2 sp] 4 times, dc in each st to end; join = 60/76/92/108/124 sts and 4 ch-2 sps

Place marker in final join to indicate the right edge of the square. Fasten off and weave in the ends.

(continued overleaf)

Square (4mm/G/6 hook)

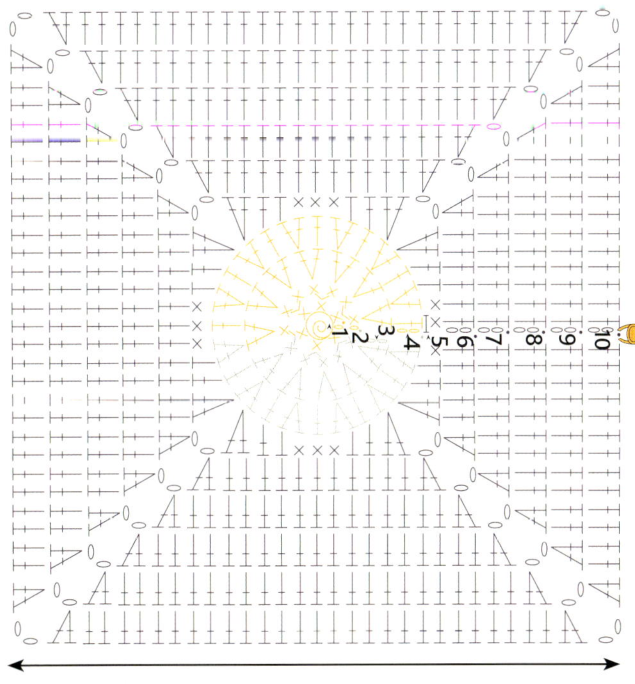

Left Ear

Work in rows with **Color 23** and a 3mm hook.

Row 1: (RS) Ch 11, skip first ch, sc2tog, sc in next 7 chs, (2 sc, ch 2, 2 sc) in last ch; work across the opposite side of the foundation ch—sc in next 8 chs, 2 sc in last ch; turn = 22 sts and ch-2 sp

Row 2: (WS) Ch 3 (counts as dc now and throughout), dc in first st, dc in next 5 sts, hdc in next 3 sts, sc in next 3 sts, (2 sc, ch 2, 2 sc) in ch-2 sp, sc in next 3 sts, hdc in next 3 sts, dc in next st, dc2tog, dc in last st; turn = 26 sts and ch-2 sp

Row 3: (RS) Ch 3, skip first st, dc in next 2 sts, hdc in next 2 sts, sc in next 6 sts, (2 sc, ch 2, 2 sc) in ch-2 sp, sc in next 7 sts, hdc in next 3 sts, dc in next 3 sts, 2 dc in next st, 3 dc in last st; fasten off, leaving a long tail for sewing; do not turn = 33 sts and ch-2 sp

Row 4: (RS) Using **Color 23**, make a slip knot and hold the yarn on WS; work surface sl sts across the inner part of the ear between Rows 2 and 3, ending at the center top; fasten off and weave in the ends = 11 sts

Right Ear

Work in rows with **Color 23** and a 3mm hook.

Row 1: (RS) Ch 11, 2 sc in second ch from hook, sc in next 8 chs, (2 sc, ch 2, 2 sc) in last ch; work across the opposite side of the foundation ch—sc in next 7 chs, sc2tog; turn = 22 sts and ch-2 sp

Row 2: (WS) Ch 3 (counts as dc), skip first st, dc2tog, dc in next st, hdc in next 3 sts, sc in next 3 sts, (2 sc, ch 2, 2 sc) in ch-2 sp, sc in next 3 sts, hdc in next 3 sts, dc in next 5 sts, 2 dc in last st; turn = 26 sts and ch-2 sp

Row 3: (RS) Ch 4, sl st in second ch from hook (counts as dc), 2 dc in first st, 2 dc in next st, dc in next 3 sts, hdc in next 3 sts, sc in next 7 sts, (2 sc, ch 2, 2 sc) in ch-2 sp, sc in next 6 sts, hdc in next 2 sts, dc in last 3 sts; fasten off, leaving a long tail for sewing; do not turn = 33 sts and ch-2 sp

Row 4: As for Left Ear.

Assembly

Hold the square with the stitch marker on the right. Outline the head by working surface sl sts between Rnds 4 and 5 with a 4mm hook using **Color 1** for the bottom of the head and **Color 23** for the top of the head; finish off seamlessly and weave in the ends (see Finishing/Surface Crochet). Holding **Color 1** on WS, outline the edge above the snout with surface sl sts by working across the bottom half between Rnds 1 and 2; fasten off and weave in the ends.

Position the ears as shown. Using **Color 23**, whipstitch across the raw edges onto the square, then backstitch across the side edges. Fasten off and weave in the ends; remove the marker from the square.

Cut out the indicated pieces from Felts A, D, E, and K, using the templates. Assemble the ear inserts (see Working With Felt) and glue them onto the ears.

Assemble the eye layers, with the exception of the black eyeliner. Position the nose, eyes, and whiskers referring to the image; use pins to mark the main points. Glue all the pieces onto the head and let them dry. Once the eyes have dried, apply a tiny amount of glue around the outer edge and attach the eyeliner layer; let the final layer dry.

Thread the needle with 3 strands of DMC floss (310) and stitch the mouth and vertical wrinkles as indicated. Use pins to mark the main points prior to stitching. Finish off and weave in the ends.

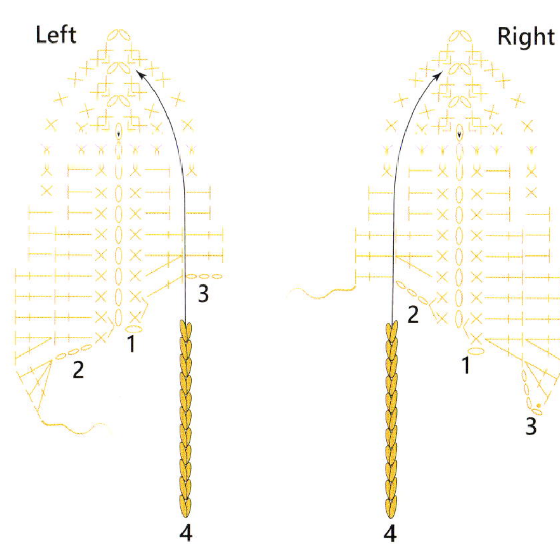

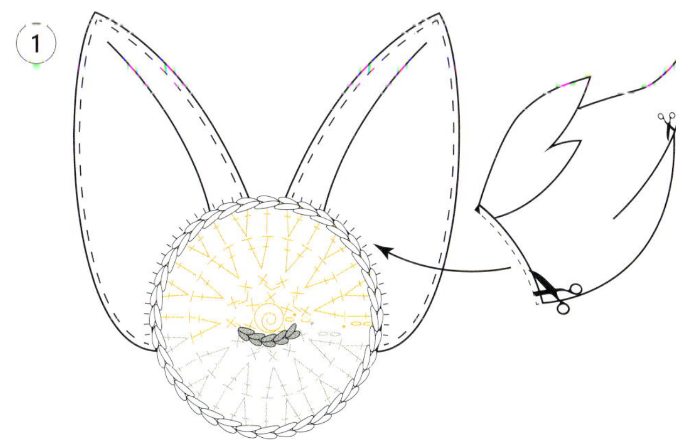

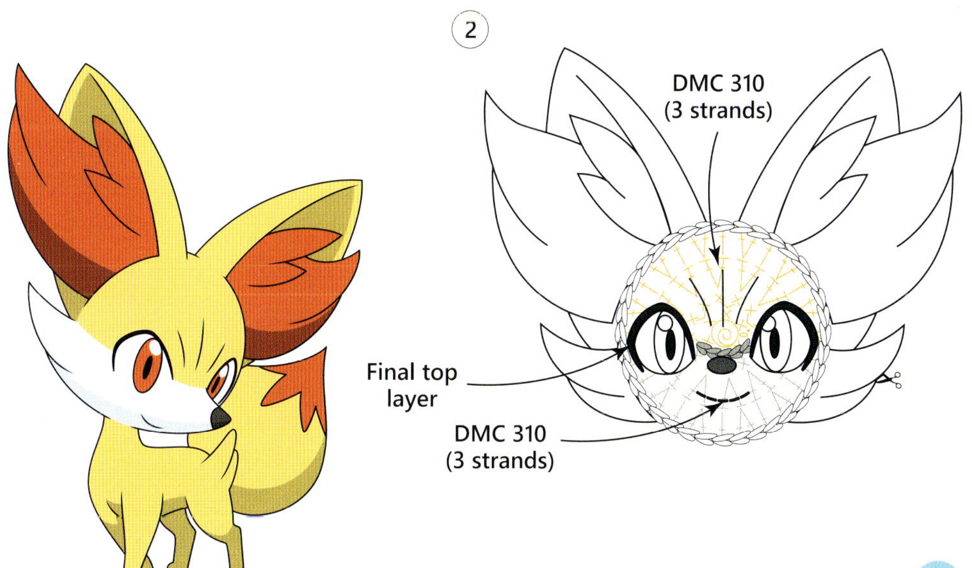

Scorbunny

Once its body has heated up, Scorbunny can use the full extent of its power. That's why it does warm-up exercises.

Key

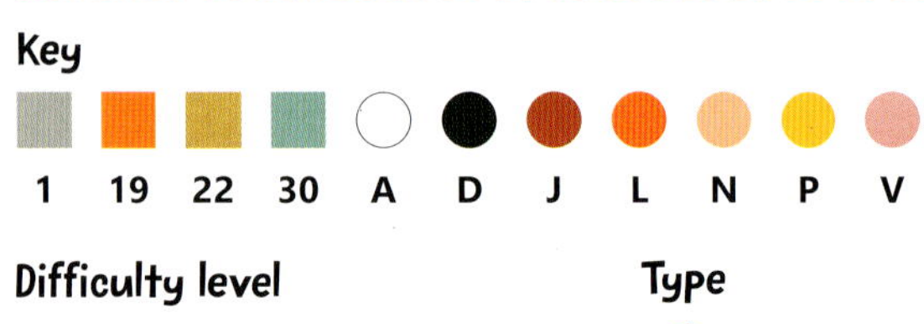

Difficulty level

Type

Square

Make one Basic Square using **Color 30** and a 4mm hook (see Basic Shapes).

Head

Make a magic ring using **Color 1** and work in the round with a 4mm hook.

Follow Rnds 1–3 of Basic Circle (see Basic Shapes).

Rnd 4: Ch 1 (does not count as a st), sc in same st as join, sc in next 2 sts, *2 sc in next st, hdc in next 2 sts, 2 hdc in next st, [dc in next st, 2 dc in next st] 2 times, dc in next st, 2 hdc in next st, hdc in next 2 sts, 2 sc in next st**, sc in next 5 sts; repeat from * to **, sc in last 2 sts; join = 48 sts

Fasten off, leaving a long tail for sewing.

Whiskers

Work in rows with **Color 1** and a 3mm hook.

Top Piece (make 2)

Row 1: (RS) Ch 5, sl st in second ch from hook, sc in next ch, hdc in last 2 chs; fasten off, leaving a long tail for sewing = 4 sts

Bottom Piece (make 2)

Row 1: (RS) Ch 9, sc in second ch from hook, hdc in next ch, dc in next ch, tr in next 2 chs, dc in next ch, hdc in next ch, sc in last ch; fasten off, leaving a long tail for sewing = 8 sts

Ear (make 2)

Work in rows with a 3mm hook.

Row 1: (WS) With **Color 1**—Ch 4, leaving a long tail at the beg for sewing; 2 hdc in second ch from hook, hdc in next ch, 2 hdc in last ch; turn = 5 sts

Row 2: (RS) Ch 1 (does not count as a st now and throughout), hdc in first st, hdc in each st across; turn

Whiskers (3mm/D/3 hook)

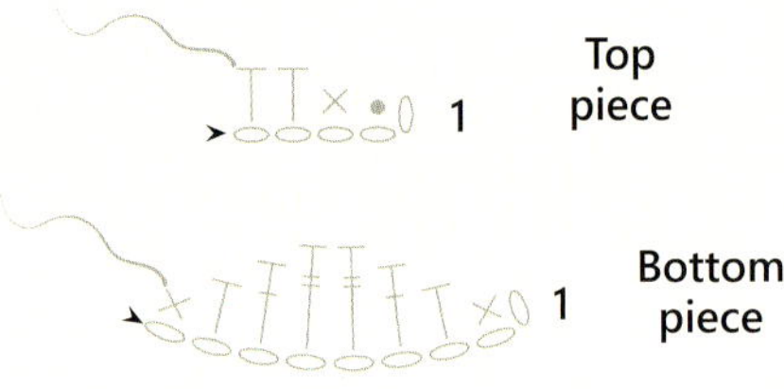

Head (4mm/G/6 hook)

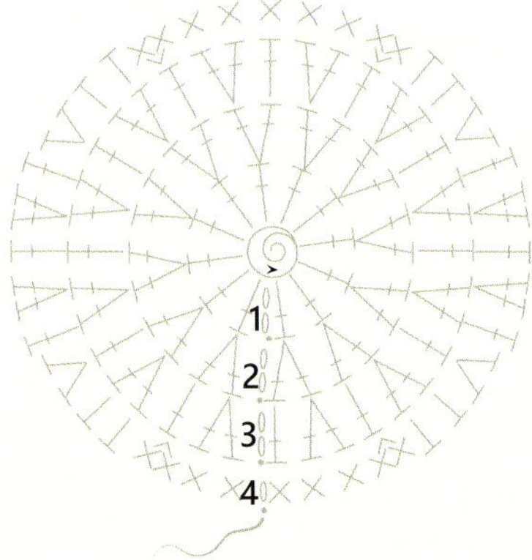

Row 3: (WS) Ch 1, 2 hdc in first st, hdc in next 3 sts, 2 hdc in last st; turn = 7 sts

Row 4: (RS) As Row 2

Row 5: (WS) Ch 1, hdc in first st, hdc in next 2 sts, 2 hdc in next st, hdc in last 3 sts; turn = 8 sts

Row 6: (RS) As Row 2

Row 7: (WS) Ch 1, sc in first st, sc in next st, hdc in next st, dc in next 2 sts, hdc in next st, sc in last 2 sts; change to **Color 22**, break off **Color 1** and turn = 8 sts

Row 8: (RS) With **Color 22**—Ch 1, hdc in first st, hdc in each st across; change to **Color 19**, break off **Color 22** and turn = 8 sts

Row 9: (WS) With **Color 19**, work in third loops only (they will be facing you)—ch 1, hdc in first st, hdc in next st, sc in next st, sc2tog, sc in next st, hdc in last 2 sts; turn = 7 sts

Rows 10–12: As Row 2

Row 13: (WS) Ch 1, do not skip first st, sc2tog, hdc in next 3 sts, sc2tog; turn = 5 sts

Row 14: (RS) Ch 3 (counts as dc), skip first st, dc3tog, dc in last st; turn = 3 sts

Row 15: (WS) Skip first st, sc2tog = 1 st

Fasten off, leaving a long tail for sewing. Make a slip knot with **Color 22** and hold the yarn on WS; work surface sl st between Rows 7 and 8 on RS. Fasten off and weave in the ends.

Right Ear Add-on

Work in rows with **Color 1** and a 3mm hook.

Row 1: (RS) Ch 11, sl st in second ch from hook, sc in next ch, hdc in next ch, dc in next 4 chs, hdc in next ch, sc in next ch, sl st in last ch = 10 sts

Fasten off, leaving a long tail for sewing.

(continued overleaf)

Felt templates

Ear (3mm/D/3 hook)

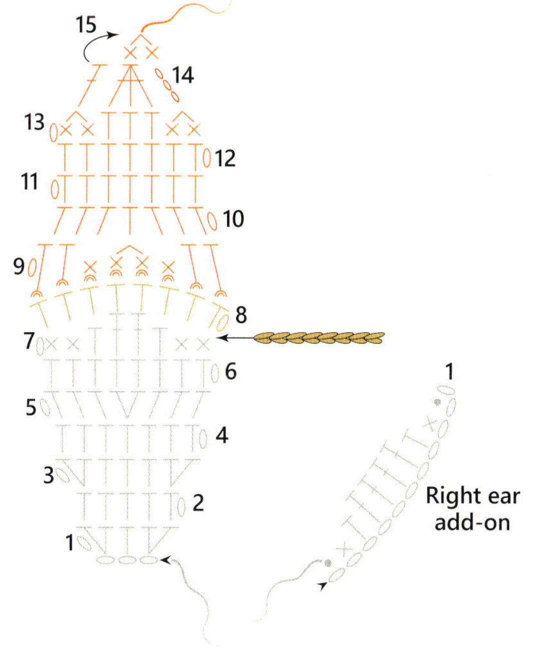

Assembly

Assembly

Position the head on the square, 1 rnd above the bottom edge and backstitch around using **Color 1**. Position the ears as shown and backstitch around onto the square using the corresponding yarn colors. Finish off and weave in the ends.

Position the right ear add-on as shown and backstitch around onto the square with **Color 1**. Position the whisker pieces as shown. Using **Color 1**, backstitch around the bottom piece partially and whipstitch across the raw edge of the top pieces onto the head; leave the points unstitched. Finish off and weave in the ends.

Cut out the indicated pieces from Felts A, D, I, L, N, P, and V, using the templates and assemble the layers to complete the mouth and eyes (see Working With Felt). Position all the felt pieces referring to the image and use pins to mark the main points. Glue the pieces onto the head and let them dry.

Thread the needle with 3 strands of black DMC floss (310) and stitch a straight line between the nose and mouth. Finish off and weave in the ends.

Totodile

This Pokémon's powerful, well-developed jaws are capable of crushing anything. Even its Trainer must be careful.

Key

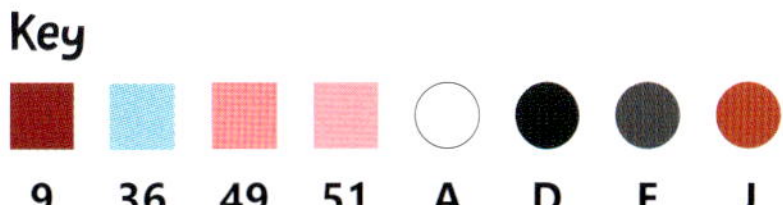

9 36 49 51 A D E J

Difficulty level

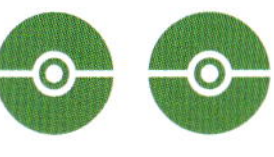

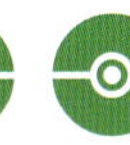

Type

Square

Make a magic ring using **Color 36** and work in the round with a 4mm hook.

Follow Rnds 1–4 of Basic Circle (see Basic Shapes).

Rnd 5: Ch 2 (does not count as a st now and throughout), dc in same st as join, 2 dc in next st, dc in next st, 2 dc in next st, [dc in next 3 sts, 2 dc in next st] 2 times, *[dc in next st, 2 dc in next st] 2 times, [dc in next 3 sts, 2 dc in next st] 2 times, repeat from * 2 more times; join and fasten off **Color 36** – 64 sts

Rnd 6: Work in BLO—join **Color 51** with a standing sc in first st, sc in next 5 sts, hdc in next st, dc in next st, (2 dc, ch 2, 2 dc) in next st, dc in next st, hdc in next st, [sc in next 11 sts, hdc in next st, dc in next st, (2 dc, ch 2, 2 dc) in next st, dc in next st, hdc in next st] 3 times, sc in last 5 sts; join = 76 sts and 4 ch-2 sps

Rnd 7: Ch 1 (does not count as a st), sc in same st as join, sc in next 3 sts, hdc in next 2 sts, dc in next 4 sts, (2 dc, ch 2, 2 dc) in next ch-2 sp, dc in next 4 sts, hdc in next 2 sts, [sc in next 7 sts, hdc in next 2 sts, dc in next 4 sts, (2 dc, ch 2, 2 dc) in next ch-2 sp, dc in next 4 sts, hdc in next 2 sts] 3 times, sc in last 3 sts; join = 92 sts and 4 ch-2 sps

Rnds 8–9: Ch 2, dc in same st as join, [dc in each st to next ch-2 sp, (2 dc, ch 2, 2 dc) in ch-2 sp] 4 times, dc in each st to end; join = 108 /124 sts and 4 ch-2 sps

Place marker in final join to indicate the right edge of the square. Fasten off and weave in the ends.

Head Shaping

Holding the square with the stitch marker on the right, work around the upper edge of the head (Rnd 5 of the square) using **Color 36** and a 4mm hook.

(continued overleaf)

Square (4mm/G/6 hook)

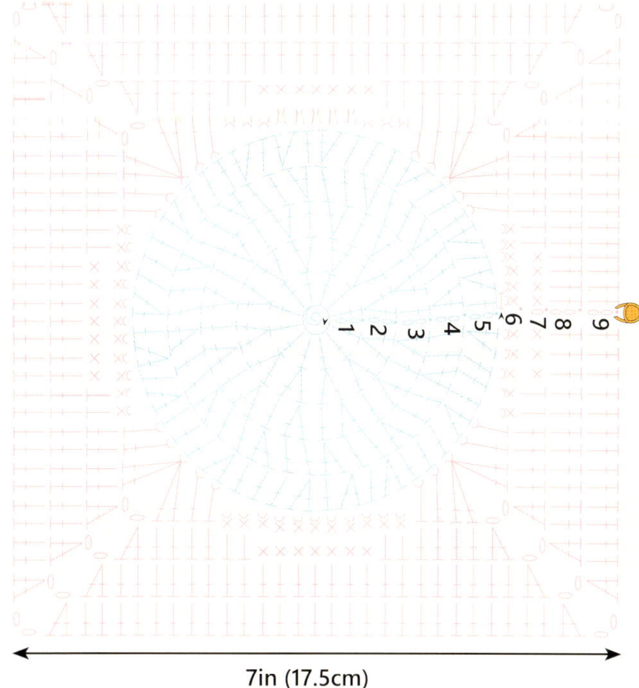

Snout (4mm/G/6 hook)

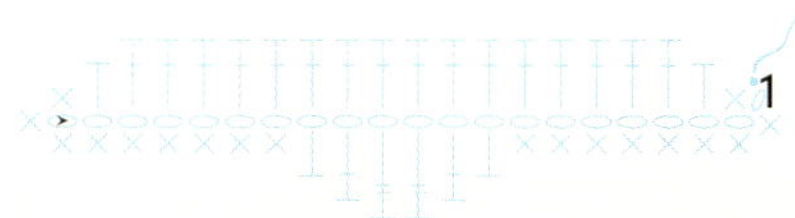

Snout outline (3.5mm/E/4 hook)

1

Head shaping (4mm/G/6 hook)

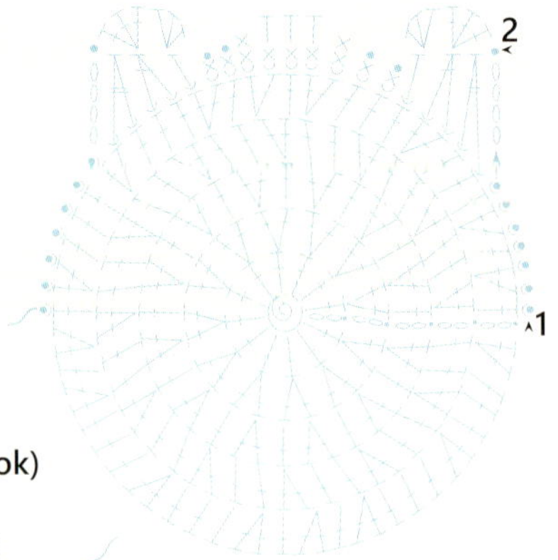

2

1

Mouth (4mm/G/6 hook)

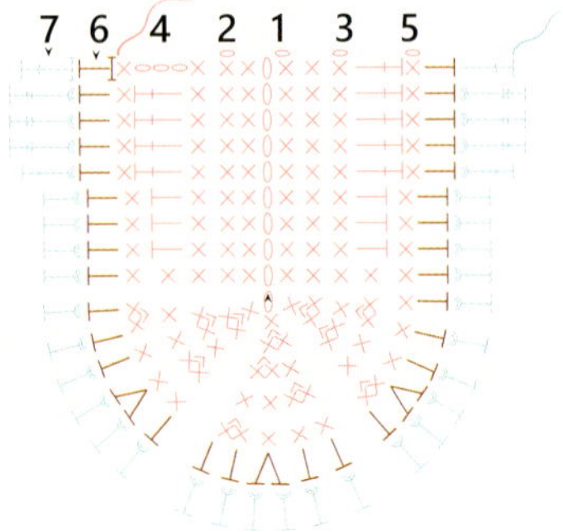

7 6 4 2 1 3 5

Eye outline (3.5mm/E/4 hook)

1

Felt templates

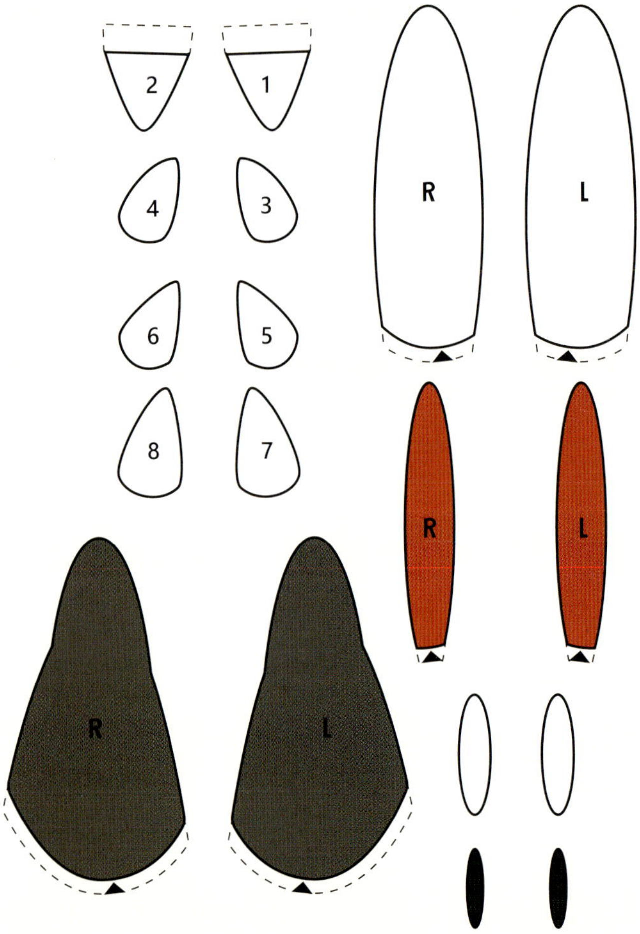

2 1

4 3

6 5

8 7

R L

R L

R L

Row 1: (RS) Work in FLO—Join yarn with a sl st in first st, sl st in next 6 sts, ch 4 (counts as tr) and place marker in last ch made, tr2tog, dc2tog, hdc in next st, sc in next 9 sts, hdc in next st, dc2tog, tr2tog, ch 4 (counts as tr), sl st in next 7 sts, leave the remaining sts unworked; fasten off, leaving a long tail for sewing = 31 sts

Row 2: (RS) Join yarn with a sl st in st with marker and remove the marker, skip next st, 3 dc in next st, 3 hdc in next st, sl st in next 2 sts, sc in next st, hdc in next 3 sts, sc in next st, sl st in next 2 sts, 3 hdc in next st, 3 dc in next st, skip st, sl st in next st; fasten off and weave in the ends = 23 sts

Snout

Work in the round with **Color 36** and a 4mm hook.

Rnd 1: Ch 21, sc in second ch from hook, hdc in next ch, dc in next 16 chs, hdc in next ch, 3 sc in last ch; work across the opposite side of the foundation ch—sc in next 6 chs, hdc in next ch, dc in next ch, tr in next 2 chs, dc in next ch, hdc in next ch, sc in next 6 chs, 2 sc in last ch; join = 42 sts

Fasten off, leaving a long tail for sewing.

Eye Outline (make 2)

Using **Color 36** and a 3.5mm hook, make an 8 d-ch crochet cord (see Stitches/Finishing). Fasten off and leave a long tail for sewing.

Snout Outline

Using **Color 36** and a 3.5mm hook, make a 13 d-ch crochet cord (see Stitches/Finishing). Fasten off, leaving a long tail for sewing.

Mouth

Begin by working in rows with **Color 49** and a 4mm hook.

Row 1: (WS) Ch 11, sc in second ch from hook, sc in next 8 chs, 3 sc in last ch; work across the opposite side of the foundation ch—sc in next 9 chs; turn = 21 sts

Row 2: (RS) Ch 1 (does not count as a st now and throughout), sc in first st, sc in next 8 sts, 2 sc in next 3 sts, sc in last 9 sts; turn = 24 sts

Row 3: (WS) Sc in first st, sc in next 8 sts, [sc in next st, 2 sc in next st] 3 times, sc in last 9 sts; turn = 27 sts

Row 4: (RS) Ch 3 (counts as dc), skip first st, dc in next 4 sts, hdc in next 3 sts, sc in next st, [sc in next 2 sts, 2 sc in next st] 3 times, sc in next st, hdc in next 3 sts, dc in last 5 sts; turn = 30 sts

Row 5: (WS) Ch 1, sc in first st, sc in next 8 sts, [sc in next 3 sts, 2 sc in next st] 3 times, sc in last 9 sts; fasten off **Color 49** leaving a long tail for sewing; turn = 33 sts

Row 6: (RS) Join **Color 9** with a standing hdc in first st, hdc in next 11 sts, [2 hdc in next st, hdc in next 3 sts] 3 times, hdc in last 9 sts and fasten off **Color 9**; do not turn = 36 sts

Row 7: (RS) Join **Color 36** with a standing dc in first st, then work in third loops only—tr in next 3 sts, dc in next st, hdc in next 26 sts, dc in next st, tr in next 3 sts, dc in last st; fasten off, leaving a long tail for sewing = 36 sts

Assembly

Hold the square with the stitch marker on the right. Using **Color 36**, backstitch around the top edge of the head onto the square. Position the mouth with its straight edge across the center of the head. Whipstitch across the top edge onto the square using **Color 49**, then backstitch around the outer edge onto the square using **Color 36**. Fasten off and weave in the ends; remove the marker from the square.

Position the snout horizontally across the center of the head. Using **Color 36**, whipstitch across the top edge and backstitch the sides and the bottom corner onto the square. Leave the bottom edge unstitched for inserting the teeth. Cut out the indicated pieces from Felts A, D, E, and J, using the templates (see Working With Felt). To assemble the eyes, align the notches and glue the pieces together; once dried, trim away the seam allowances from all three layers. Position and glue the eyes and teeth onto the head. Do not trim away the seam allowances from teeth 1 and 2; insert them under the snout edge when gluing.

Thread the needle with 4 ply black yarn and stitch the nostrils. Position the snout outline and eye outlines as shown and whipstitch across each piece onto the head. Fasten off and weave in the ends.

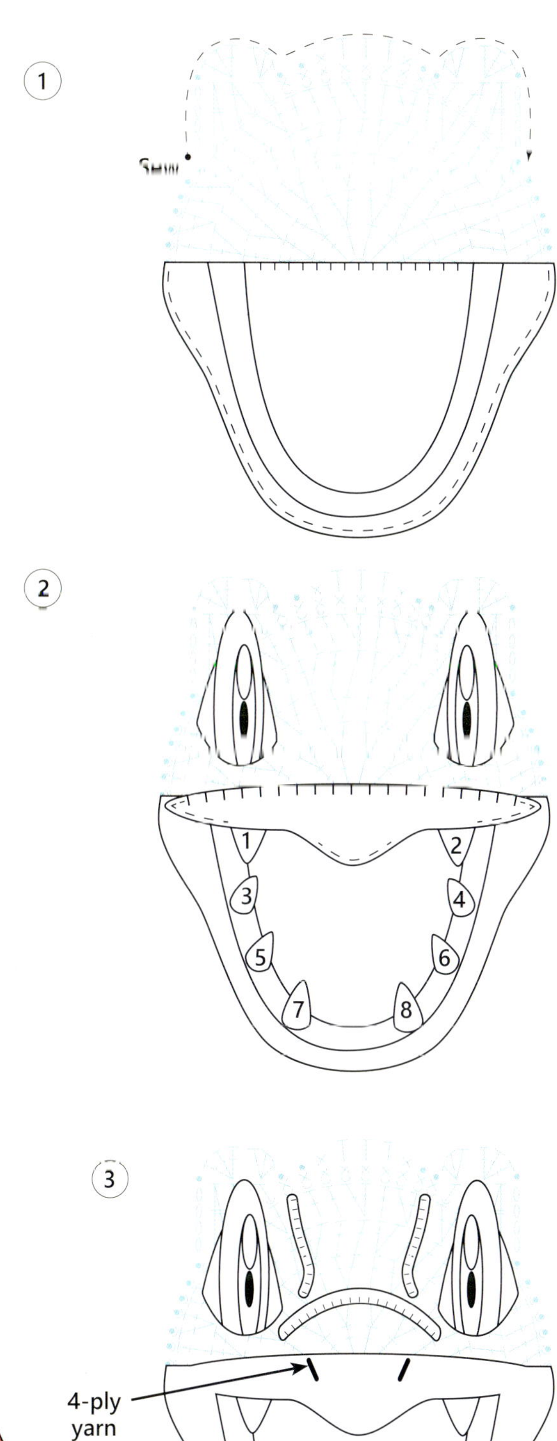

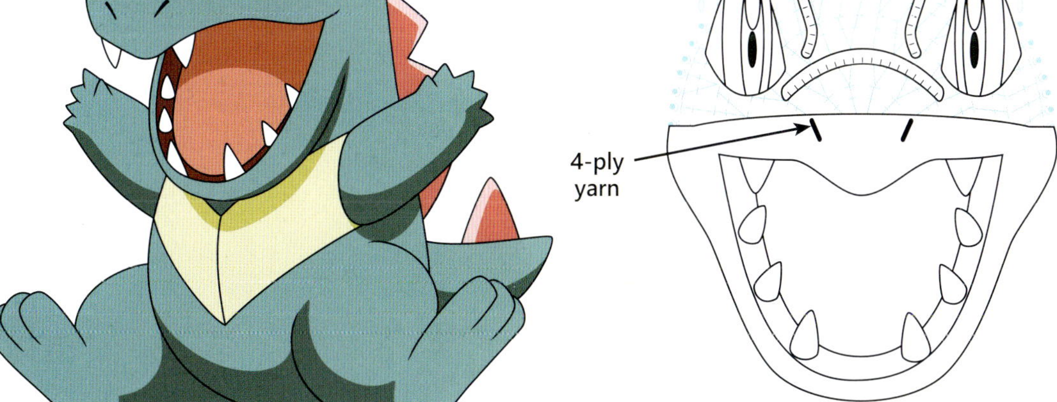

Tamato Berry

This large, pointy berry is very spicy. Twice the size of a Sitrus Berry, Tamato Berries are known to make Pokémon very friendly.

Key

8 23 27

Difficulty level

Square (4mm/G/6 hook)

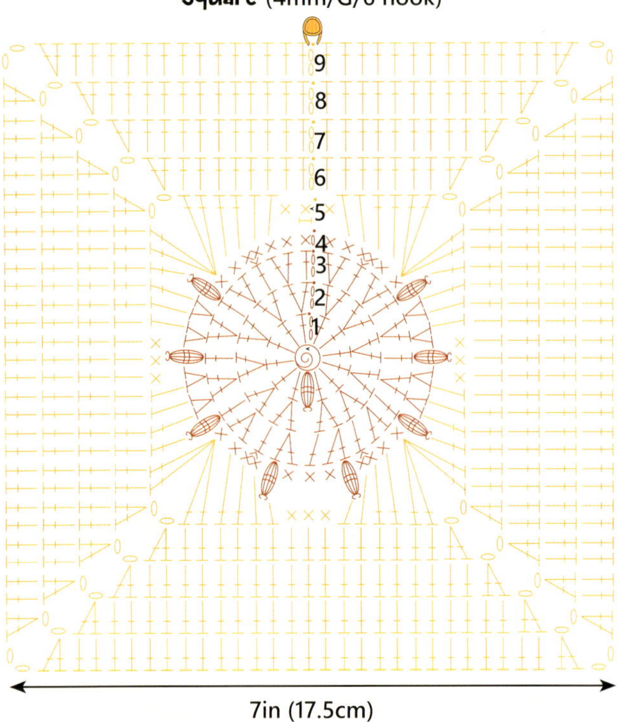

Square

Make a magic ring using **Color 8** and work in the round with a 4mm hook.

Rnd 1: Ch 2 (does not count as a st now and throughout), (6 dc, 5-tr PC, 6 dc) in ring; join = 13 sts

Rnd 2: Ch 2, 2 dc in same st as join, 2 dc in next 5 sts, skip PC, 2 dc in next 6 sts; join = 24 sts

Rnd 3: Ch 2, dc in same st as join, 2 dc in next st, [dc in next st, 2 dc in next st] 11 times; join = 36 sts

Rnd 4: Ch 1 (does not count as a st now and throughout), sc in same st as join, sc in next 2 sts, *2 sc in next st, sc in next 2 sts, [5-tr PC in next st, 2 hdc in next 2 sts] 2 times, 5-tr PC in next st, sc in next 2 sts, 2 sc in next st**; 5-tr PC in next st, sc in next 3 sts, 5-tr PC in next st; repeat from * to **, sc in last 2 sts; join and fasten off without breaking off **Color 8**, hold it on WS (see Finishing/ Surface Crochet) = 48 sts

Rnd 5: Join **Color 23** with a standing sc in first st, sc in next st, hdc in next 2 sts, dc in next 2 sts, (2 dc, ch 2, 2 dc) in next st; [dc in next 2 sts, hdc in next 2 sts, sc in next 3 sts, hdc in next 2 sts, dc in next 2 sts, (2 dc, ch 2, 2 dc) in next st] 3 times; dc in next 2 sts, hdc in next 2 sts, sc in last st; join = 60 sts and 4 ch-2 sps

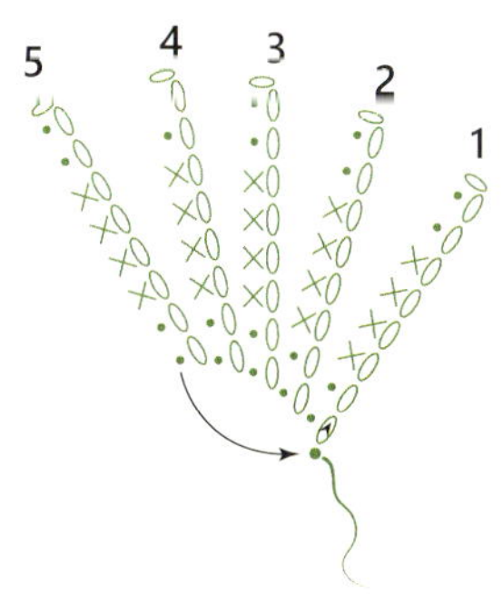

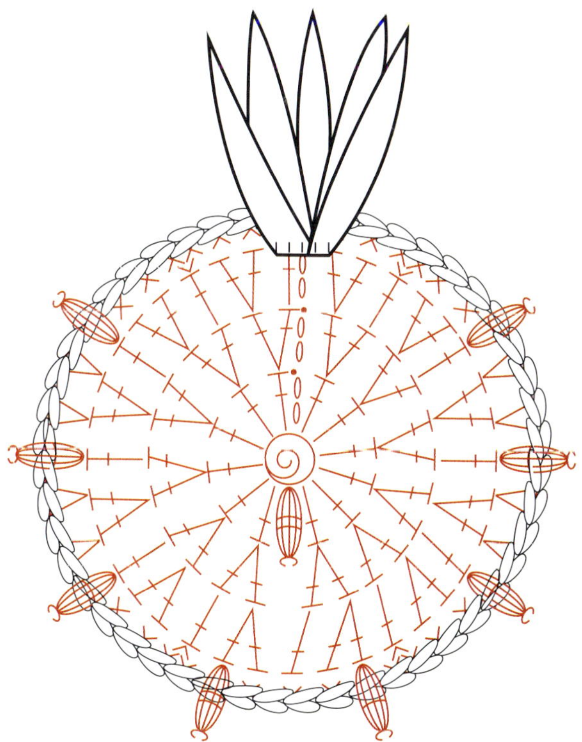

Rnd 6: Ch 2, dc in same st as join, *dc in each st to next ch-2 sp, (2 dc, ch 2, 2 dc) in ch-2 sp; dc in next 5 sts, hdc in next 5 sts, dc in next 5 sts, (2 dc, ch 2, 2 dc) in next ch-2 sp**; repeat from * to **, dc in each st to end; join = 76 sts and 4 ch-2 sps

Rnds 7–9: Ch 2, dc in same st as join, [dc in each st to next ch-2 sp, (2 dc, ch 2, 2 dc) in ch-2 sp] 4 times, dc in each st to end; join = 92/108/124 sts and 4 ch-2 sps

Place marker in final join to indicate the top of the square. Fasten off and weave in the ends.

Leaves

Work in rows with **Color 27** and a 2.5mm hook.

Rows 1–5: (RS) Ch 9, sl st in second ch from hook, sl st in next ch, sc in next 4 chs, sl st in last 2 chs; do not turn = 8 sts

Sl st in Row 1 and fasten off, leaving a long tail for sewing.

Assembly

Outline the berry with **Color 8** by working surface sl sts between Rnds 4 and 5 with a 4mm hook, holding yarn on WS (see Finishing/ Surface Crochet). Position the leaves on the top of the berry and whipstitch across the base, leaving the tips of the leaves unstitched. Fasten off and weave in the ends; remove the marker from the square.

Torchic

This Pokémon has a sac filled with burning fire in its belly, so that Torchic feels as warm as a hot water bottle if you hug it.

Key

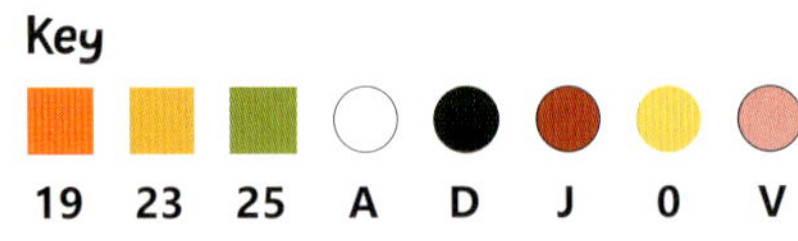

19 23 25 A D J 0 V

Difficulty level

Type

Square (4mm/G/6 hook)

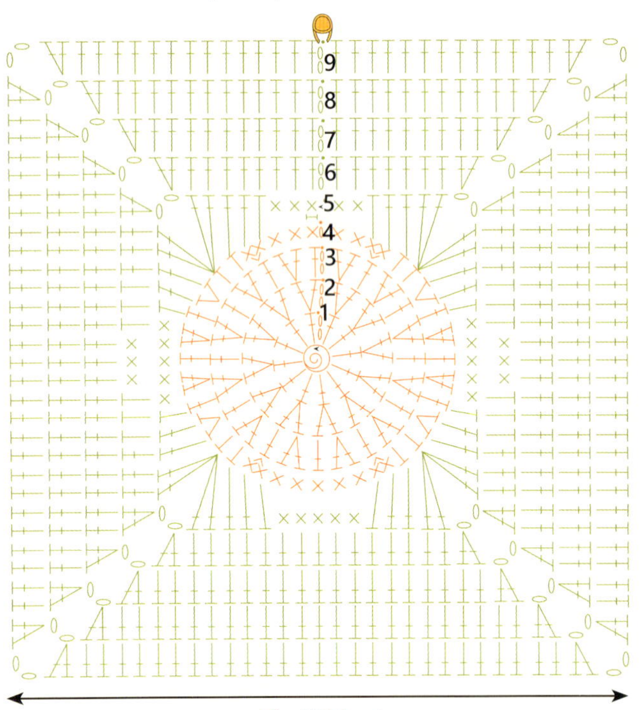

Front feathers
(3mm hook)

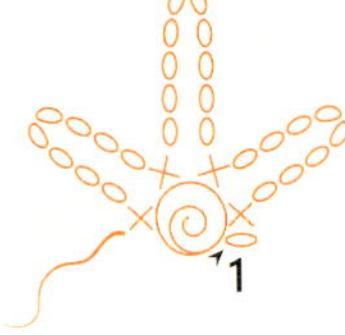

Side feathers
(3.5mm/E/4 hook)

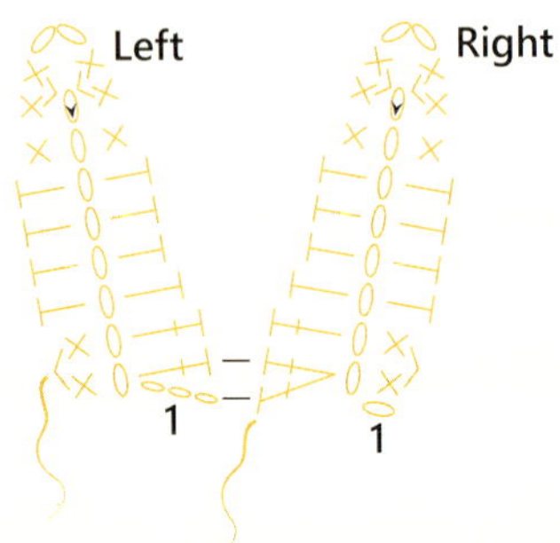

Square

Make a magic ring using **Color 19** and work in the round with a 4mm hook.

Follow Rnds 1–3 of Basic Circle (see Basic Shapes).

Rnd 4: Ch 1 (does not count as a st), sc in same st as join, sc in next 2 sts, *2 sc in next st, hdc in next 2 sts, 2 hdc in next st, [dc in next st, 2 dc in next st] 2 times, dc in next st, 2 hdc in next st, hdc in next 2 sts, 2 sc in next st**, sc in next 5 sts; repeat from * to **, sc in next 2 sts; join and fasten off without breaking off **Color 19**, hold it on WS (see Finishing/Surface Crochet) = 48 sts

Rnd 5: Join **Color 25** with a standing sc in first st, sc in next 2 sts, hdc in next st, dc in next 2 sts, (2 dc, ch 2, 2 dc) in next st; [dc in next 2 sts, hdc in next st, sc in next 5 sts, hdc in next st, dc in next 2 sts, (2 dc, ch 2, 2 dc) in next st] 3 times; dc in next 2 sts, hdc in next st, sc in last 2 sts; join = 60 sts and 4 ch-2 sps

Rnd 6: Ch 2 (does not count as a st now and throughout), dc in same st as join, *dc in each st to next ch-2 sp, (2 dc, ch 2, 2 dc) in ch-2 sp, dc in next 3 sts, hdc in next 3 sts, sc in next 3 sts, hdc in next 3 sts, dc in next 3 sts, (2 dc, ch 2, 2 dc) in next ch-2 sp, repeat from *, dc in each st to end; join = 76 sts and 4 ch-2 sps

Rnds 7–9: Ch 2, dc in same st as join, [dc in each st to next ch-2 sp, (2 dc, ch 2, 2 dc) in ch-2 sp] 4 times, dc in each st to end; join = 92/108/124 sts and 4 ch-2 sps

Place marker in final join to indicate the top of the square. Fasten off and weave in the ends.

Front Feathers

Make a magic ring using **Color 19** and work in ring with a 3mm hook—Ch 1 (does not count as a st), sc, ch 8, sc, ch 10, sc, ch 8, sc; fasten off, leaving a long tail for sewing = 3 sts and 3 loops

Center Feather

Work in rows with **Color 23** and a 3.5mm hook.

Row 1: (WS) Ch 10, sc in second ch from hook, *hdc in next 2 chs, dc in next 2 chs, hdc in next 2 chs, sc in next ch**, (2 sc, ch 2, 2 sc) in last ch; work across the opposite side of the foundation ch—sc in next ch, repeat from * to **; turn = 20 sts and 1 ch-2 sp

Row 2: (RS) Ch 1 (does not count as a st), sc in first st, sc in next 9 sts, (2 sc, ch 2, 2 sc) in ch-2 sp, sc in each st to end = 24 sts and 1 ch-2 sp

Fasten off, leaving long tail for sewing.

Side Feathers

Work in rows with **Color 23** and a 3.5mm hook.

Left Feather: (RS) Ch 11, dc in fourth ch from hook (the skipped chs count as dc), dc in next ch, hdc in next 4 chs, sc in next ch, (2 sc, ch 2, 2 sc) in last ch; work across the opposite side of the foundation ch—sc in next ch, hdc in next 4 chs, sc2tog; fasten off, leaving a long tail for sewing = 18 sts and 1 ch-2 sp

Right Feather: (RS) Ch 9, skip turning ch, sc2tog, hdc in next 4 chs, sc in next ch, (2 sc, ch 2, 2 sc) in last ch; work across the opposite side of the foundation ch—sc in next ch, hdc in next 4 chs, dc in next ch, 2 dc in last ch; fasten off, leaving a long tail for sewing. Using this tail, whipstitch the final 2 sts of the right feather and the first 2 sts of the left feather together to join them; weave in the end = 18 sts and 1 ch-2 sp

Assembly

Hold the square with the stitch marker at the top. Outline the head with **Color 19** by working surface sl sts between Rnds 4 and 5 with a 4mm hook, holding yarn on WS. Finish off seamlessly and weave in the end (see Finishing/Surface Crochet). Position the center feather as shown. Using **Color 23**, whipstitch across the bottom edge onto the square, then backstitch across the side edges partially leaving the top edge unstitched. Finish off and weave in the end; remove the marker from the square.

Position the side feathers as shown. Using **Color 23**, whipstitch across the bottom edge onto the square, then backstitch across the center of each feather, leaving the side edges unstitched. Finish off and weave in the end.

Position the front feathers as shown and whipstitch across the bottom edge onto the head using **Color 19**; finish off and weave in the end. Cut out the indicated pieces from Felts A, D, J, O, and V, using the templates and assemble to complete the beak and eyes (see Working With Felt).

Position the beak and eyes on the head as shown in the image; use pins to mark the main points. Glue the pieces onto the head and leave to dry.

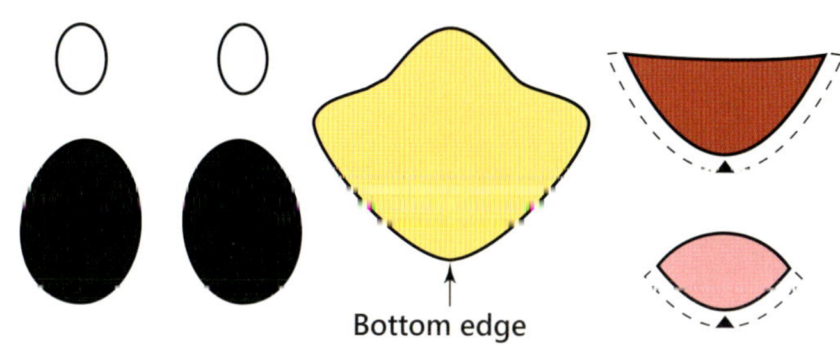

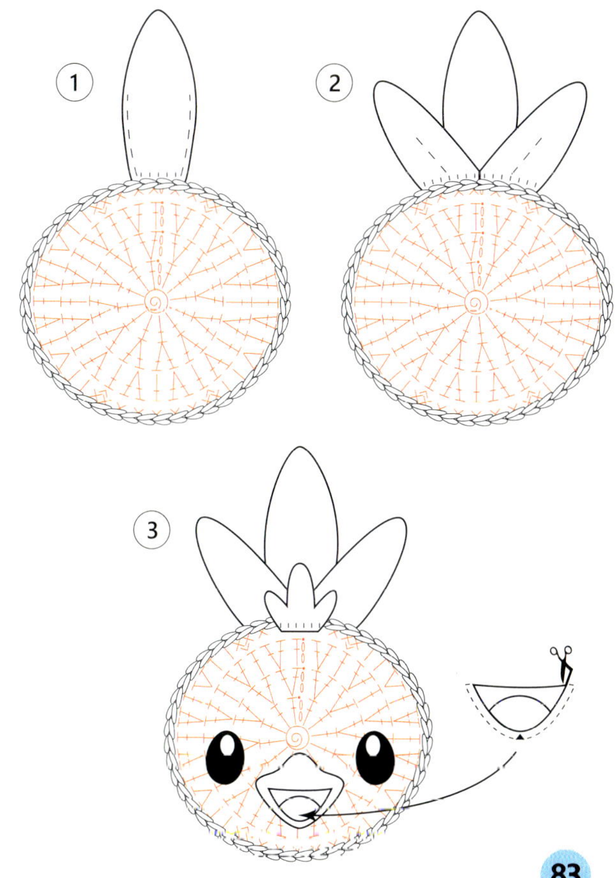

Chikorita

This Pokémon loves to bask in the sunlight. It uses the leaf on its head to seek out warm places.

Key

27 29 51 A J V

Difficulty level

Type

Square (4mm/G/6 hook)

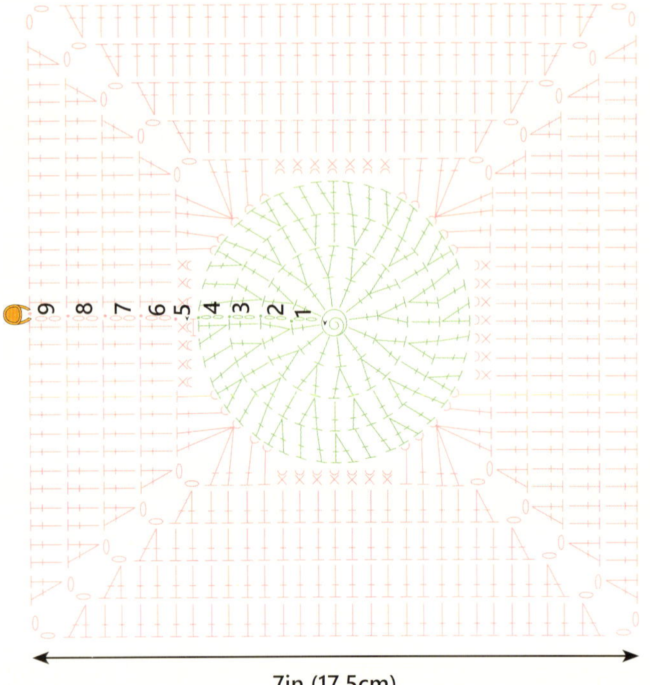

7in (17.5cm)

Bud (3mm hook)

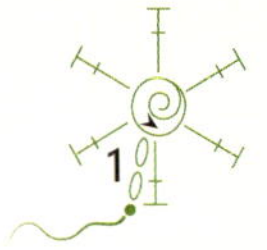

Square

Make the square as for Chimchar, but using **Color 29** for the center, and **Color 51** for the background. Place marker in final join to indicate the left edge of the square.

Head Shaping

Holding the square with the stitch marker on the left, work around the head edge (Rnd 4 of the square) using **Color 29** and a 4mm hook.

Rnd 1: (RS) Work in FLO—Join yarn with a standing sl st in first st, sl st in next 3 sts, ch 3, dc in next 4 sts, hdc in next 9 sts, dc in next 4 sts, ch 3, sl st in each st to end; join and fasten off, leaving a long tail for sewing = 48 sts and 2 ch-3

Row 2: (RS) Skip 4 sts and ch-3, join yarn with a standing dc in next st, dc in next 16 sts, leave the remaining sts unworked; fasten off and weave in the ends = 17 sts

Backstitch the bottom edges onto the square using **Color 29** from Rnd 1. Finish off and weave in the ends.

Bud (make 5)

Make a magic ring using **Color 27** and work in the round with a 3mm hook.

Rnd 1: Ch 2 (does not count as a st), 6 dc in ring; join = 6 sts

Fasten off, leaving a long tail for sewing. Apply a small drop of fabric glue inside each bud to secure the end from the center.

Leaf

Begin by working in the round with **Color 27** and a 4mm hook.

Rnd 1: Ch 41, sc in second ch from hook, sc in next 4 chs, hdc in next 4 chs, 2 hdc in next ch, [dc in next 4 chs, 2 dc in next ch] 3 times, dc in next 5 chs, hdc in next 5 chs, sc in next 4 chs, 2 sc in last ch and place marker in st just made, ch 2, 2 sc in same ch; work across the opposite side of the foundation ch—sc in next 2 chs, hdc in next 2 chs, dc in next 3 chs, dc2tog, [tr in next 3 chs, tr2tog] 3 times, dc in next 3 chs, dc2tog, hdc in next 3 chs, [sc2tog] 2 times, sc in next 2 chs, 2 sc in last ch; join, fasten off and weave in the end = 80 sts and 1 ch-2 sp

Row 2: Join **Color 27** with a standing dc in st with marker and remove the marker, (hdc, sc) in next ch-2 sp, sl st in next 5 sts, sc in next 3 sts, hdc in next 2 sts, dc2tog, dc in next 3 sts, tr in next 5 sts, [dc2tog, dc in next 3 sts] 2 times, hdc in next st, sc in next st, sl st in next 2 sts; work stem—ch 7, dc in fifth ch from hook, sc in next 2 chs; skip st on the leaf, sl st in join; leave the remaining sts unworked = 35 sts and stem

Fasten off, leaving a long tail for sewing.

(continued overleaf)

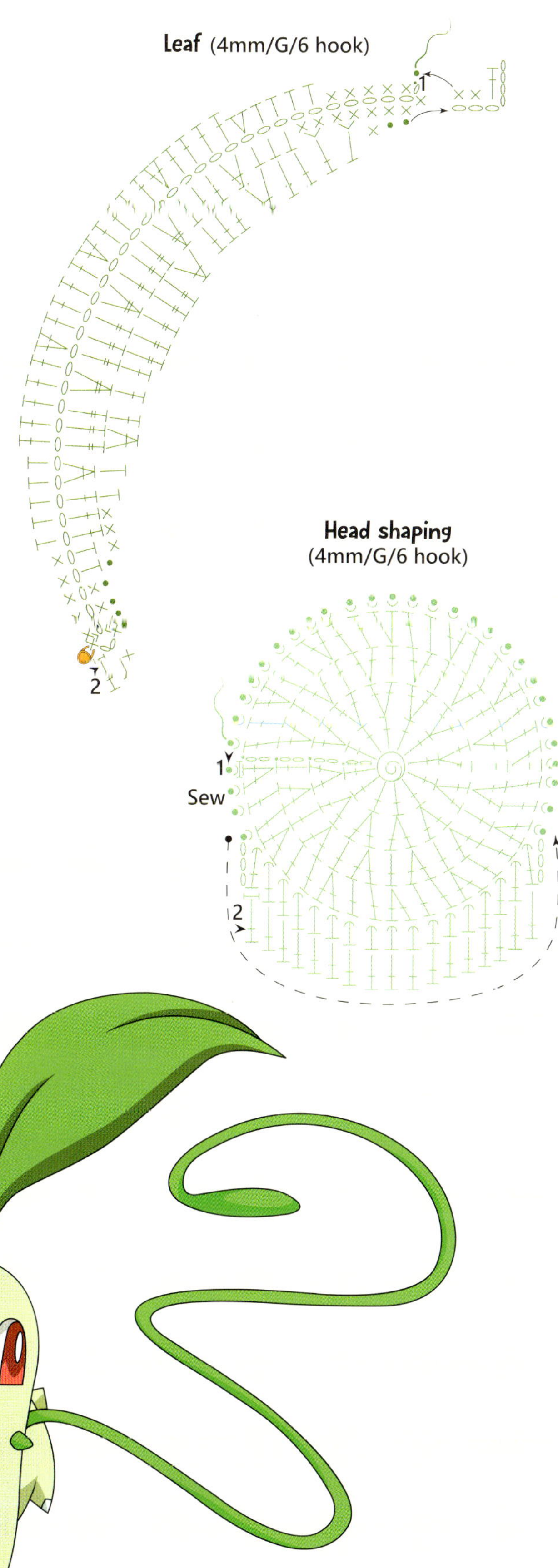

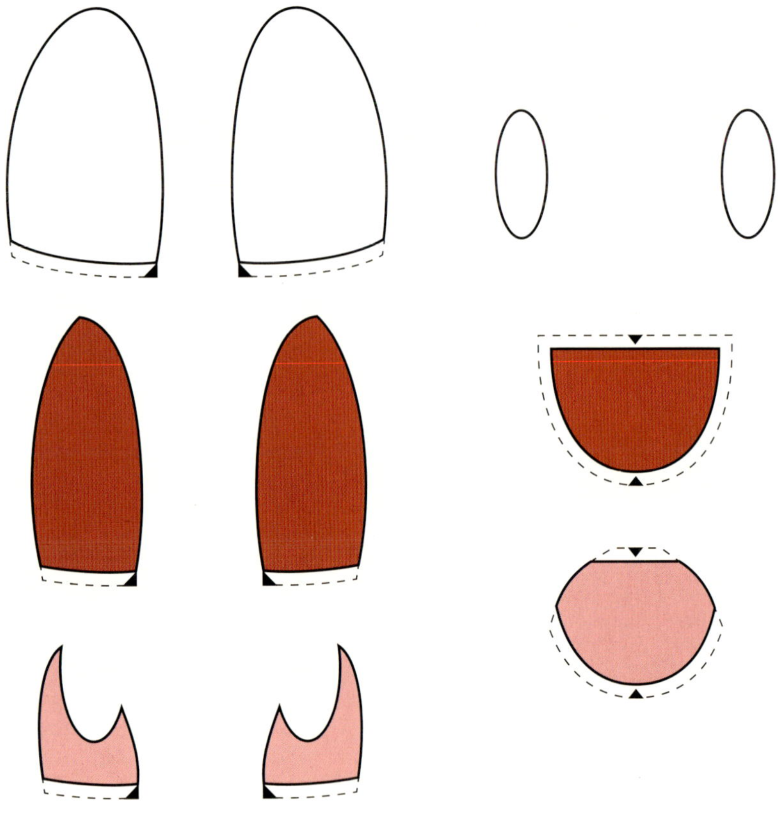

Assembly

Holding the square with the stitch marker on the left, position the leaf on the top of the head with WS facing you. Using **Color 27**, backstitch around the stem, then flip the leaf to RS and backstitch across the edges indicated on the diagram, leaving the remaining edges unstitched. Position the buds as shown and whipstitch around their edges onto the head using **Color 27**. Fasten off and weave in the ends; remove the marker from the square.

Cut out the indicated pieces from Felts A, J, and V, using the templates and assemble the layers to complete the mouth and eyes (see Working With Felt). Position and glue the eyes and mouth onto the head, using pins to mark the main points. Let the glue dry.

Thread the needle with 3 strands of black DMC floss (310) and backstitch a line on the leaf as shown. Finish off and weave in the ends.

Sobble

This Pokémon gets berries to eat by shooting them down with bullets of water it spurts from its mouth. Its aim is perfect.

Key

20 23 36 37 42 A U

Difficulty level

Type

Square

Make one Basic Square using **Color 20** and a 4mm hook (see Basic Shapes).

Head

Make a magic ring using **Color 37** and work in the round with a 3.5mm hook. Follow Rnds 1–4 of Basic Circle (see Basic Shapes).

Rnd 5: Ch 1 (does not count as a st), sc in same st as join, sc in next 3 sts, hdc in next 2 sts, 2 hdc in next st, [dc in next 2 sts, 2 dc in next st] 2 times, hdc in next 2 sts, 2 hdc in next st, sc in next 3 sts, sl st in next 11 sts, sc in next 3 sts, 2 hdc in next st, hdc in next 2 sts, [2 dc in next st, dc in next 2 sts] 2 times, 2 hdc in next st, hdc in next 2 sts, sc in next 3 sts; join and fasten off, leaving a long tail for sewing = 56 sts.

Cheek (make 2)

Make cheeks as for Pikachu but using **Color 42** and a 3mm hook.

Snout

Begin by working in the round using **Color 36** and a 3.5mm hook.

Rnd 1: Ch 13, dc in third ch from hook (the skipped chs do not count as a st), dc in next 9 chs, 6 dc in last ch; work across the opposite side of the foundation ch—dc in next 4 chs, 2 dc in next ch, dc in next 4 chs, 5 dc in last ch; join = 31 sts

Rnd 2: Ch 2 (does not count as a st), 2 dc in same st as join, dc in next 9 sts, 2 dc in next 3 sts, 2 hdc in next st, 2 sc in next st, sc in next 12 sts, 2 sc in next st, 2 hdc in next st, 2 dc in last 2 sts; join = 41 sts

(continued overleaf)

Head (3.5mm/E/4 hook)

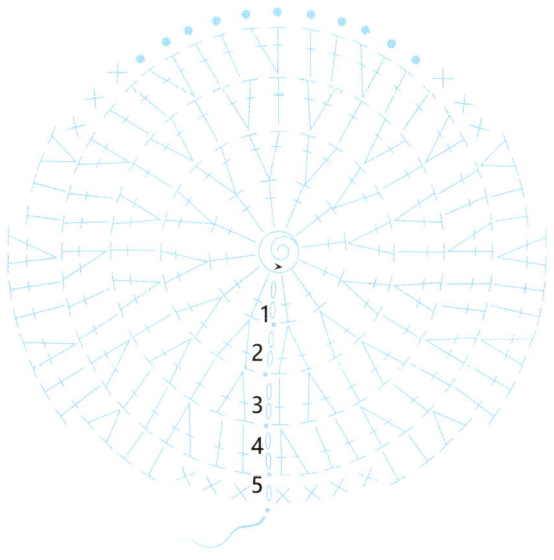

Cheek (3mm/D/3 hook)

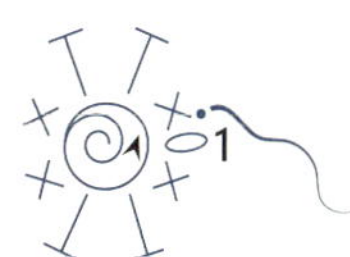

Snout (3.5mm/E/4 hook)

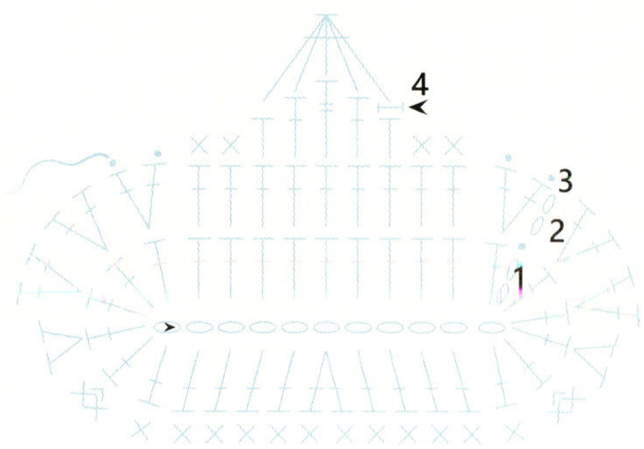

Fin (3.5mm/E/4 hook)

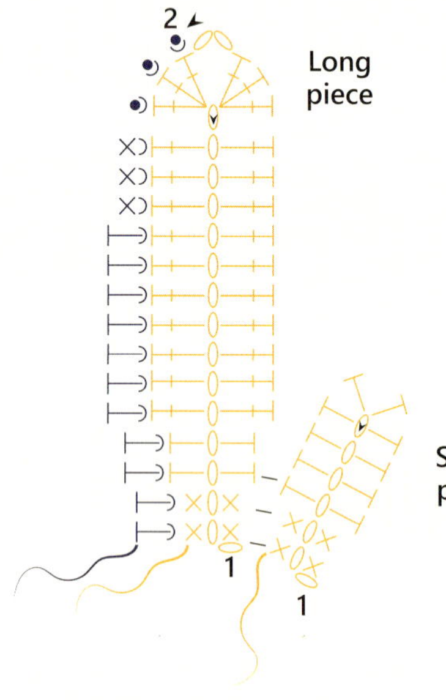

Row 3: (RS) Sl st in next st after join, sc in next 2 sts, hdc in next st and place marker in st just made, dc in next st, tr in next st, dc in next st, hdc in next st, sc in next 2 sts, sl st in next 2 sts; leave the remaining sts unworked; fasten off, leaving a long tail for sewing; do not turn = 13 sts including join

Row 4: (RS) Make a slip knot with **Color 36** and hold it on the hook; dc5tog, placing the first standing st in hdc with marker; leave the remaining sts unworked = 1 st

Fasten off and weave in the end; remove the marker.

Fin

Work in rows with a 3.5mm hook.

Long Piece

Row 1: With **Color 23**—Ch 16, sc in second ch from hook, sc in next ch, hdc in next 2 chs, dc in next 10 chs, (3 dc, ch 2, 3 dc) in last ch; work across the opposite side of the foundation ch—dc in next 10 chs, hdc in next 2 chs, sc in last 2 chs; fasten off **Color 23**, leaving a long tail for sewing = 34 sts and 1 ch-2 sp

Row 2: Work in BLO—join **Color 42** with a sl st in dc after ch-2 sp, sl st in next 2 sts, sc in next 3 sts, hdc in last 11 sts; fasten off **Color 42**, leaving a long tail for sewing = 17 sts

Short Piece

Row 1: With **Color 23**—Ch 7, sc in second ch from hook, sc in next ch, hdc in next 3 chs, 4 hdc in last ch; work across the opposite side of the foundation ch—hdc in next 3 chs, sc in last 2 chs; fasten off, leaving a long tail for sewing = 14 sts

Finishing Fin

Position the 2 pieces side by side with their yellow edges touching. Using **Color 23** from the short piece, whipstitch across 3 sts to join them; finish off and weave in the end.

Assembly

Position the head on the square, 1 rnd above the bottom edge, and backstitch around using **Color 37**.

Position the snout as shown, aligning its bottom edge with the head; backstitch around onto the head using **Color 36**.

Position the fin on the top of the head as shown. Using **Color 23**, whipstitch across the bottom edge and backstitch along the center of the short piece; leave the remaining edges unstitched. Bring **Color 42** to WS and work surface sl sts along the corresponding color edge to join it to the square. Finish off and weave in the ends.

Cut out the indicated felt pieces using the templates and assemble the layers to complete each eye (see Working With Felt). Position and glue the eyes onto the head. Position the cheeks as shown. Using **Color 42**, backstitch around each cheek onto the head. Finish off and weave in the ends.

Thread the needle with a 4-ply black yarn and stitch the mouth and nose as indicated. Finish off and weave in the ends.

Felt templates

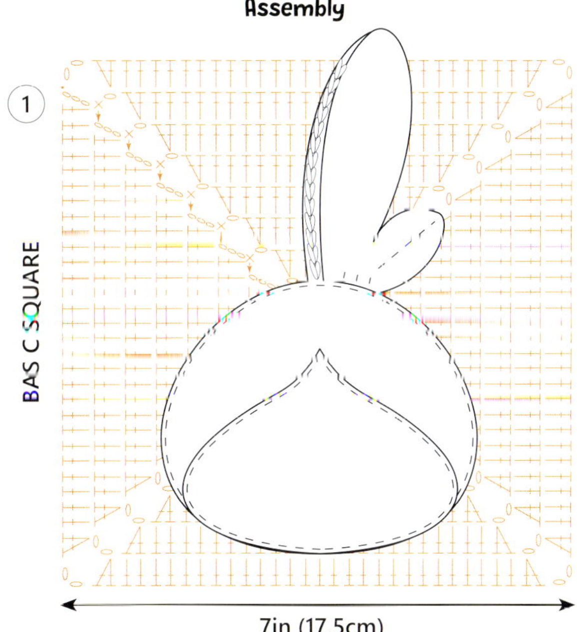

Charmander

The flame on the tip of this Pokémon's tail shows the strength of its life-force. If Charmander is healthy, the flame burns vigorously.

Key

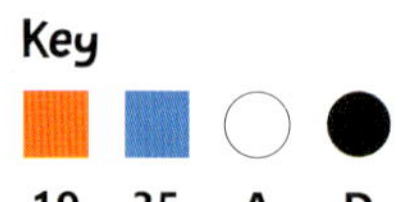

19 35 A D R

Difficulty level

Type

Square (4mm/G/6 hook)

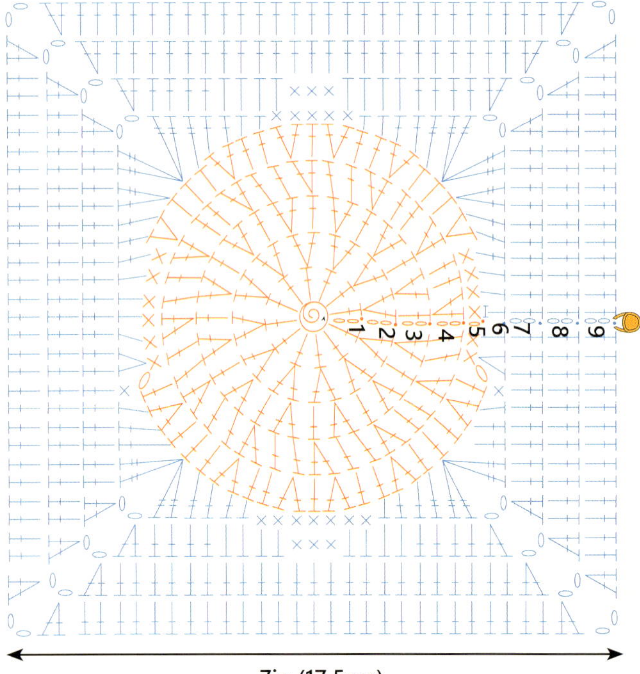

7in (17.5cm)

Square

Make a magic ring using **Color 19** and work in the round with a 4mm hook.

Follow Rnds 1–4 of Basic Circle (see Basic Shapes).

Rnd 5: Ch 1 (does not count as a st), sc in same st as join, sc in next 3 sts, 2 hdc in next st, hdc in next 3 sts, *2 dc in next st, dc in next 2 sts, 2 dc in next st, dc in next st, 2 dc in next st, dc in next 2 sts, 2 dc in next st**, hdc in next 3 sts, 2 hdc in next st, sc in next 6 sts, ch 1, dc in next st, 2 dc in next st, dc in next 3 sts, repeat from * to **, dc in next 3 sts, 2 dc in next st, dc in next st, ch 1, sc in last 2 sts; join and fasten off without breaking off **Color 19**, hold it on WS (see Finishing/Surface Crochet) = 60 sts and 2 chs

Rnd 6: Join **Color 35** with a standing hdc in first st, hdc in next 2 sts, dc in next 3 sts, (dc, tr) in next st, (2 tr, ch 2, 2 tr) in next st; tr in next st, dc in next 2 sts, hdc in next 2 sts, sc in next 5 sts, hdc in next 2 sts, dc in next 2 sts, tr in next st, (2 tr, ch 2, 2 tr) in next st; (tr, dc) in next st, dc in next 3 sts, hdc in next 4 sts, 2 hdc in next st, skip ch, sc in next st, hdc in next st, dc in next 2 sts, (2 tr, ch 2, 2 tr) in next st; tr in next st, dc in next 2 sts, hdc in next st, sc in next 7 sts, hdc in next st, dc in next 2 sts, tr in next st, (2 tr, ch 2, 2 tr) in next st; dc in next 2 sts, hdc in next st, sc in next st, skip ch, 2 hdc in next st, hdc in last st; join = 76 sts and 4 ch-2 sps

Rnd 7: Ch 2 (does not count as a st now and throughout), dc in same st as join, *dc in each st to next ch-2 sp, (2 dc, ch 2, 2 dc) in ch-2 sp, dc in next 4 sts, hdc in next 4 sts, sc in next 3 sts, hdc in next 4 sts, dc in next 4 sts, (2 dc, ch 2, 2 dc) in ch-2 sp, repeat from *, dc in each st to end; join = 92 sts and 4 ch-2 sps

Rnds 8–9: Ch 2, dc in same st as join, [dc in each st to next ch-2 sp, (2 dc, ch 2, 2 dc) in ch-2 sp] 4 times, dc in each st to end; join – 108/124 sts and 4 ch-2 sps.

Place marker in final join to indicate the right edge of the square. Fasten off and weave in the ends.

Assembly

Hold the square with the stitch marker on the right.

Outline the head with **Color 19** by working surface sl sts between Rnds 5 and 6 with a 4mm hook, holding yarn on WS. Finish off seamlessly and weave in the end (see Finishing/Surface Crochet).

Cut out the indicated pieces from Felts A, D, and R, using the templates and assemble the layers to complete each eye (see Working With Felt). Position the eyes referring to the image; use pins to mark the main points. Glue the eyes onto the head and leave them to dry. Thread the needle with a 4-ply white yarn and stitch the eye highlights as indicated. Finish off and weave in the ends.

Thread the needle with a 4-ply black yarn and stitch the mouth, nostrils, and eyebrows as indicated. Use straight pins to mark the main points prior to stitching. Finish off and weave in the ends; remove the marker from the square.

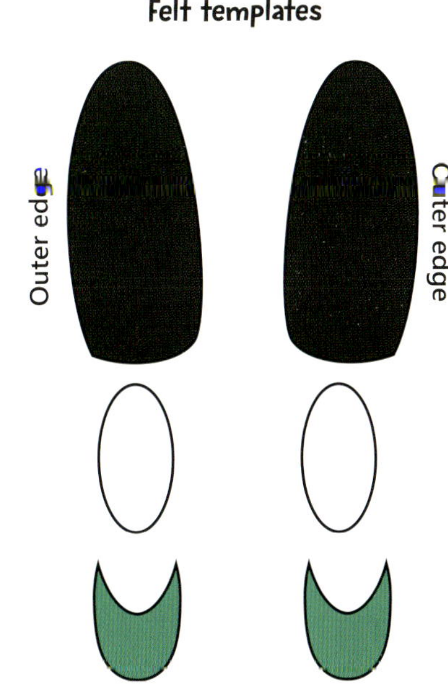

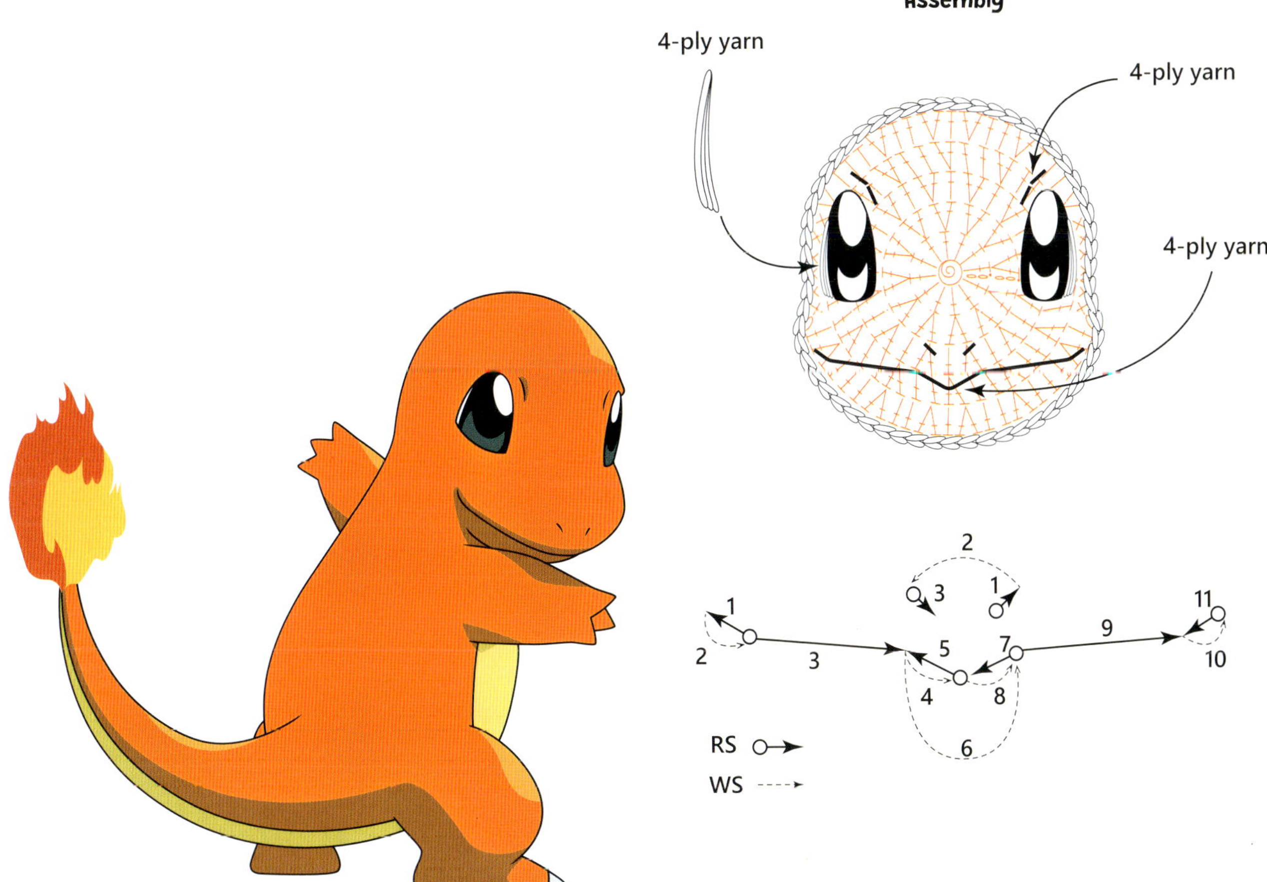

Bulbasaur

This Pokémon carries a seed on its back right from birth. It uses the nutrients that are packed into the seed to grow.

Key

17 31 A I S

Difficulty level

Type

Square (4mm/G/6 hook)

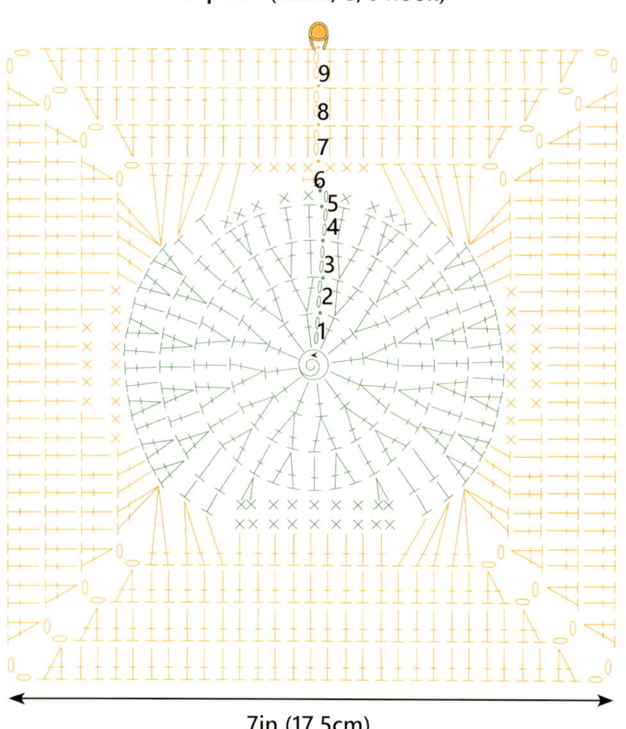

7in (17.5cm)

Ear (3mm/D/3 hook)

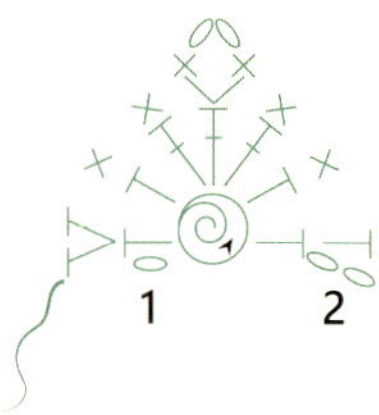

Square

Make a magic ring using **Color 31** and work in the round with a 4mm hook.

Follow Rnds 1–3 of Basic Circle (see Basic Shapes).

Rnd 4: Ch 2 (does not count as a st now and throughout), dc in same st as join, [dc in next 2 sts, 2 dc in next st] 2 times, [dc in next st, 2 dc in next st] 3 times, hdc in next 2 sts, 2 sc in next st, sc in next 5 sts, 2 sc in next st, hdc in next 2 sts, [2 dc in next st, dc in next st] 3 times, [2 dc in next st, dc in next 2 sts] 2 times; join = 48 sts

Rnd 5: Ch 1 (does not count as a st), sc in same st as join, sc in next 4 sts, *hdc in next 2 sts, 2 dc in next 2 sts, dc in next st, 2 dc in next st, dc in next 3 sts, 2 dc in next st, dc in next st, 2 dc in next 2 sts, hdc in next 2 sts**, sc in next 9 sts; repeat from * to **, sc in next 4 sts; join and fasten off without breaking off **Color 31**, hold it on WS (see Finishing/Surface Crochet) = 60 sts

Rnd 6: Join **Color 17** with a standing sc in first st, sc in next 3 sts, hdc in next 2 sts; *2 dc in next st, (2 dc, ch 2, 2 dc) in next st, dc in next 2 sts, hdc in next st, sc in next 9 sts, hdc in next st, dc in next 2 sts, (2 dc, ch 2, 2 dc) in next st, 2 dc in next st**, dc in next 11 sts; repeat from * to **, hdc in next 2 sts, sc in last 3 sts; join = 76 sts and 4 ch-2 sps

Rnd 7: Ch 2, dc in same st as join, *dc in each st to next ch-2 sp, (2 dc, ch 2, 2 dc) in ch-2 sp; dc in next 4 sts, hdc in next 3 sts, sc in next 5 sts, hdc in next 3 sts, dc in next 4 sts, (2 dc, ch 2, 2 dc) in next ch-2 sp; repeat from *, dc in each st to end; join = 92 sts and 4 ch-2 sps

Rnds 8–9: Ch 2, dc in same st as join, [dc in each st to next ch-2 sp, (2 dc, ch 2, 2 dc) in ch-2 sp] 4 times, dc in each st to end; join = 108/124 sts and 4 ch-2 sps

Place marker in final join to indicate the top of the square. Fasten off and weave in the ends.

Ear (make 2)

Make a magic ring using **Color 31** and work in rows with a 3mm hook.

Row 1: (WS) Ch 1 (does not count as a st); work in ring—2 hdc, 3 dc, 2 hdc; turn without joining = 7 sts

Row 2: (RS) Ch 2 (counts as hdc), hdc in first st, sc in next 2 sts, (sc, ch 2, sc) in next st, sc in next 2 sts, 2 hdc in last st = 10 sts and 1 ch-2 sp

Fasten off, leaving a long tail for sewing.

Assembly

Outline the head with **Color 31** by working surface sl sts between Rnds 5 and 6 with a 4mm hook, holding yarn on WS. Finish off seamlessly and weave in the end (see Finishing/Surface Crochet).

Holding the square with the stitch marker at the top, position the ears referring to the image. Using **Color 31** whipstitch across the bottom edge of each ear onto the square and through the center of the ears; leave the remaining edges unstitched. Finish off and weave in the ends; remove the marker from the square.

Cut out the indicated pieces from Felts A, I, and S, using the templates; assemble the layers to complete each eye (see Working With Felt). Position the eyes and patches referring to the image; use pins to mark the main points. Glue all pieces onto the head and leave to dry.

Thread the needle with a 4-ply black yarn and stitch the mouth, nostrils, and eyebrows as indicated. Use straight pins to mark the main points prior to stitching. Finish off and weave in the ends.

Felt Templates

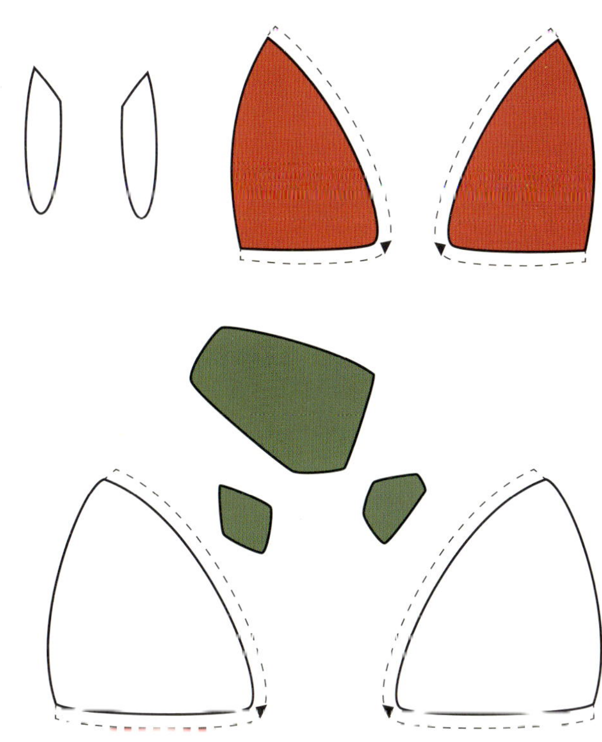

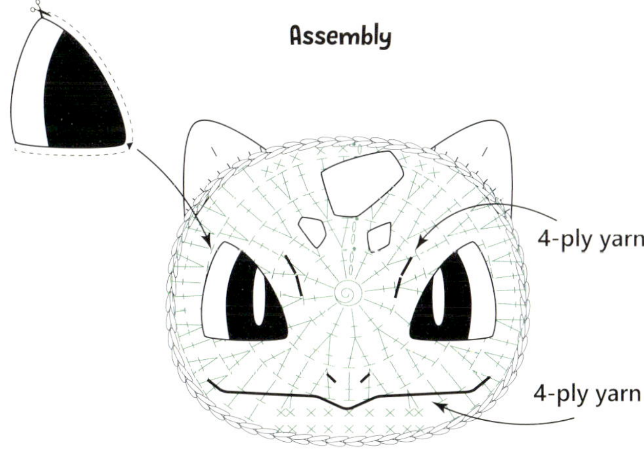

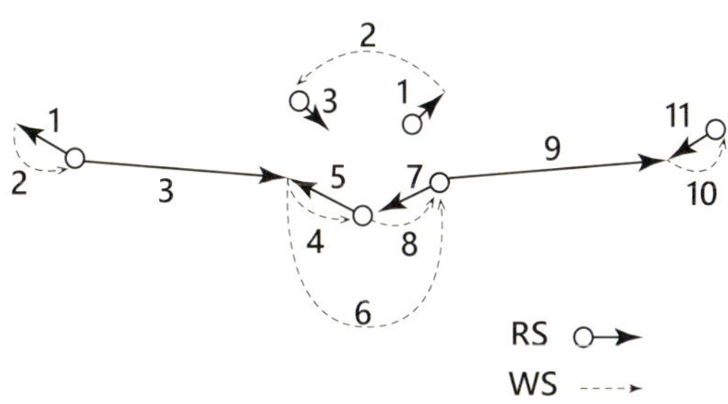

Snivy

The leaf on Snivy's tail generates energy when exposed to sunlight, making the Pokémon swifter and adding an edge to its moves.

Key

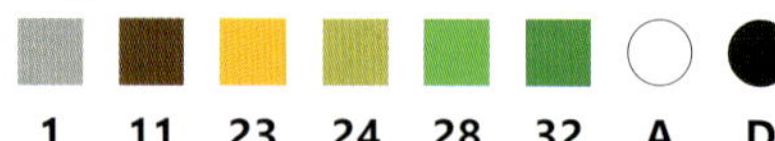

1 11 23 24 28 32 A D

Difficulty level

Type

Eye (3.5mm/E/4 hook)

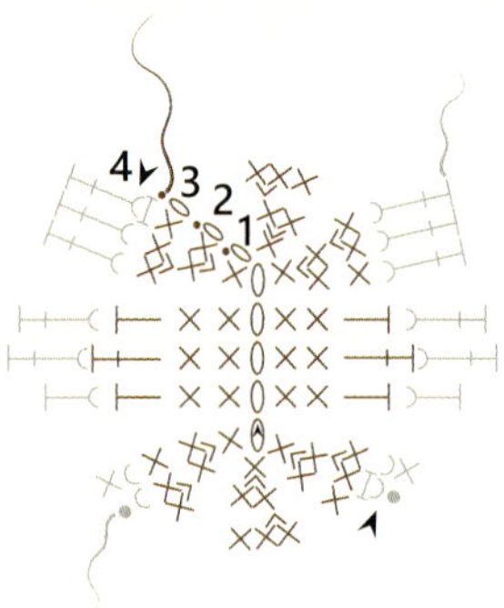

Eyelid (3.5mm/E/4 hook)

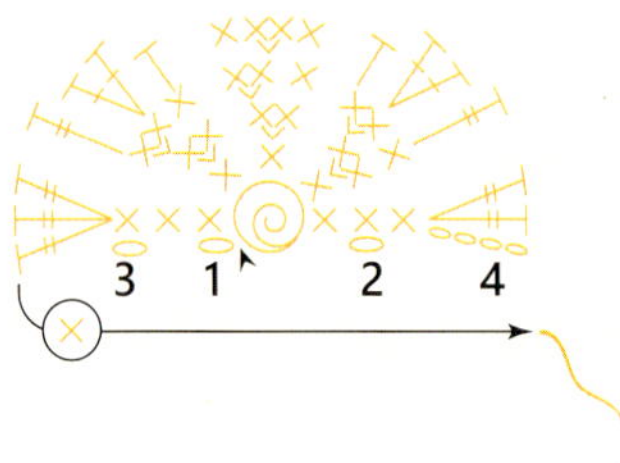

Square

Make one Basic Square using **Color 28** and a 4mm hook (see Basic Shapes).

Head and Snout

Make a magic ring using **Color 32** and work in the round with a 3.5mm hook.

Follow Rnds 1–4 of Basic Circle (see Basic Shapes).

Rnd 5: Ch 2, dc in same st as join, dc in next 2 sts, 2 dc in next st, [dc in next 3 sts, 2 dc in next st] 11 times; join = 60 sts

Row 6: Sl st in next st, sc in next 4 sts, hdc in next 4 sts; work the snout—ch 14, sl st in second ch from hook, sl st in next ch, sc in next 2 chs, hdc in next 2 chs, 3 dc in next ch, tr in next 3 chs, tr3tog, tr in post of hdc before the snout, skip 3 sts on the head, sl st in next st; leave the remaining sts unworked; fasten off, leaving a long tail for sewing = 9 sts and snout

Chin

Begin by working in rows across the snout edge, using **Color 24** and a 3.5mm hook.

Row 1: (RS) Work in BLO of the snout—Join **Color 24** with a sl st in first st, sc in each of next 13 sts, ch 17; turn = 14 sts and ch-17

Row 2: (WS) Dc in fourth ch from hook (the skipped chs count as dc), dc in next ch, [2 dc in next ch, dc in next 2 chs] 4 times; dc in next 4 sts, hdc in next 3 sts, sc in next 2 sts, skip 2 sts, dc in next st; turn, leaving the remaining sts unworked = 29 sts

Row 3: (RS) Skip dc just made, sc2tog, 2 hdc in next st, dc in each st across; turn = 28 sts

Row 4: (WS) Ch 3 (counts as dc), skip first st, dc2tog, dc in next 15 sts, hdc in next 3 sts, sc in next 2 sts, skip 2 sts, dc in next st; turn, leaving the remaining sts unworked = 23 sts

Row 5: (RS) Skip dc just made, sc2tog, sc in next 5 sts, hdc in next 5 sts, sc in next 8 sts, dc2tog and place marker in st just made; do not turn = 20 sts

Row 6: (RS) Work across the raw edge of the chin—2 sc in each of next 4 rows; rotate and continue to work across the opposite side of the foundation ch—ch 2 (counts as dc), dc in next 11 chs, hdc in next ch, sc in next ch, sl st in last ch; fasten off **Color 24**, leaving a long tail for sewing; do not turn = 23 sts

Row 7: (RS) Work in BLO—join **Color 23** with a sl st in st with marker and remove the marker, sl st in next st, sc in next 2 sts, hdc in next 2 sts, 2 dc in next st, tr in next st, 2 tr in next st, leave the remaining sts unworked; fasten off **Color 23**, leaving a long tail for sewing = 11 sts

Eye

Begin by working in the round using **Color 11** and a 3.5mm hook.

Rnd 1: Ch 6, sc in second ch from hook, sc in next 3 chs, 3 sc in last ch; work across the opposite side of the foundation ch—sc in next 3 chs, 2 sc in last ch; join = 12 sts

Rnd 2: Ch 1 (does not count as a st now and throughout), 2 sc in same st as join, sc in next 3 sts, 2 sc in next 3 sts, sc in next 3 sts, 2 sc in last 2 sts; join = 18 sts

Rnd 3: Ch 1, sc in same st as join, 2 sc in next st, *hdc in next st, dc in next st, hdc in next st**, [sc in next st, 2 sc in next st] 3 times, repeat from * to **, [sc in next st, 2 sc in next st] 2 times; join and break off **Color 11**, leaving a long tail for sewing =24 sts

Rnd 4: Work in BLO—join **Color 1** with a standing dc in first st, dc in next 4 sts, hdc in next st, sc in next st, sl st in next st; fasten off **Color 1**, leaving a long tail for sewing; skip 5 sts and and continue working in BLO—join **Color 1** with a standing sl st in next st, sc in next st, hdc in next st, dc in next 5 sts; leave the remaining sts unworked; fasten off **Color 1**, leaving a long tail for sewing = 14 sts and 2 long tails

Eyelid

Make a magic ring using **Color 23** and work in rows with a 3.5mm hook.

Row 1: (WS) Ch 1 (does not count as a st now and throughout), 5 sc in ring; turn = 5 sts

Row 2: (RS) Ch 1, sc in first st, 2 sc in next 3 sts, sc in last st; turn = 8 sts

Row 3: (WS) Ch 1, sc in first st, [2 sc in next st, sc in next st] 3 times, sc in last st; turn = 11 sts

(continued overleaf)

Head (3.5mm/E/4 hook)

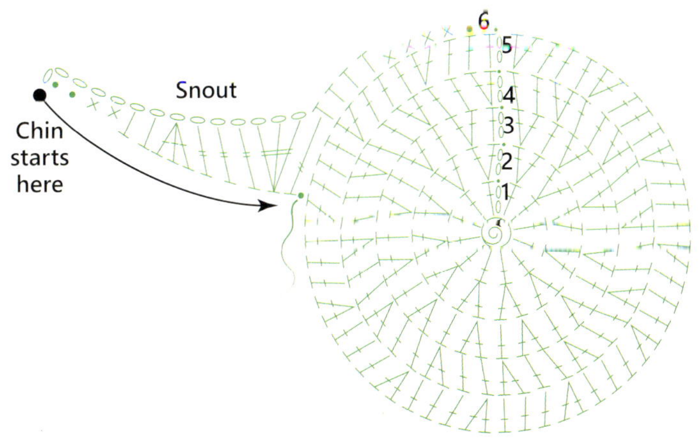

Chin (3.5mm/E/4 hook)

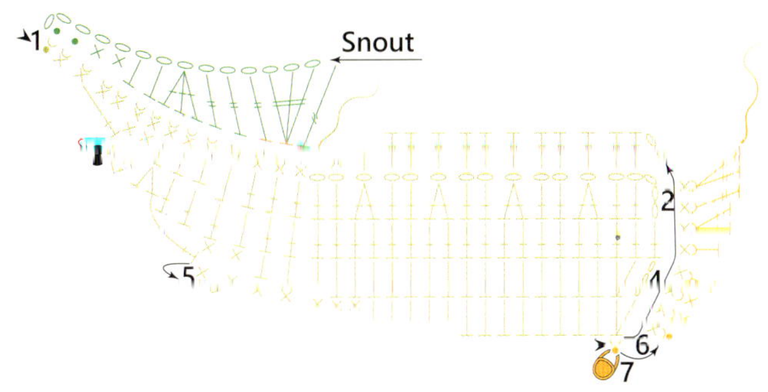

Felt templates

Assembly

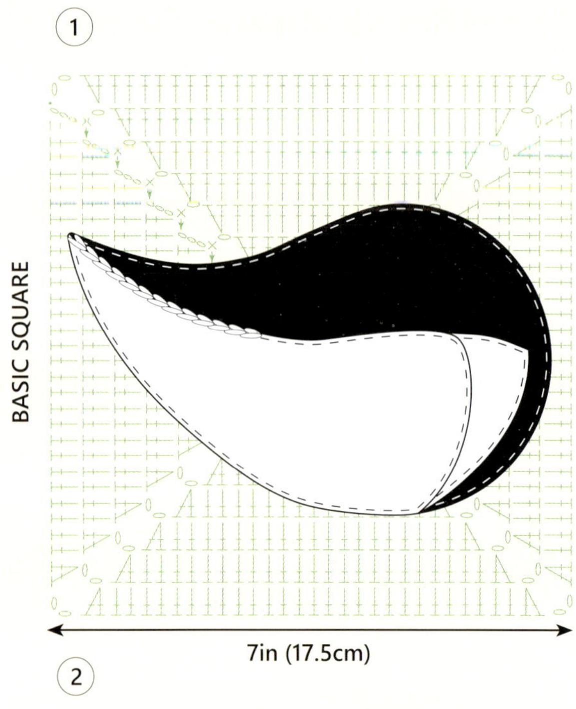

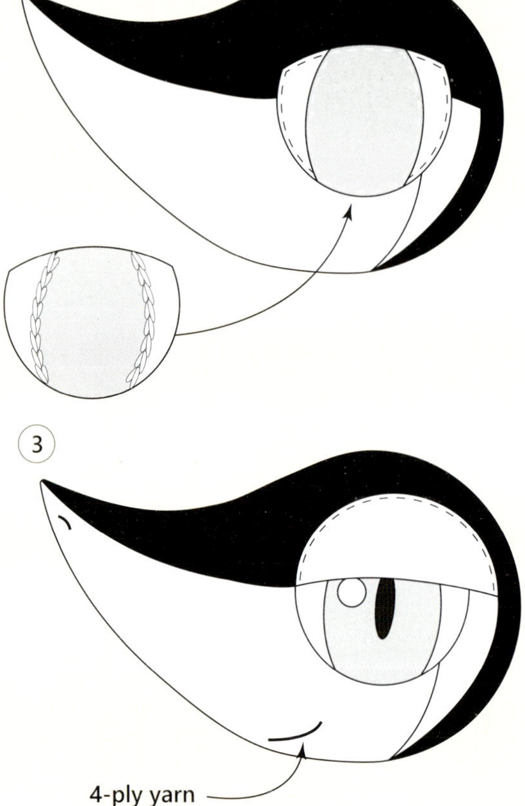

Row 4: (RS) Ch 4 (counts as tr), 2 tr in first st, tr in next st, 2 dc in next st, hdc in next st, sc in next st, 2 sc in next st, sc in next st, hdc in next st, 2 dc in next st, tr in next st, 3 tr in last st = 18 sts

Edging: Work sc evenly across the raw edge; fasten off, leaving a long tail for sewing.

Assembly

Using **Color 24** and a 3.5mm hook, work surface sl sts across the connected edge of the chin and snout. Sew the chin onto the head, then sew the finished head onto the square; finish off and weave in the ends.

Using **Color 1** and a 3.5mm hook, work surface sl sts between Rnds 3 and 4 of the eye. Sew the eye onto the head as shown; Finish off and weave in the ends.

Cut out and glue the felt pieces onto the eye, then sew the eyelid as shown. Stitch the mouth and nostril with 4-ply black yarn. Finish off and weave in the ends.

The Projects

In this section, you will find some fun project ideas to make using the Pokémon squares from this book. Make a cozy throw blanket with a coordinating pillow, a cute mug rug, a handy wall hanging with pockets, a stylish banner, and colorful play cubes. Let your creativity run wild by mixing Pokémon of the same type in your favorite projects.

Lap Blanket

Get cozy with this colorful blanket that features all 36 squares from the book. You can snuggle up for a night or just dive into your favorite Pokémon tales while reading in style. If you wish to expand your blanket, you'll find helpful tips to make it just the way you like it.

Assembly

Key

40

Difficulty level

Materials

- Stylecraft Special DK (100% acrylic), 5½oz (160g) of **Color 40** for edging
- 4mm (G/6) hook
- 36 completed Pokémon squares (1 of each)

Size

48 x 48in (122 x 122cm)

To Begin

Make 36 Pokémon squares (1 of each).

Edging and Assembly

Using **Color 40** and a 4mm hook, work around each square. Join squares as you go while adding the edging (placing squares as shown in the diagram), or use an alternative joining technique after finishing the edging around each square (see Finishing/ Joining Squares).

Square Edging

Join **Color 40** with a standing dc in any corner, (2dc, ch 2, 3 dc) in same sp, [ch 1, skip 3 sts, 3 dc in next st] 7 times, ch 1, skip 3 sts; *(3 dc, ch 2, 3 dc) in next ch-2 sp, [ch 1, skip 3 sts, 3 dc in next st] 7 times, ch 1, skip 3 sts; repeat from * around; join = 108 sts, 32 ch-1 sps and 4 ch-2 sps

Fasten off and weave in the ends.

Blanket Edging

Work around the blanket edge with **Color 40** and a 4mm hook.

Join **Color 40** with a sl st in any ch-1 sp, [ch 2, 2 dc in same sp, skip 3 dc, sl st in next sp] around = 192 points

Fasten off and weave in the ends.

Square edging (4mm/G/6 hook)

Blanket edging (4mm/G/6 hook)

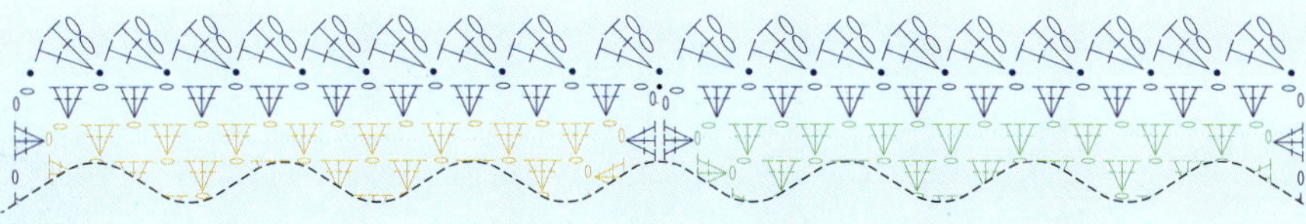

RESIZING TIP

If you want to make your blanket larger, you can add basic squares between the Pokémon squares (see Basic Shapes) or enlarge each Pokémon square by adding additional rounds of granny edging. Simply work (3 dc, ch 2, 3 dc) in each corner and (3 dc, ch 1) in each ch-1 sp around.

Pillow

Join your favorite squares together into a playful pebble-pillow for a themed bedroom where your Pokémon dreams will come to life. We recommend grouping any four Pokémon by type or consider pairing Pikachu with the three first partners of a single region (see Pokémon Grouping Considerations).

Key

43

Difficulty level

Materials

- Stylecraft Special DK (100% acrylic): 4¼oz (120g) of **Color 43** for the pillow back and edging, plus a small amount of colorful yarn scraps for the pebbles
- 4mm (G/6) hook
- 4 Pokémon squares
- 4 toggle buttons (for closure)
- Polyester stuffing
- Pillow insert, 17–18¾in (43–48cm)

Size

17 x 17in (43 x 43cm)

Front

Make four Pokémon squares, referring to the Pokémon grouping considerations (in the sample, I used three first partners of the Paldea region plus Pikachu).

Work around each square with **Color 43** and a 4mm hook, as for the blanket, joining them as you go (see Finishing/Joining Squares). Fasten off and weave in the ends. Now, work around the entire edge of your four-square unit.

Rnd 1: Join **Color 43** with a standing dc in any corner, (2 dc, ch 2, 3 dc) in same sp, *ch 1, skip 3 dc, [3 dc in next sp, ch 1, skip 3 dc] to next corner, (3 dc, ch 2, 3 dc) in next ch-2 sp**; repeat from * to ** 2 more times; ch 1, skip 3 dc, [3 dc in next sp, ch 1, skip 3 dc] to end; join = 228 sts, 72 ch-1 sps and 4 corners

Fasten off and weave in the ends.

Back

Make two rectangular units. To complete each unit, first make two granny squares and join them as you go across one side while working the last round of the second square (see Finishing/Joining Squares).

Granny Square

Work in the round with a 4mm hook or any hook size needed to obtain gauge. To prevent distortion in the corners, change the direction of your work in every round.

To begin: Ch 4, sl st in last ch from hook to form a ring.

Rnd 1: (RS) Ch 3 (counts as dc now and throughout), work in ring—2 dc, [ch 2, 3 dc] 3 times; ch 2, sl st in top of beg ch-3; turn = 12 sts and 4 corners

Rnd 2: (WS) Ch 3, (2 dc, ch 2, 3 dc) in first ch-2 sp, ch 1, skip 3 dc, [(3 dc, ch 2, 3 dc) in next ch-2 sp, ch 1, skip 3 dc] 3 times; sl st in top of beg ch-3; turn = 24 sts, 4 ch-1 sps and 4 corners

Rnd 3: (RS) Ch 3, 2 dc in first ch-1 sp, ch 1, skip 3 dc, (3 dc, ch 2, 3 dc) in next ch-2 sp; [ch 1, skip 3 dc, 3 dc in next ch-1 sp, ch 1, skip 3 dc, (3 dc, ch 2, 3 dc) in next ch-2 sp] 3 times; ch 1, skip 3 dc; sl st in top of beg ch-3; turn = 36 sts, 8 ch-1 sps and 4 corners

Back (4mm/G/6 hook)

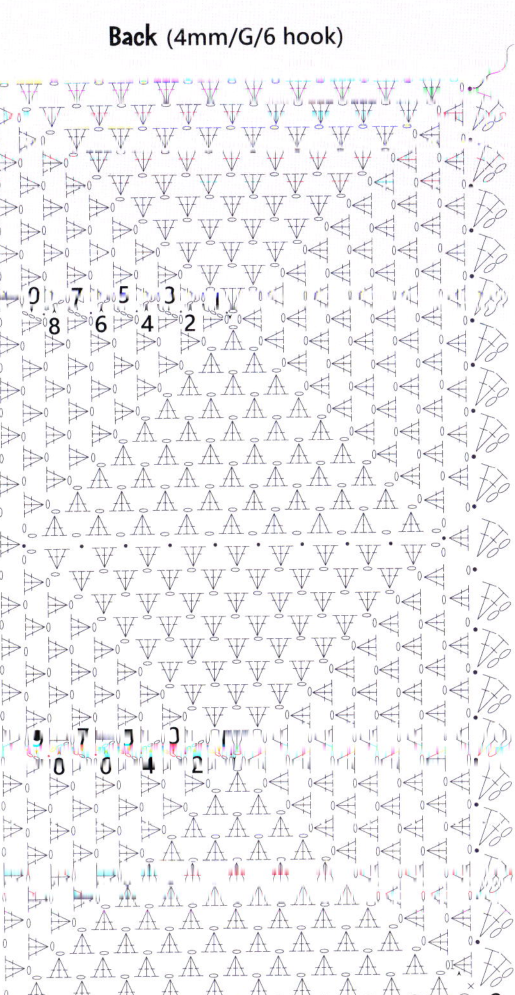

9in (23cm)

Front (4mm/G/6 hook)

17in (43cm)

Rnd 4: (WS) Ch 3, 2 dc in first ch-1 sp, ch 1, skip 3 dc; *(3 dc, ch 2, 3 dc) in next ch-2 sp, ch 1, skip 3 dc, [3 dc in next ch-1 sp, ch 1, skip 3 dc] to next corner**; repeat from * to ** 2 more times; (3 dc, ch 2, 3 dc) in next ch-2 sp, ch 1, skip 3 dc, 3 dc in next ch-1 sp, ch 1, skip 3 dc; sl st in top of beg ch-3; turn = 48 sts, 12 ch-1 sps and 4 corners

Rnd 5: (RS) Ch 3, 2 dc in first ch-1 sp, ch 1, skip 3 dc, 3 dc in next ch-1 sp, ch 1, skip 3 dc; *(3 dc, ch 2, 3 dc) in next ch-2 sp, ch 1, skip 3 dc, [3 dc in next ch-1 sp, ch 1, skip 3 dc] to next corner**; repeat from * to ** 2 more times; (3 dc, ch 2, 3 dc) in next ch-2 sp, ch 1, skip 3 dc, 3 dc in next ch-1 sp, ch 1, skip 3 dc; sl st in top of beg ch-3; turn = 60 sts, 16 ch-1 sps and 4 corners

Rnd 6: (WS) Ch 3, 2 dc in first ch-1 sp, ch 1, skip 3 dc, 3 dc in next ch-1 sp, ch 1, skip 3 dc; *(3 dc, ch 2, 3 dc) in next ch-2 sp, ch 1, skip 3 dc, [3 dc in next ch-1 sp, ch 1, skip 3 dc] to next corner**; repeat from * to ** 2 more times; (3 dc, ch 2, 3 dc) in next ch-2 sp, ch 1, skip 3 dc, [3 dc in next ch-1 sp, ch 1, skip 3 dc] to end; sl st in top of beg ch-3; turn = 72 sts, 20 ch-1 sps and 4 corners

Rnds 7–9: Ch 3, 2 dc in first ch-1 sp, ch 1, skip 3 dc; *[3 dc in next ch-1 sp, ch 1, skip 3 dc] to next corner, (3 dc, ch 2, 3 dc) in next ch-2 sp, ch 1, skip 3 dc**; repeat from * to ** 3 more times; [3 dc in next ch-1 sp, ch 1, skip 3 dc] to end; sl st in top of beg ch-3; turn = 84/96/108 sts, 24/28/32 ch-1 sps and 4 corners

Fasten off and weave in the ends.

(continued overleaf)

Edging

Work around the entire edge of the rectangular unit, holding it vertically.

Rnd 1: (RS) Join **Color 43** with a standing dc in bottom right corner, 2 dc in same sp, *ch 1, skip 3 dc, [3 dc in next sp, ch 1, skip 3 dc] to next corner, (3 dc, ch 2, 3 dc) in next ch-2 sp**; repeat from * to ** 2 more times; ch 1, skip 3 dc, [3 dc in next ch-1 sp, ch 1, skip 3 dc] to end; 3 dc into same corner as your standing dc, ch 1, sc in first st to join = 174 sts, 54 ch-1 sps and 4 corners

Rnd 2: (RS) Ch 2, 2 dc in same corner, skip 3 sts, sl st in ch-1 sp, [ch 2, 2 dc in same sp, skip 3 sts, sl st in ch-1 sp] to next corner; leave the remaining edges unworked = 19 points

Fasten off, leaving a long tail for sewing.

Finishing

Position your two back pieces on WS of the front piece, with their pointy edges overlapping vertically in the center by one round. Using the long tail from each back piece, sew the sides to the front using the mattress stitch (see Finishing/Joining Squares). Leave the pointy edges in the center unstitched. Finish off and weave in the ends. Sew four toggle buttons, evenly spaced along one side of the center back. Insert the pillow and button it up on the back.

Pebbles

Using colorful yarn scraps, make seven large pebbles, four medium pebbles, and five small pebbles.

Large Pebble

Make a magic ring using any color and work in spiral rounds with a 4mm hook.

Rnd 1: Ch 1 (does not count as a st), 6 sc in ring; do not join now and throughout = 6 sts

Rnd 2: 2 sc in each st around = 12 sts

Rnd 3: [Sc in next st, 2 sc in next st] 6 times = 18 sts

Rnd 4: [Sc in next 2 sts, 2 sc in next st] 6 times = 24 sts

Rnd 5: [Sc in next 3 sts, 2 sc in next st] 6 times = 30 sts

Rnds 6–10: Sc in each st around = 30 sts

Rnd 11: [Sc in next 3 sts, sc2tog] 6 times = 24 sts

Rnd 12: [Sc in next 2 sts, sc2tog] 6 times = 18 sts

Rnd 13: [Sc in next st, sc2tog] 6 times; stuff pebble = 12 sts

Rnd 14: [Sc2tog] 6 times; add more stuffing = 6 sts

Skip st, sl st in next st and fasten off, leaving a long tail for sewing. Using a tapestry needle, close the opening.

Pokémon Grouping Considerations

When picking which Pokémon to pair for your project, we recommend grouping them by type or by choosing the three first partners of a single region. Of course, Pikachu is always welcome when a fourth Pokémon is needed for your craft!

Kanto: Bulbasaur, Charmander, Squirtle

Johto: Chikorita, Cyndaquil, Totodile

Hoenn: Treecko, Torchic, Mudkip

Sinnoh: Turtwig, Chimchar, Piplup

Unova: Snivy, Tepig, Oshawott

Kalos: Chespin, Fennekin, Froakie

Alola: Rowlet, Litten, Popplio

Galar: Grookey, Scorbunny, Sobble

Paldea: Sprigatito, Fuecoco, Quaxly

Medium Pebble

Make a magic ring using any color and work in spiral rounds with a 4mm hook.

Rnds 1–4: Work as for Large pebble

Rnds 5–8: Sc in each st around = 24 sts

Rnd 9: [Sc in next 2 sts, sc2tog] 6 times = 18 sts

Rnd 10: [Sc in next st, sc2tog] 6 times; stuff pebble = 12 sts

Rnd 11: [Sc2tog] 6 times; add more stuffing = 6 sts

Skip st, sl st in next st and fasten off, leaving a long tail for sewing. Using a tapestry needle, close the opening.

Small Pebble

Make a magic ring using any color and work in spiral rounds with a 4mm hook.

Rnds 1–3: Work as for Large pebble

Rnds 4–6: Sc in each st around = 18 sts

Rnd 7: [Sc in next st, sc2tog] 6 times; stuff pebble = 12 sts

Rnd 8: [Sc2tog] 6 times; add more stuffing = 6 sts

Skip st, sl st in next st and fasten off, leaving a long tail for sewing. Using a tapestry needle, close the opening.

Finishing

Position the pebbles in random order around the pillow edges and attach them with a whipstitch using the long tail from each pebble. Finish off and weave in the ends.

Banner

Add a touch of fun to your Pokémon parties with a stylish banner that will catch your guests' attention. Simply join together three Pokémon squares and four triangular flags to complete your colorful banner.

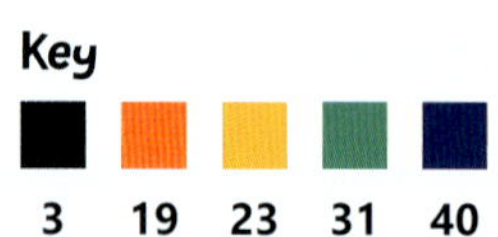

Difficulty level

Square flag edging (4mm/G/6 hook)

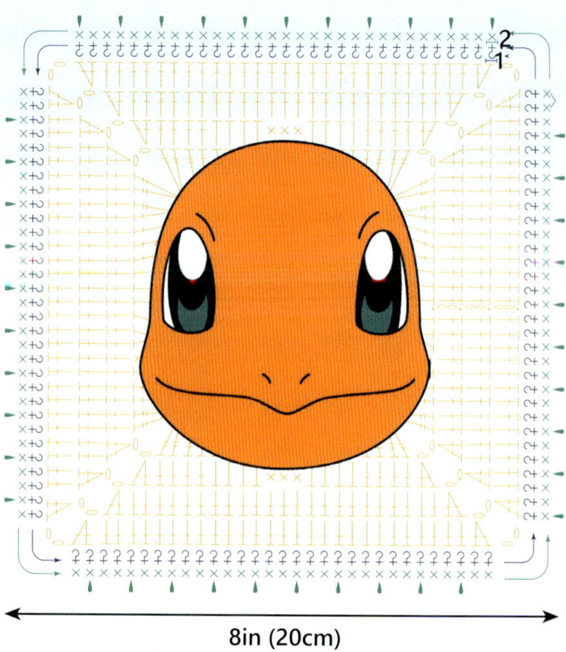

Materials

- Stylecraft Special DK (100% acrylic): ⅓–⅔oz (10–20g) each of the 5 listed yarn colors, or use your own colors
- 4mm (G/6) hook
- 3 Pokémon squares

Size

58in (147cm) excluding ties

To Begin

Make three Pokémon squares of the same type or three first partners of a single region (see Pillow/Pokémon Grouping Considerations). Bulbasaur (Grass), Charmander (Fire), and Squirtle (Water) are from the Kanto region. Add edging to each Pokémon square to complete square flags.

Square Flag Edging

Work in the round with a 4mm hook, starting across the top edge of the square.

Rnd 1: Begin at the top right corner and work across the top edge—join **Color 40** with a standing bpsc in first dc, [bpsc in each st to next corner, skip corner sp] around; join and fasten off **Color 40** = 124 sts

Rnd 2: Join color of your choice with a standing sc in first st, picot, [sc in next 3 sts, picot] to last 3 sts; sc in next st, sc2tog; join = 123 sts and 41 picots

Fasten off and weave in the ends.

Triangular Flags

Make four flags using the indicated colors or choose your own. Work in the round with a 4mm hook.

To begin: Using **Color 3**—Ch 4, sl st in last ch from hook to form a ring

Rnd 1: (RS) Ch 3 (counts as dc), work in ring—3 dc, [ch 3, 4 dc] 2 times; ch 3, sl st in top of beg ch-3; fasten off **Color 3** and turn = 12 sts and 3 corners

Rnd 2: (WS) Join **Color 31** with a standing dc in any corner, (3 dc, ch 3, 4 dc) in same sp, [ch 1, skip 4 dc, (4 dc, ch 3, 4 dc) in next corner] 2 times, ch 1, skip 4 dc; join, fasten off **Color 31** and turn = 24 sts, 3 ch-1 sps and 3 corners

Rnd 3: (RS) Join **Color 23** with a standing dc in any corner, (3 dc, ch 3, 4 dc) in same sp, ch 1, skip 4 dc, 4 dc in next ch-1 sp, ch 1, skip 4 dc; *(4 dc, ch 3, 4 dc) in next corner, ch 1, skip 4 dc, 4 dc in next ch-1 sp, ch 1, skip 4 dc; repeat from *; join, fasten off **Color 23** and turn = 36 sts, 6 ch-1 sps and 3 corners

Continue working as established, turning and changing colors in every rnd (**Color 40**/**Color 19**/**Color 31**/**Color 3**).

Rnds 4–7: Join **Color 40** with a standing dc in any corner, (3 dc, ch 3, 4 dc)

in same sp, ch 1, skip 4 dc, [4 dc in next ch-1 sp, ch 1, skip 4 dc] to next corner, *(4 dc, ch 3, 4 dc) in corner, ch 1, skip 4 dc, [4 dc in next ch-1 sp, ch 1, skip 4 dc] to next corner; repeat from *; join, fasten off and turn (all but last rnd) = 48/60/72/84 sts, 9/12/15/18 ch-1 sps and 3 corners

Rnd 8: (RS) With **Color 3**—Ch 1 (does not count as a st), sc in first 2 sts, picot, sc in next 2 sts, picot, [2 sc, picot] twice in corner, *[sc in next 2 sts, picot] to next corner, skipping ch-1 sps, [2 sc, picot] twice in corner; repeat from *, [sc in next 2 sts, picot] to end, skipping ch-1 sps; join = 108 sts and 48 picots

Fasten off and weave in the ends.

Assembly

Position the seven flags in a row, alternating the square and triangular flags. Join the flags into a banner by working across the top edge of each flag with **Color 3** and a 4mm hook.

Row 1: Ch 120, *work across the top edge of triangular flag—sl st in corner picot, ch 1, [sl st in next picot, ch 1] 16 times; work across the top edge of square flag—sl st in first picot, [ch 2, sl st in next picot] 10 times, ch 1; repeat from *, ending after last triangular flag; ch 120.

Fasten off and make a knot on each side to finish ties; trim off the ends.

Triangular flag (4mm/G/6 hook)

8.5in (21.5cm)

Mug Rug

Wake up with the coziest of companions! Using some colorful yarn scraps you can turn your favorite Pokémon square into a cute mug rug for your morning beverage and it will keep you huddled under the covers for just a little longer.

Key

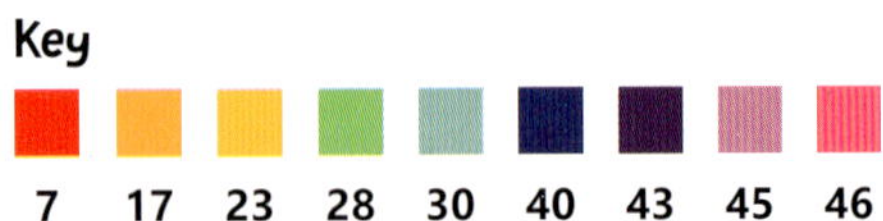

Difficulty level

Materials

- Stylecraft Special DK (100% acrylic): a small amount of each of the 9 listed yarn colors, or use your own colors
- 4mm (G/6) hook
- 1 Pokémon square of your choice

Size

7½ x 14½in (19 x 37cm)

Mini pebble square (4mm/G/6 hook)

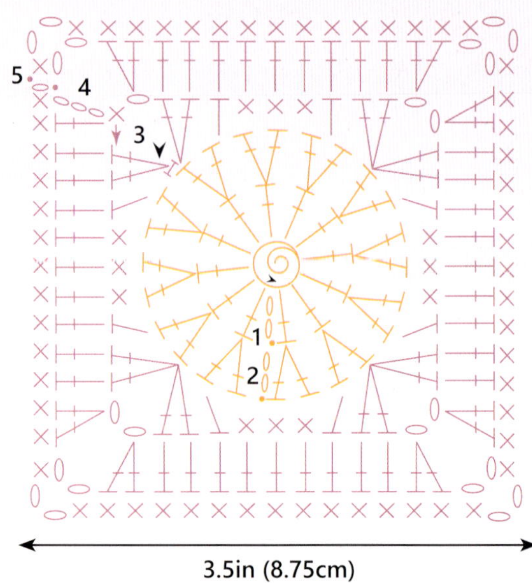

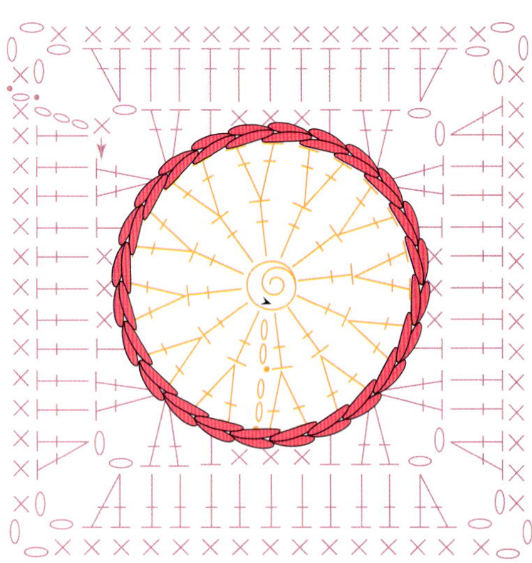

Assembly

1

2

To Begin

Make one Pokémon square of your choice and put it aside.

Mini Pebble Squares

Make four mini pebble squares using three colors of your choice, or as shown in the assembly for each square.

Make a magic ring using the first color—work in the round with a 4mm hook.

Rnd 1: Ch 2 (does not count as a st now and throughout), 12 dc in ring; join = 12 sts

Rnd 2: Ch 2, 2 dc in each st around; join and fasten off the first color = 24 sts

Rnd 3: Join the second color with a standing dc in any st, dc in same st, hdc in next st, sc in next 3 sts, hdc in next st; *(2 dc, ch 2, 2 dc) in next st, hdc in next st, sc in next 3 sts, hdc in next st; repeat from * 2 more times; 2 dc in same st as first st, ch 1, sc in top of beg st (counts as last corner) = 36 sts and 4 corners

Rnd 4: Ch 3 (counts as dc), dc in same sp, [dc in each st to next corner, (2 dc, ch 2, 2 dc) in ch-2 sp] 3 times; dc in each st to last corner, 2 dc in last ch-sp; ch 2, sl st in top of beg ch-3 = 52 sts and 4 corners

Rnd 5: Ch 1 (does not count as a st), sc in first st, [sc in each st to next corner, (sc, ch 2, sc) in corner] 4 times; join = 60 sts and 4 corners

Fasten off and weave in the ends. Holding the third color on WS, outline the circle with surface sl sts by working between Rnds 2 and 3 with a 4mm hook; finish off seamlessly and weave in the ends (see Finishing/Surface Crochet).

Assembly

Work with **Color 40** and a 4mm hook. Position four mini pebble squares as shown in the diagram and join them together with surface crochet, working through BLO to create one unit (1) (see Finishing/Surface Crochet Join).

Position your Pokémon square on the left or right of the pebble unit and join them with surface crochet through BLO using the same yarn and hook. Do not break off your working yarn.

Work the edging in the round using **Color 40** and a 4mm hook (2).

Rnd 1: Ch 1, sc in each st around, placing 3 sc in corners; join.

Rnd 2: Ch 1, fpsc in each st around; join.

Fasten off and weave in the ends.

Play Cubes

Keep your little ones entertained with a colorful set of Pokémon play cubes. They are easy to make and fun to play with while learning about color, texture, and identifying different Pokémon.

Key

46

Difficulty level

Assembly

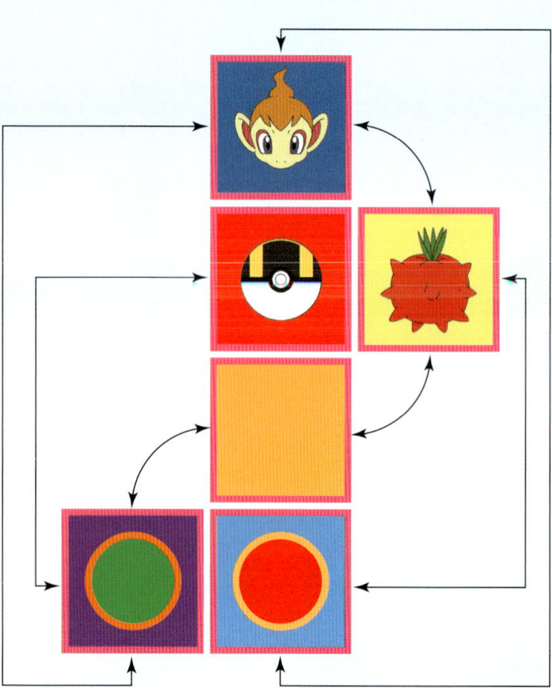

Materials

- For one cube: Stylecraft Special DK (100% acrylic): ½oz (15g) of **Color 46** (or any other) for edging, ⅓–½oz (10–16g) each of 3–5 additional colors of your choice for filler squares.
- 4mm (G/6) hook
- 3 Pokémon squares
- 6 pieces of medium-weight felt (3–4mm)
- Polyester stuffing
- Fabric glue

Size

7in (17.5cm) across each side

Square edging (4mm/G/6 hook)

7in (17.5cm)

Pebble square (4mm/G/6 hook)

7in (17.5cm)

To Begin

Make three Pokémon squares as indicated or choose your own (see Pillow/Pokémon Grouping Considerations).

Filler Squares

Using colors of your choice make three basic squares (see Basic Shapes) or combine basic and pebble squares as shown in the diagram.

Pebble Square

Make a magic ring using any desired color—work in the round with a 4mm hook.

Follow Rnds 1–4 of Basic Circle (see Basic Shapes).

Rnd 5: Join second color of your choice with a standing sc in any st, sc in next 3 sts, hdc in next st, dc in next st, (2 dc, ch 2, 2 dc) in next st; [dc in next st, hdc in next st, sc in next 7 sts, hdc in next st, dc in next st, (2 dc, ch 2, 2 dc) in next st] 3 times; dc in next st, hdc in next st, sc in next 3 sts; join = 60 sts and 4 ch-2 sps

Rnds 6–9: Ch 2, dc in same st as join, [dc in each st to next ch-2 sp, (2 dc, ch 2, 2 dc) in ch-2 sp] 4 times, dc in each st to end; join = 76/92/108/124 sts and 4 ch-2 sps

Fasten off and weave in the ends. Using a third color of your choice, outline the pebble with surface sl sts by holding the yarn on WS. Finish off seamlessly and weave in the ends (see Finishing/Surface Crochet).

Square Edging

Finish each Pokémon square and filler square with one round of edging, using **Color 46** and a 4mm hook.

Rnd 1: Begin in the st after any corner—join **Color 46** with a standing bpsc in first dc, [bpsc in each st to next corner, skip corner sp] around; join = 124 sts

Fasten off leaving a long tail for sewing.

Assembly

Cut six squares from medium-weight felt, slightly smaller than your crocheted squares—6¾ x 6¾in (17 x 17cm). Apply fabric glue to one side of the felt pieces, covering the entire surface evenly and glue them onto the WS of your crochet squares. Let the glue dry. This will stabilize the sides and prevent your cube from stretching.

Join squares as shown in the diagram using the long tails from the edging. Using the mattress stitch, sew from corner to corner (see Finishing/Joining Squares). When there are two sides left to sew, stuff your cube with polyester stuffing, then complete sewing. Finish off and weave in the ends.

Wall Hanging

This colorful wall hanging is like a burst of sunshine for your room! The pockets between Pokémon squares are fun and functional. They will help you organize your essentials and store all your little trinkets and treasures in one place.

Assembly

Key

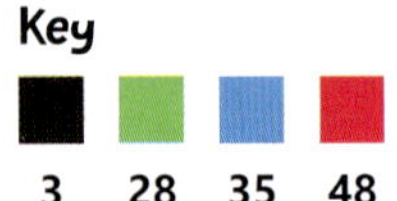

3 28 35 48

Difficulty level

Materials

- Stylecraft Special DK (100% acrylic): 1⅛oz (30g) each of four main colors for the back/front pockets and edging, plus 10–15 additional colors of your choice for the accents (a small amount of each)
- 4mm (G/6) hook
- 3 Pokémon squares
- 19in (48.5cm) wooden dowel
- 6 pieces of thin felt (1–1.2mm)
- Polyester stuffing
- Fabric glue

Size

14 x 24½in (35.5 x 62.5cm) excluding trimmings

To Begin

Make three Pokémon squares as indicated or choose your own (see Pillow/Pokémon Grouping Considerations).

Pocket Squares (back)

Make three basic squares (see Basic Shapes) using **Colors 48**, **35**, and **28**.

Pocket Squares (front)

Make three pebble squares (as for the Play Cubes), using any colors of your choice for the pebbles and **Colors 48**, **35**, and **28** for the background. Finish the square edging as for the Play Cubes, using the corresponding background colors. Leave a long tail at the end for sewing.

Top Banner

Make four mini pebble squares as for the Mug Rug, using additional colors of your choice.

Pebbles

Using any colors of your choice, make seven small pebbles, two medium, and two large, as for the Pillow. Do not close the openings in the large pebbles yet.

Cord

Using black yarn and a 4mm hook, make a 2yd (1.8m) d-ch cord (see Techniques/Finishing).

Assembly

Position three Pokémon squares, three basic squares, and four mini pebble squares as shown in the diagram. Join the squares with surface crochet through BLO using **Color 3** and a 4mm hook (see Finishing/Joining Squares). Finish off and weave in the ends.

Join **Color 3** yarn with a sl st in any corner and work edging with a 4mm hook—[ch 2, 2 dc in same st, skip 3 dc, sl st in next st] around; fasten off and weave in the ends.

Position 3 front pocket squares on top of the 3 corresponding back pocket squares and whipstitch the sides and bottom edges together, leaving the top edge unstitched. Finish off and weave in the ends.

Cut six squares from the thin felt, slightly smaller than your crocheted squares—6¾ x 6¾in (17 x 17cm). Apply fabric glue to one side of the felt pieces, covering the entire surface evenly and glue them onto WS of each Pokémon and basic square to stabilize them.

Position the wooden dowel at the top edge. Thread the needle with a long piece of **Color 3** and whipstitch across the edge, attaching the dowel. Finish off and weave in the ends.

Sew five small pebbles across the bottom edge. Finish off and weave in the ends.

Attach the cord to the dowel by tying a firm knot and a bow on each side. Glue the knotted sides to the dowel to prevent them from sliding and shifting; let the glue dry.

Insert the ends of the cord into the large pebbles and sew them in place; skip 5in (13cm) and sew a medium pebble on each side; skip 5in (13cm) and sew the remaining small pebbles. Finish off and weave in the ends.

Edging (4mm hook)

Techniques

Here is a complete list of techniques used in this book, including basic crochet stitches, special stitches, and finishing techniques, as well as sewing stitches for assembling your squares.

Basic Crochet Stitches

Slip Knot

Loop the yarn end around the hook, catch the working yarn, and draw it through the loop; pull the yarn end to tighten the knot.

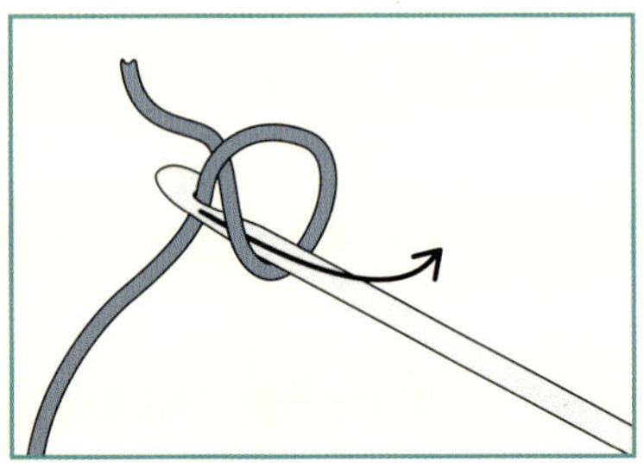

Chain (Ch)

Yarn over (1) and pull through the loop on the hook (2).

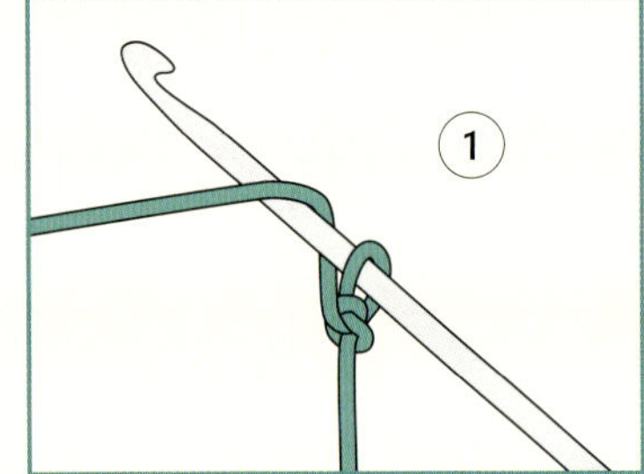

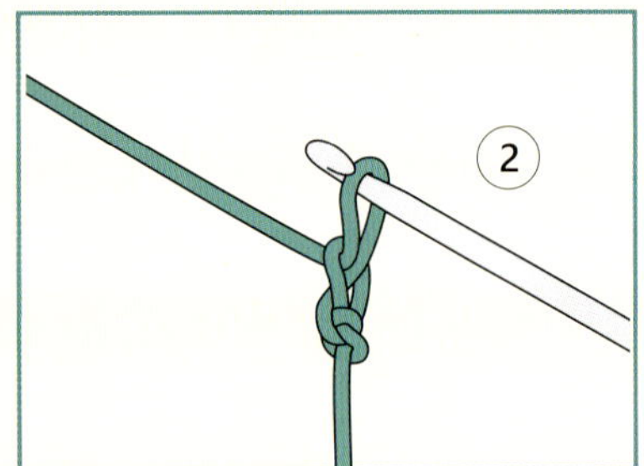

Slip Stitch (Sl st)

Insert the hook in the stitch, yarn over, and pull through the stitch and the loop on the hook.

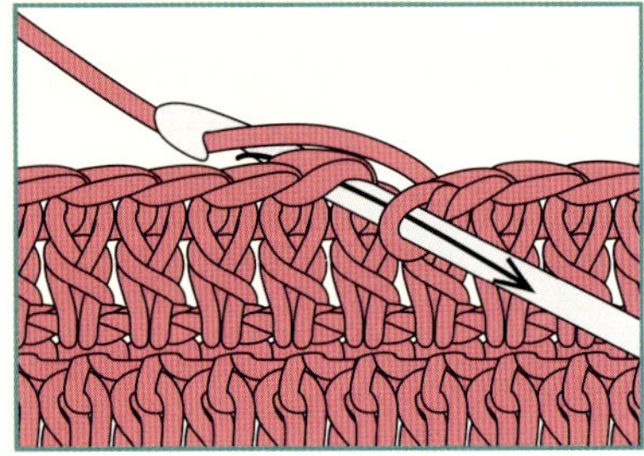

Chain Ring

Make the number of chains indicated in the pattern, insert the hook into the first ch, and complete sl st to create the ring.

Single Crochet (Sc)

Insert the hook into the stitch, yarn over (1) and pull up a loop, yarn over and pull through all loops on the hook (2).

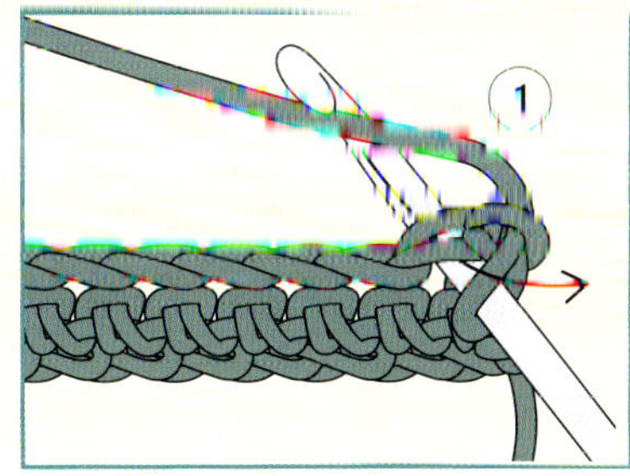

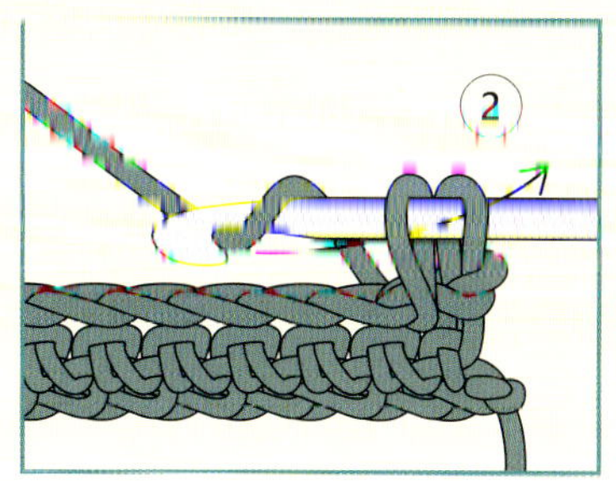

Half Double Crochet (Hdc)

Yarn over, insert the hook into the stitch (1), yarn over and pull up a loop (2), yarn over and pull through all loops on the hook.

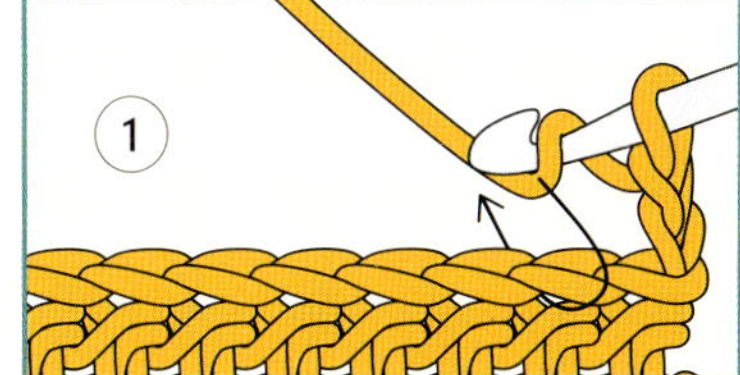

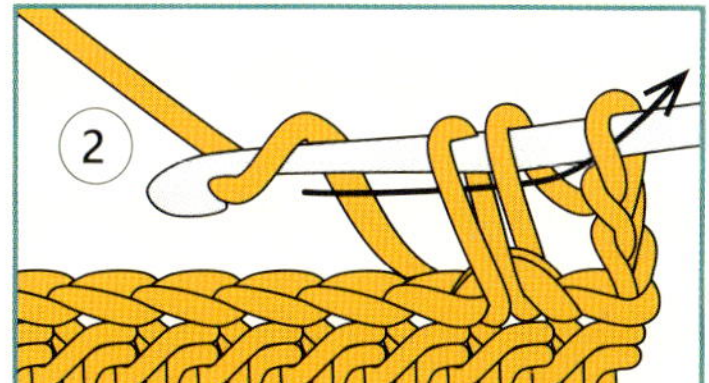

Double Crochet (Dc)

Yarn over, insert the hook into the stitch, yarn over and pull up a loop (1), [yarn over and pull through 2 loops on the hook] 2 times (1, 2).

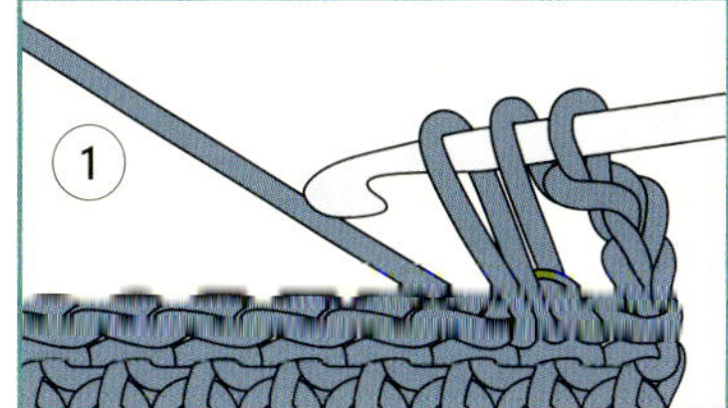

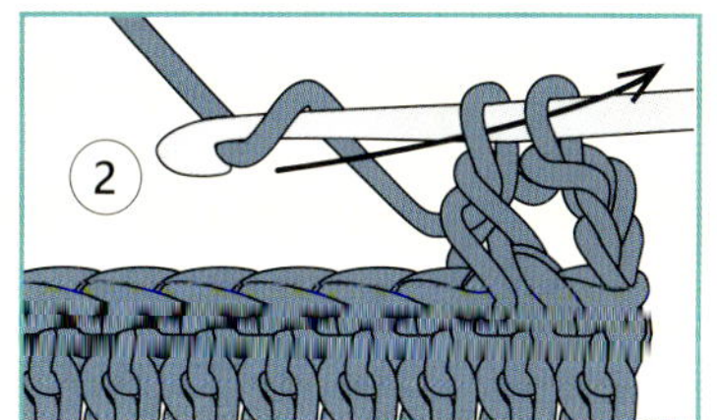

Treble Crochet (Tr)

Yarn over twice, insert the hook into the stitch (1), yarn over and pull up a loop, [yarn over and pull through 2 loops on the hook] 3 times (2).

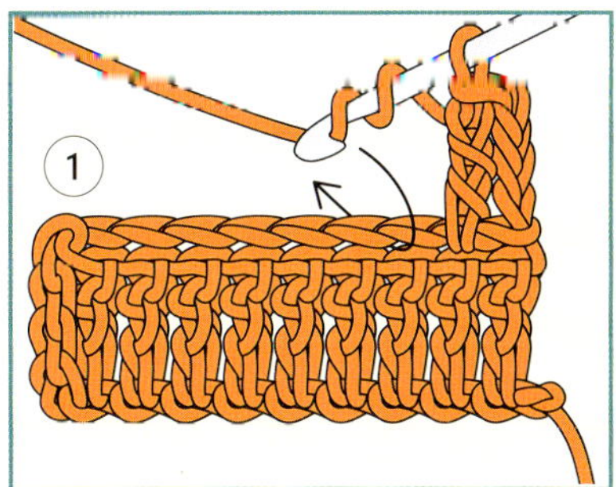

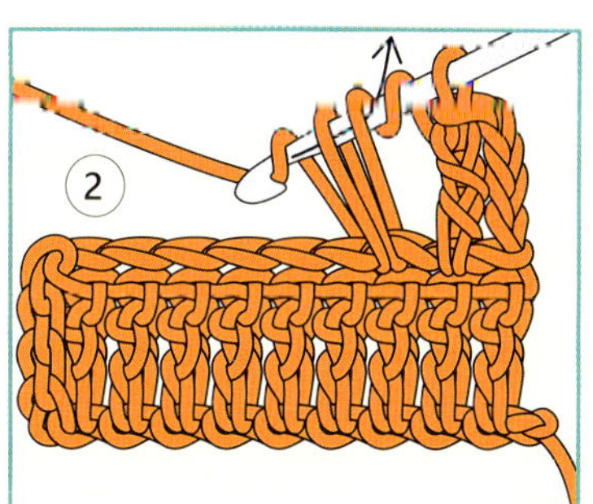

Magic Ring

Wrap the yarn around your finger creating a ring (1), insert the hook into the ring, yarn over (2) and pull up a loop; work into the ring as indicated in the pattern (3), then pull the yarn end tightly to close the ring.

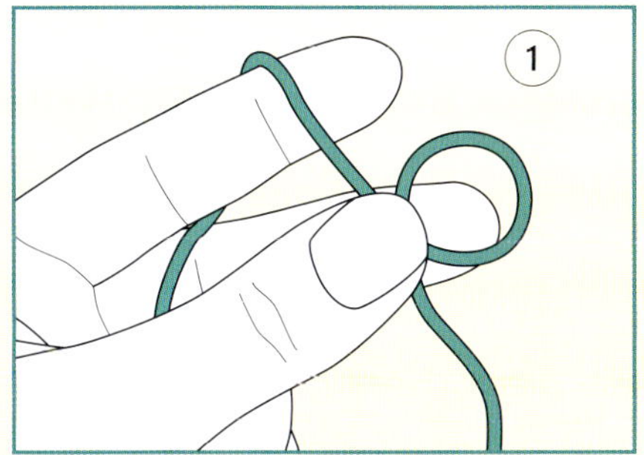

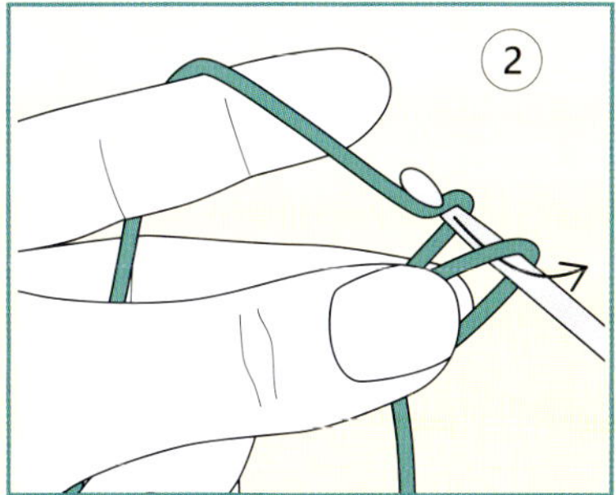

Special Stitches

Picot

Ch 3, insert the hook through the base of the previously made stitch (1), yarn over and pull through all loops on the hook (2).

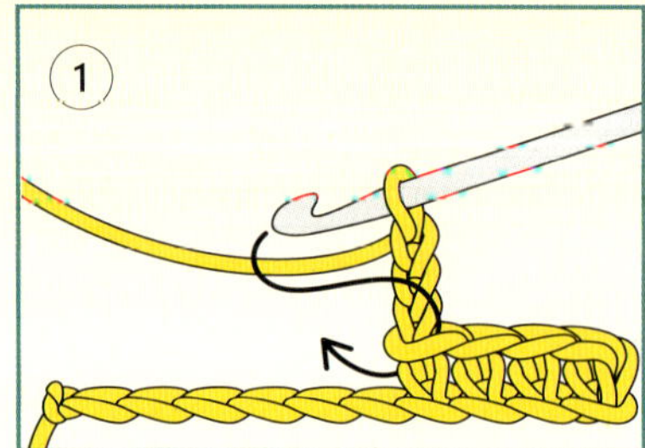

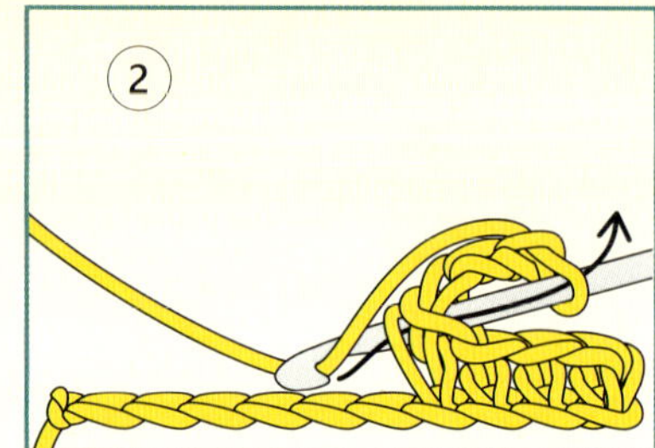

Large Popcorn (5-tr PC)

Work 5 tr into the same stitch (1), remove the hook from the loop and insert it from front to back through the top of the first tr, replace the loop on the hook (from the last tr) and pull it through (2).

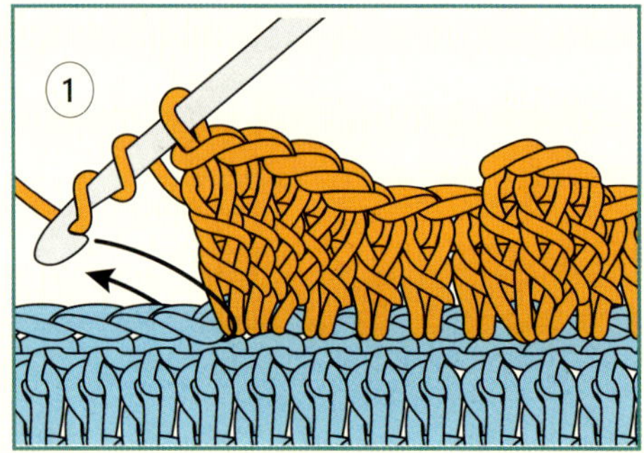

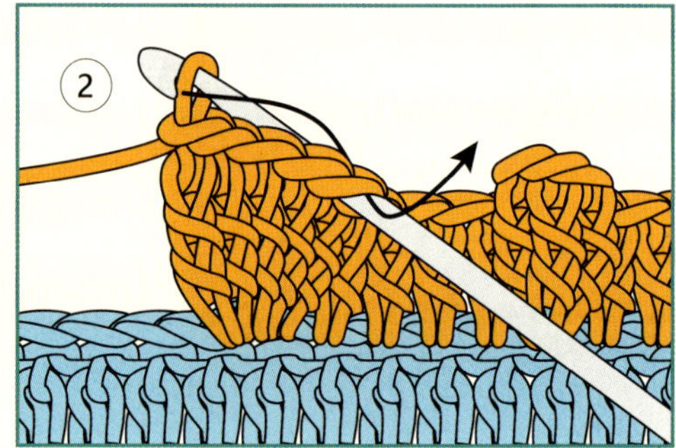

Decreases

Single Crochet 2 Together (Sc2tog)

[Insert the hook in next stitch, yarn over and pull up a loop] 2 times (1), yarn over and pull through all loops on the hook (2).

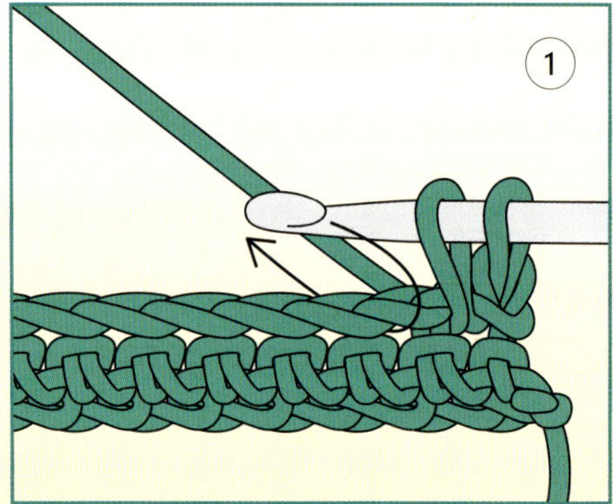

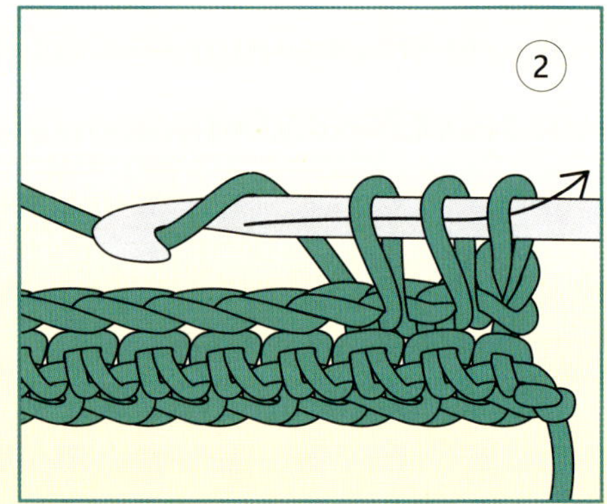

Double Crochet 2 (3/4/5) Together (Dc2[3/4/5]tog)

Double crochet decreases work by starting with partial double crochet stitches and then finishing them as one stitch. You can use the same technique for decreasing 2, 3, 4, or 5 dc stitches to 1 by repeating the sequence in square brackets.

Double crochet decease: [Yarn over, insert the hook in next stitch, yarn over and pull up a loop, yarn over and pull through 2 loops on the hook] 2/3/4/5 times (1), yarn over and pull through all loops on the hook (2).

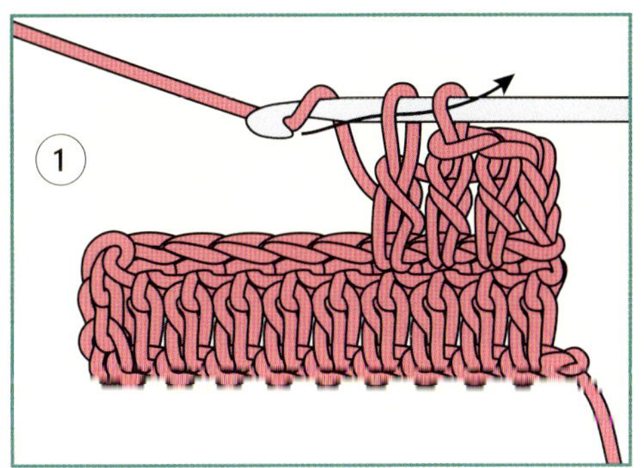

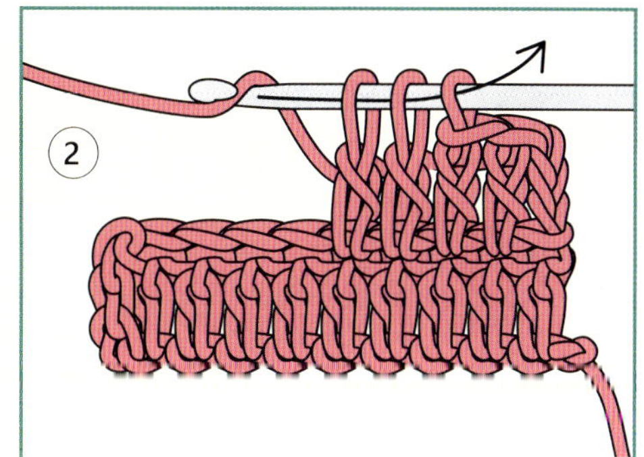

Treble Crochet 2 (3) Together (Tr2[3]tog)

As for a dc decrease, treble crochet decreases are worked by starting with a number of partial stitches and then finishing them as 1 stitch. You can use the same technique for decreasing 2 or 3 tr stitches to 1 by repeating the sequence in square brackets.

Treble crochet decease: *Yarn over twice, insert the hook in next stitch (1), yarn over and pull up a loop [yarn over and pull through 2 loops on the hook] 2 times**; repeat from * to ** 1 more time (for single decrease/tr2tog) or 2 more times (for double decrease/ tr3tog); yarn over and pull through all loops on the hook (2)

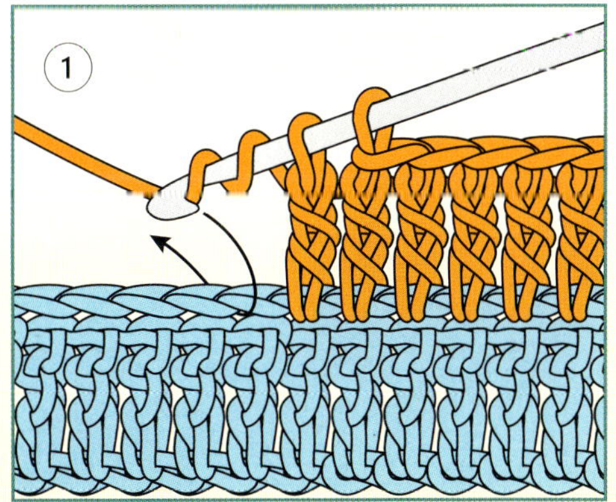

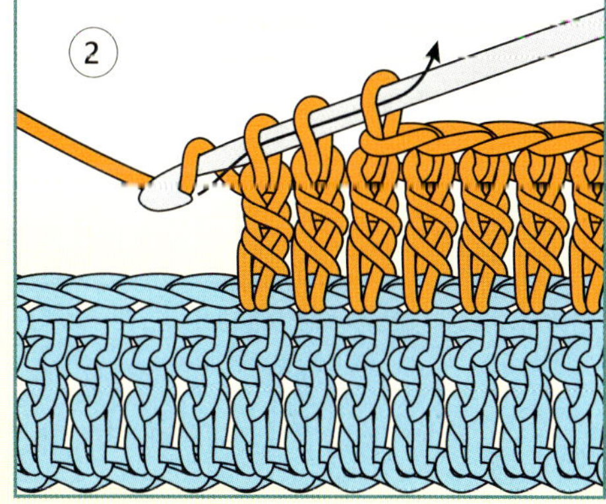

Back and Front Post Stitches

Front Post Slip Stitch (Fpslst)

Insert the hook from front to back to front around the post of the stitch (1), yarn over, and pull through all loops on the hook (2).

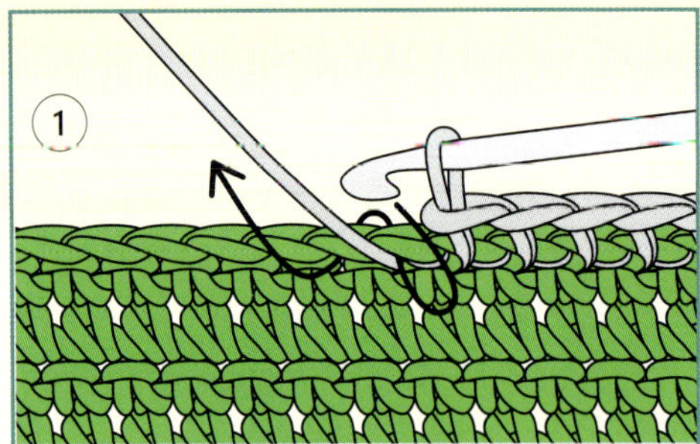

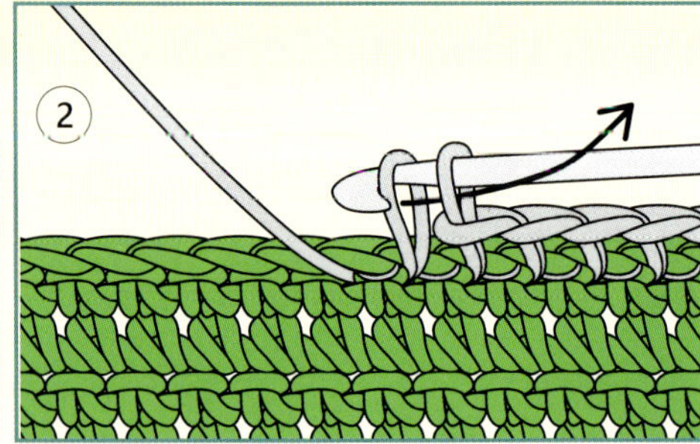

Back Post Single Crochet (Bpsc)

Insert the hook from back to front to back around the post of the stitch (1), yarn over and complete sc as usual (2).

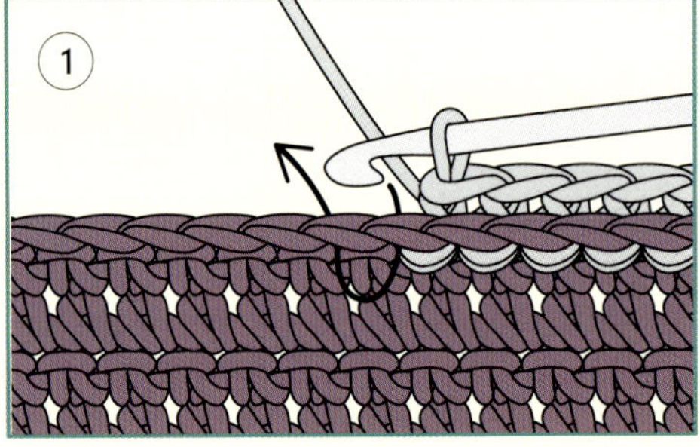

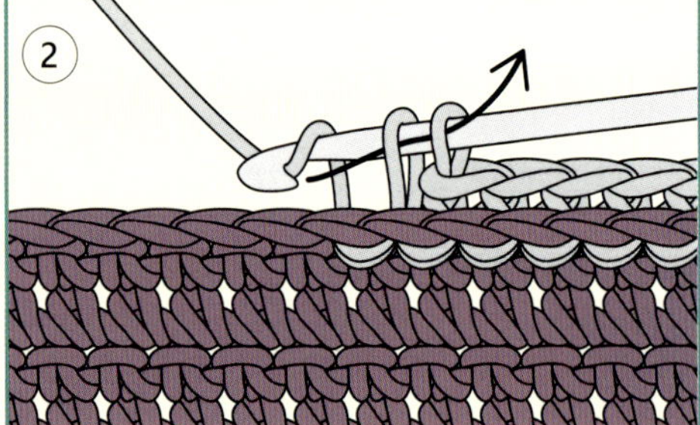

Front Post Single Crochet (Fpsc)

Insert the hook from front to back to front around the post of the stitch (1), yarn over and complete sc as usual (2).

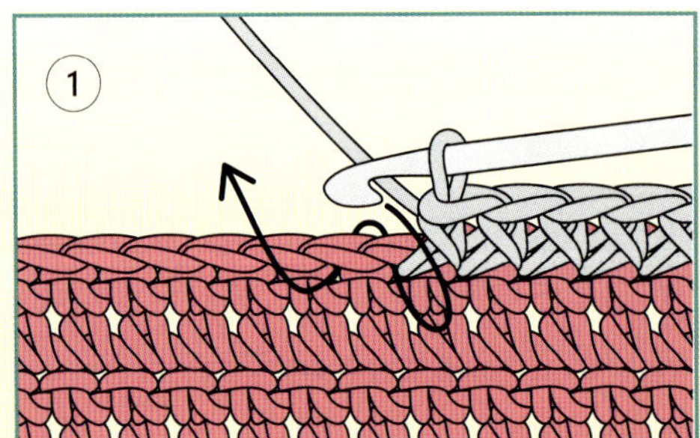

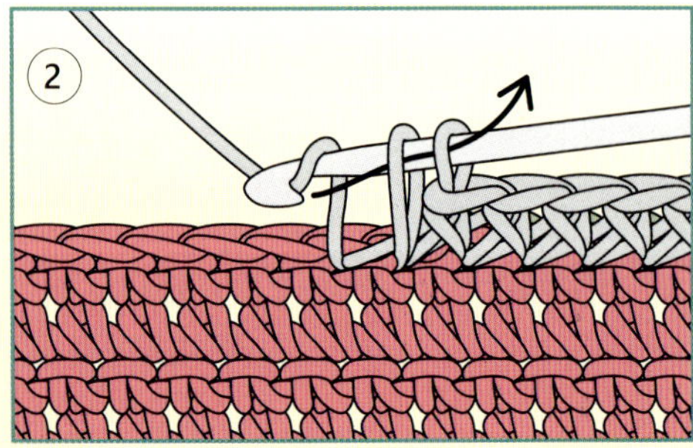

Back Post Half Double Crochet (Bphdc)

Yarn over, insert the hook from back to front to back around the post of the stitch (1), yarn over and complete hdc as usual (2).

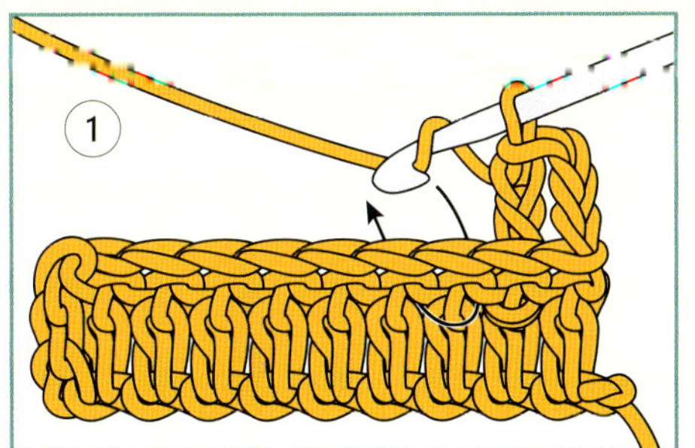

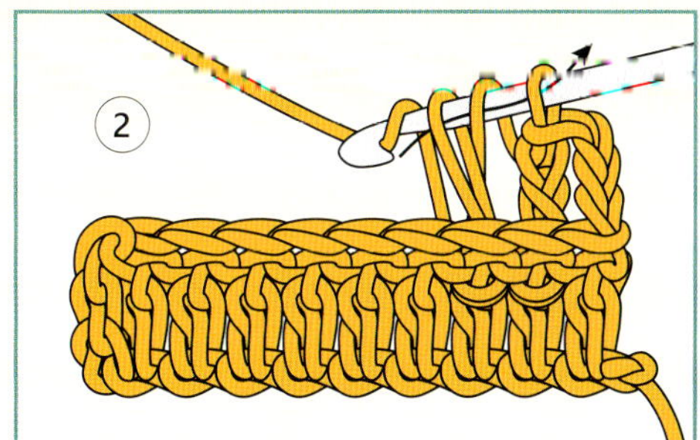

Front Post Half Double Crochet and Double Crochet (Fphdc/Fpdc)

Yarn over, insert the hook from front to back to front around the post of the stitch (1), yarn over and complete hdc (dc) as usual.

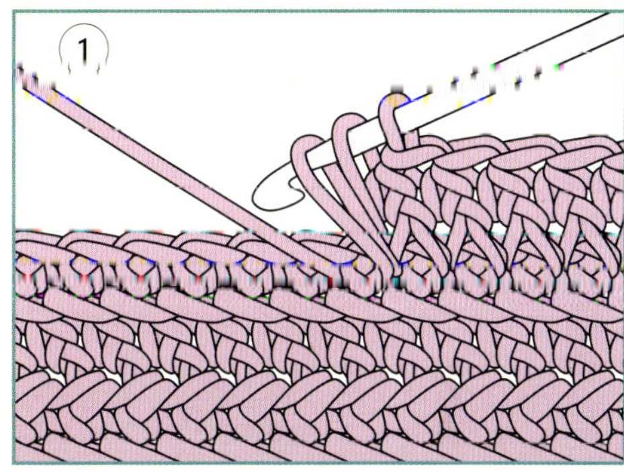

Front Post Treble Crochet (Fptr)

Yarn over twice, insert the hook from front to back to front around the post of the stitch (1), yarn over and complete tr as usual (2).

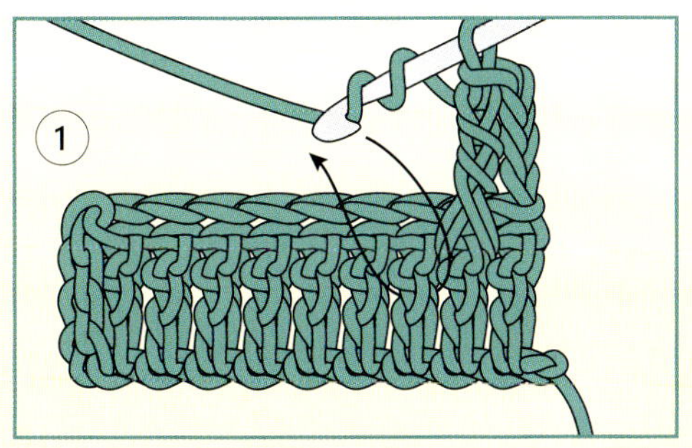

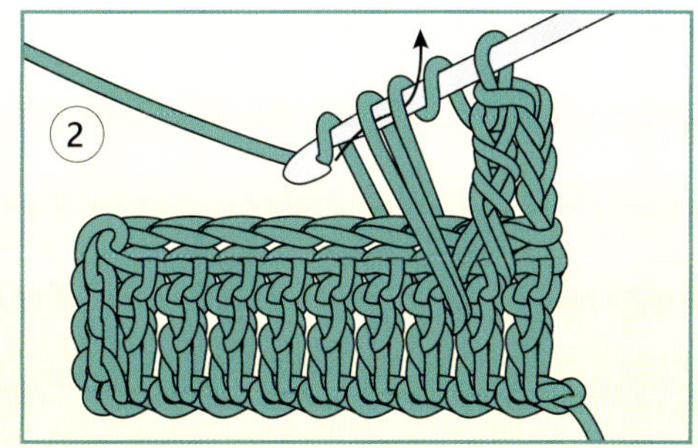

Back and Front Loops

Working in Back Loop Only (BLO)

Insert the hook in the back loop of the stitch instead of both loops.

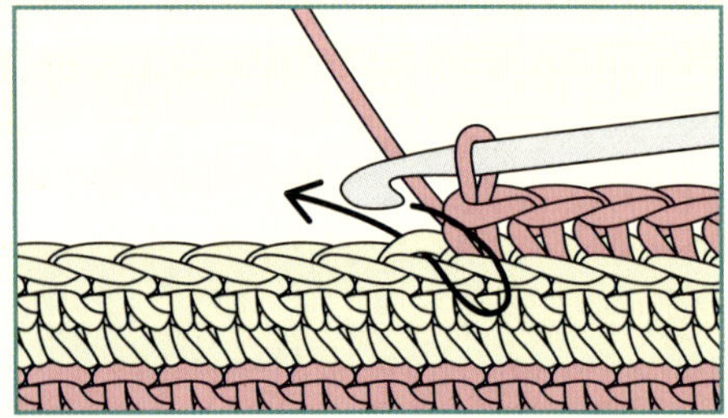

Working in Front Loop Only (FLO)

Insert the hook in the front loop of the stitch instead of both loops.

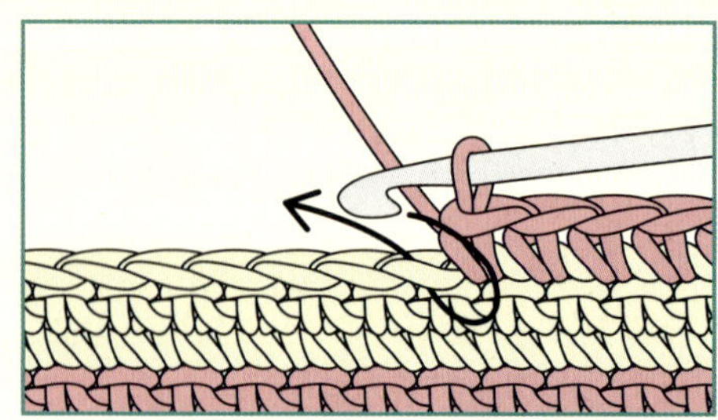

Working in Third Loop On WS

Insert the hook in the third (hidden) loop behind the stitch instead of the top 2 loops.

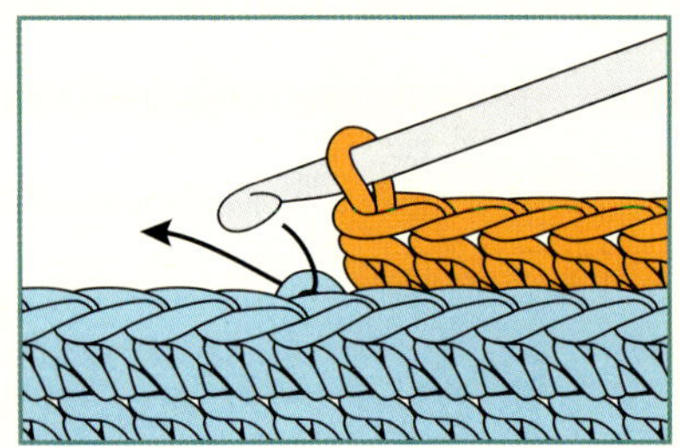

Working in Third Loop On RS

Insert the hook in the third (hidden) loop in front of the stitch instead of the top 2 loops.

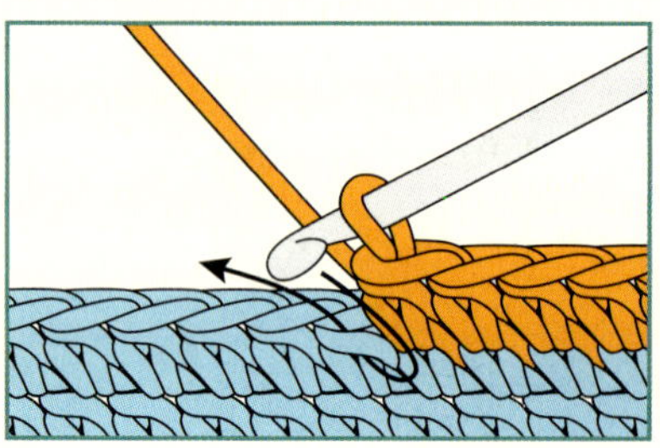

Joining New Yarn

Changing Colors In The Middle Of The Row/Round

Leave the stitch before the color change unfinished. With 2 loops on the hook, drop the working yarn and pick up the new color (1), pulling it through the remaining loops on the hook (2). Continue to work the next st(s) with the new color (3).

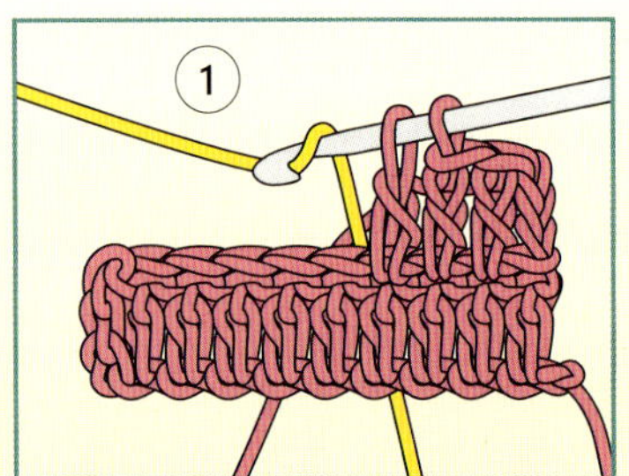

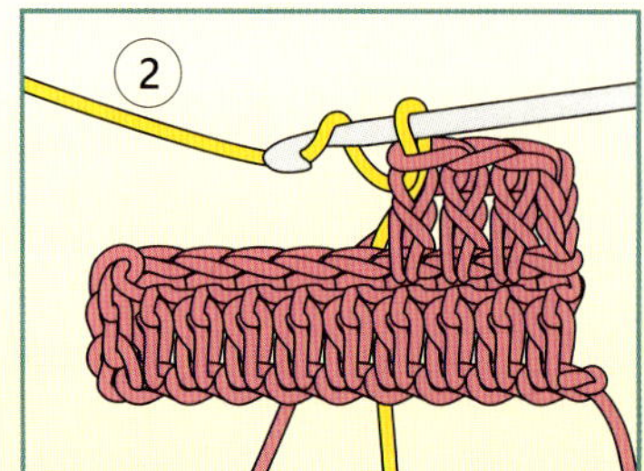

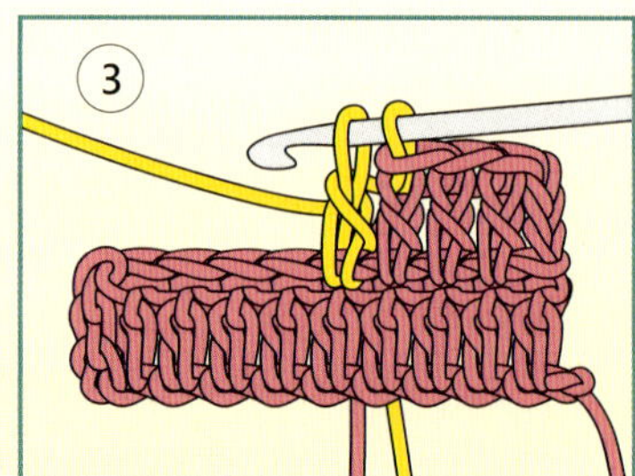

Standing Stitches

Standing stitches allow you to begin a new row/round with a different yarn, omitting chains at the beginning. Simply make a slip knot and hold the loop on the hook; complete the stitch as usual.

Standing Slip Stitch (sl st) and Single Crochet (Sc)

Make a slip knot and hold the loop on the hook, insert the hook into the stitch and complete sl st (sc) as usual.

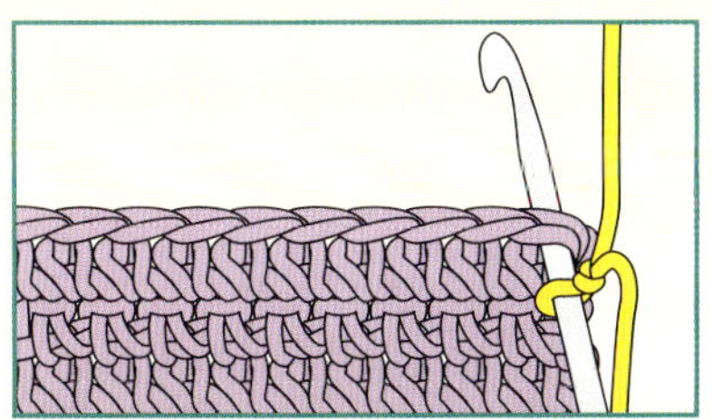

Standing Half Double Crochet (Hdc) or Double Crochet (dc)

Make a slip knot and hold the loop on the hook; yarn over, insert the hook into the stitch and complete hdc (dc) as usual.

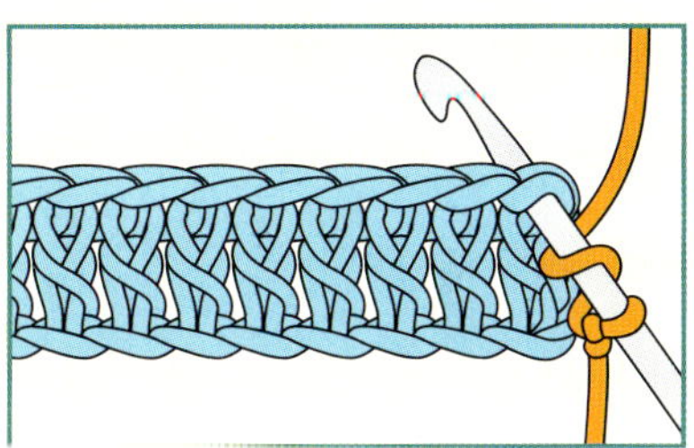

Standing Treble Crochet (Tr)

Make a slip knot and hold the loop on the hook; yarn over twice, insert the hook into the stitch and complete tr as usual.

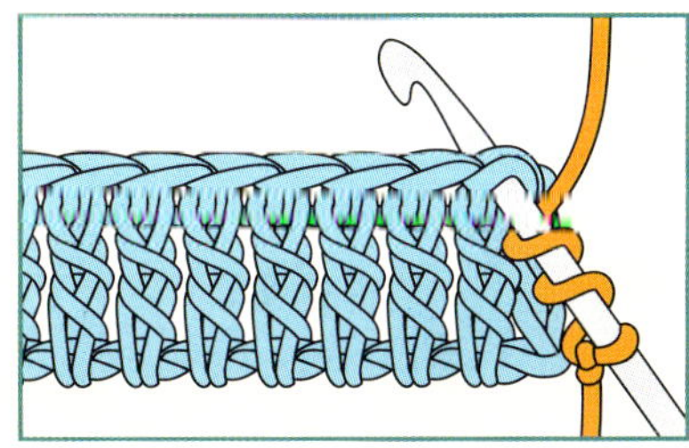

Crocheting In The Round

Working Into Ring

Make a chain ring (or magic ring); following the pattern, insert the hook in the center of the ring, and complete stitches as usual.

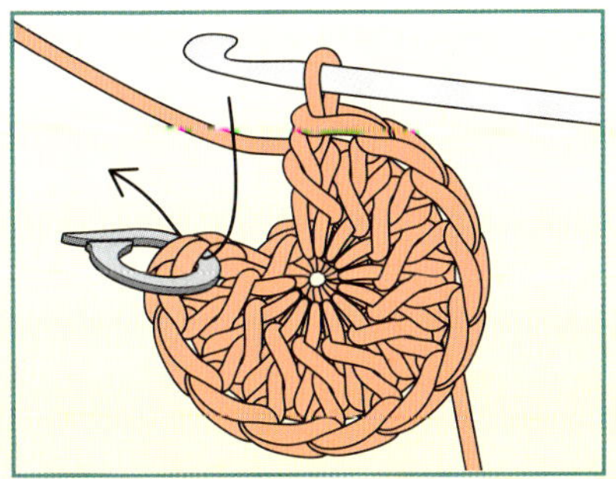

Working On Both Sides of The Foundation Chain

Complete all the required stitches, working in each chain across the foundation chain and place the increase stitches in the last chain; rotate your work and crochet along the bottom loops of the foundation chain as indicated.

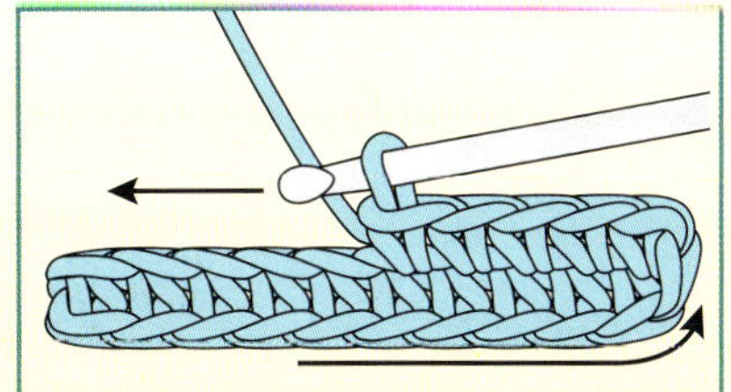

Finishing Crochet

Surface Slip Stitch (surface sl st)

Holding the yarn behind your work, insert the hook through the fabric from front to back; catch the yarn and pull up a loop to the front (1); *insert the hook into the next st from front to back, yarn over (2) and pull up a loop through the fabric and the loop on the hook (3); repeat from *.

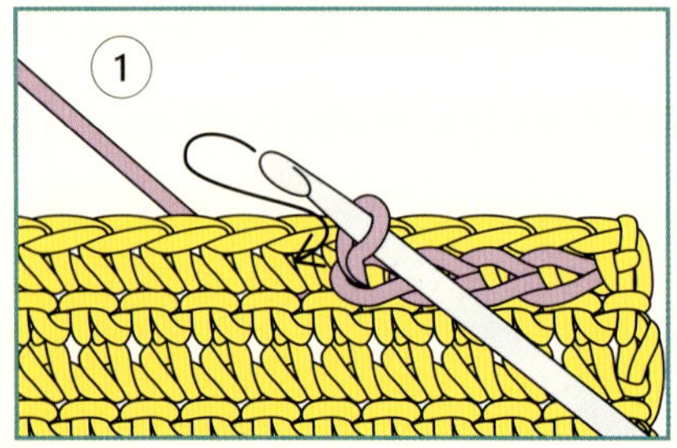

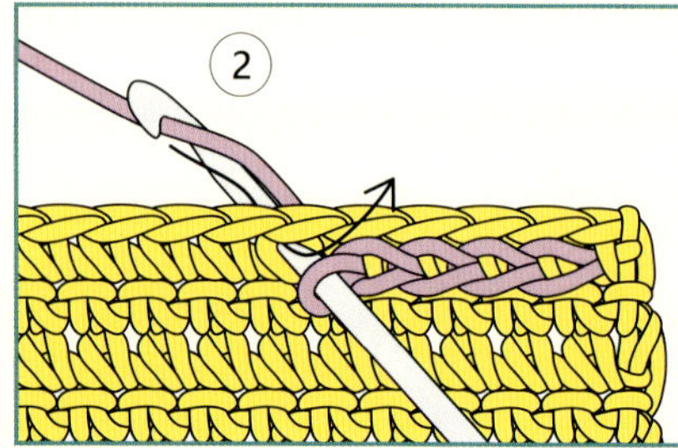

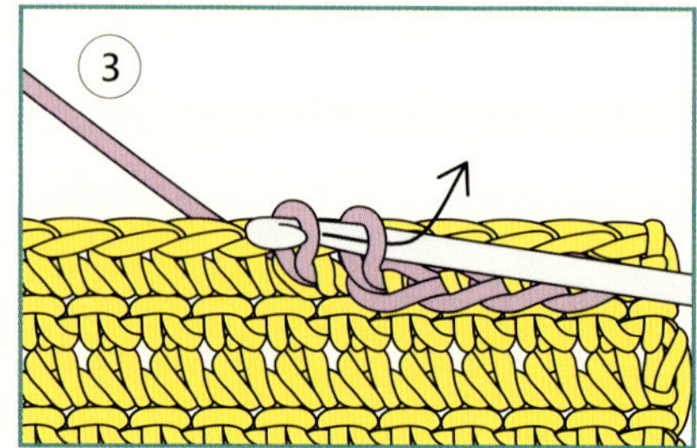

Fasten Off

Cut working yarn, leaving a 6in (15cm) tail; draw the end through the loop on the hook and pull up tight.

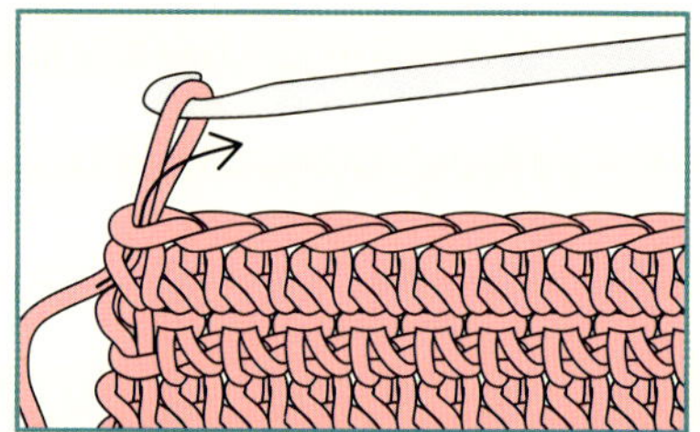

Join and Fasten Off

Make a sl st to join (1), then cut working yarn and pull it through (2); insert the hook from back to front through the same st and pull the end to the wrong side.

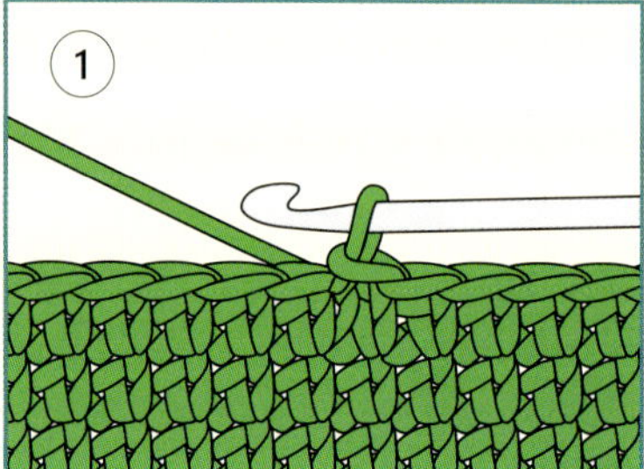

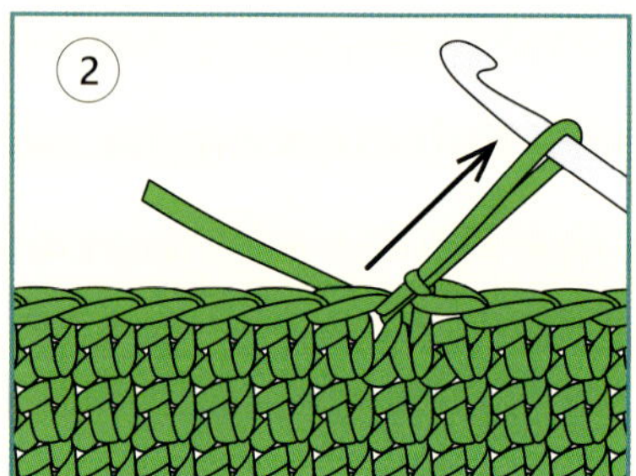

Weaving In The End

Thread the yarn end into a tapestry needle; with the wrong side facing you, weave in the end by pulling the needle through the base of the sts several times in different directions, skipping a few threads between the steps.

Double Chain Crochet Cord (D-ch cord)

Leaving a long yarn tail at the beginning, make a slip knot to create the first chain. Holding the working yarn around your index finger, tail over the hook from front to back (1). Grab working yarn and draw it through both loops on the hook (2). Repeat to the required length (3).

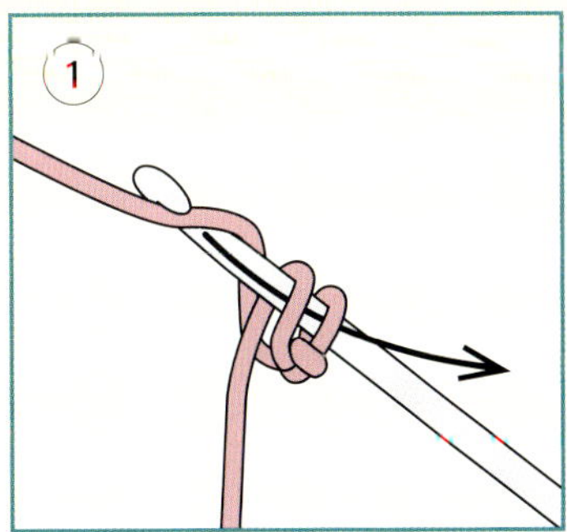

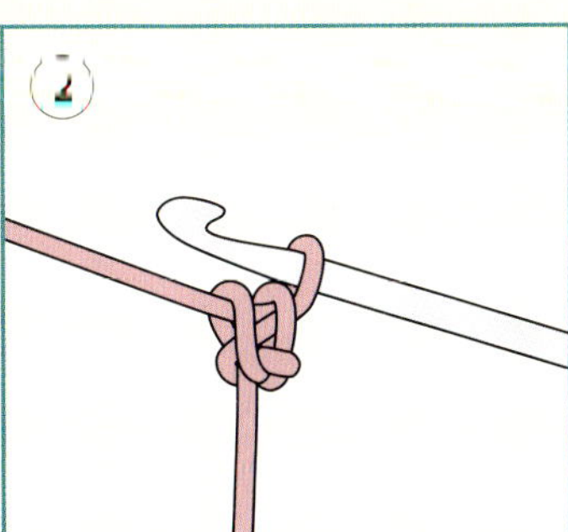

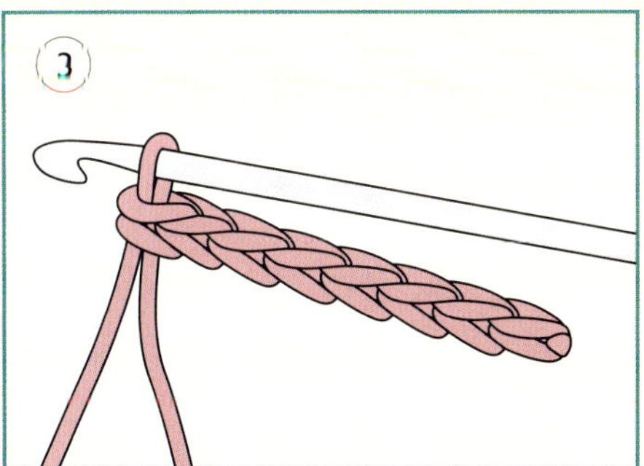

Sewing Stitches

When sewing, guide the needle through the stitches when possible, without pulling it to the WS. It will help to prevent contrasting color yarn from showing on the back and ensure your work looks clean.

Backstitch

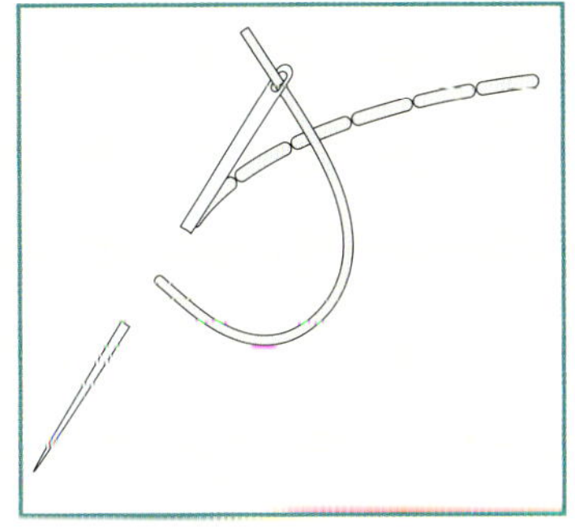

Whipstitch

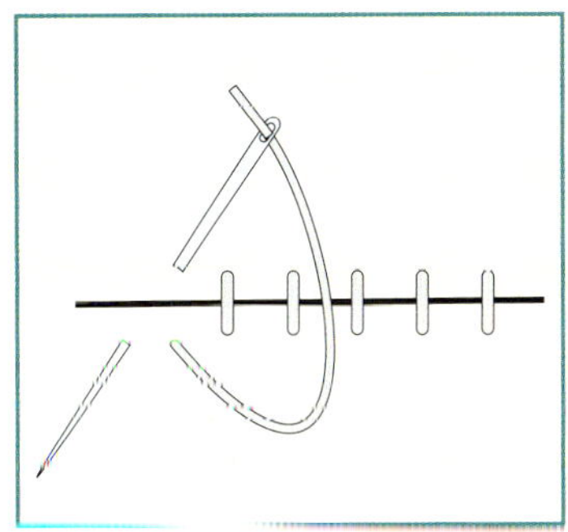

Straight Stitch

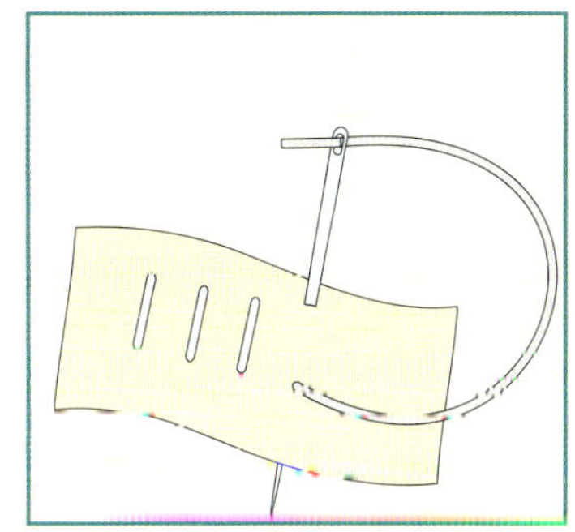

Satin Stitch

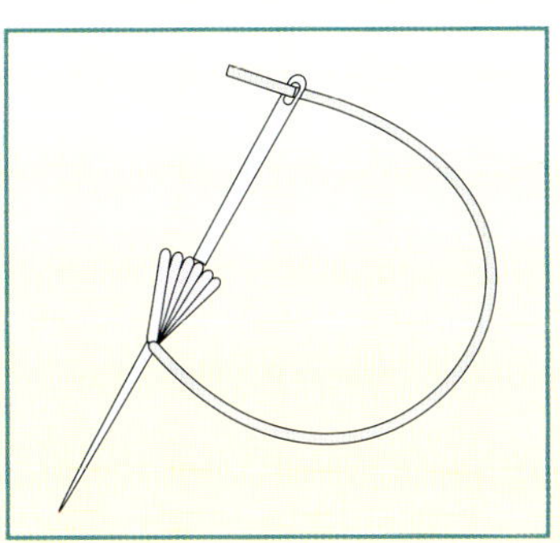

French Knot

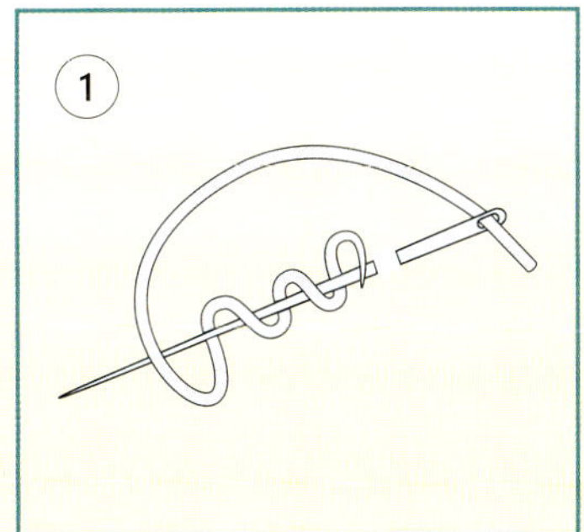

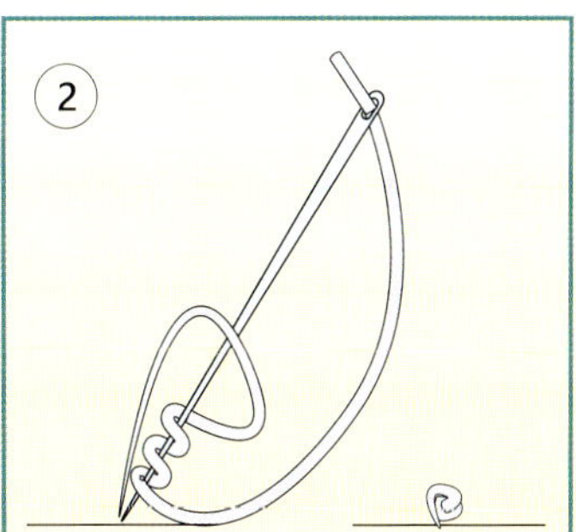

Working With Felt

Felt shapes are added to many of the Pokémon crochet squares in this book to add intricate features effectively. Below, you'll find a guide to creating and attaching these felt pieces.

Tools and Materials

To make small parts out of felt, you will need a few essential tools and materials:

- Wool blend felt sheets (1–1.2mm) for creating shapes
- Permanent fabric glue for attaching felt to squares
- Freezer paper for tracing and cutting templates
- Basic iron for bonding freezer paper to felt
- Sharp mechanical pencil for tracing
- Fabric snips for cutting
- Precision tweezers for holding small felt pieces

Using the Templates

The templates included with the square patterns are produced actual size on the page, designed for 7 x 7in (17.5 x 17.5cm) squares. There's no need to resize or adjust them, just make sure your Pokémon squares are spot-on!

Freezer paper makes using templates simple and precise. To begin, trace the pattern pieces onto the dull side of the freezer paper so that the shiny side is facing down when you draw. Freezer paper is translucent, which makes it easy to see the lines of the pattern when tracing. Follow every line, including any special markings, such as notches and seam allowances. To make it easier to trace, you can tape freezer paper to the pattern page with masking tape.

With the shiny side facing down, position your traced templates onto the felt and press with a hot iron (1); do not use steam. The shiny side of freezer paper is slightly adhesive and will stick to the felt temporarily, but be careful not to stick it to the hot iron by mistake.

Now, you can cut out your felt templates, following the lines on the freezer paper (2). Use sharp fabric snips and cut slowly with precision. The felt pieces are now ready but do not remove the freezer paper yet.

Using Fabric Glue

The templates have already been mirrored for your convenience. So, the side with the freezer paper is where you need to apply fabric glue. Simply position all pieces on your square with the paper side facing down, then glue them as follows:

Use tweezers to hold small felt pieces. They will help you to keep your fingers clean and maneuver the shapes. Clean the glue from your tools after every use.

Peel the freezer paper off the felt and apply fabric glue evenly, covering the entire surface (3).

Glue the shape onto the square. If a shape has multiple layers, glue all the layers together first (see Tips and Tricks).

Let the glue dry, then check the edges to ensure they are attached all the way around. If needed, add extra glue carefully without overfilling the edges and let it dry again.

Tips and Tricks

Some shapes have multiple layers. Assemble these shapes and let them dry before gluing them onto the square (4). In multi-layered shapes, you may also find seam allowances that need to be aligned. Trim these seam allowances from all fully assembled layers when the glue is dry (5). This will provide a perfectly aligned edge.

If multi-layered shapes have notches (dark triangular marks), cut them out of each shape carefully, without cutting through the solid line (6). Align these notches when assembling the shape, then cut away the seam allowances with notches when the glue is dry (7).

When gluing your felt pieces onto the square, first position them as indicated in the pattern. Add pins into the fabric to secure the correct placement, marking the main points for each shape (8). Pick up the first shape and apply the glue while the pins are still in the fabric. Put the shape back between the pins and remove the pins. Repeat the process with the remaining shapes and let the glue dry.

1
2
3
4
5
6
7
8
TITANIUM CERAMIC
FABRIC FUSE

Finishing

Surface crochet, blocking, and different joining techniques are some of the methods used to give the squares and projects in this book those essential finishing touches.

Surface Crochet

For some of the Pokémon squares, you will be working surface sl sts to outline the center part of the square. To avoid unnecessary rejoining of the same color yarn, do not cut the yarn after you change to the background color. Simply enlarge the last loop to the size of your yarn ball and pull the ball through the loop without cutting the yarn (1). Keep this yarn on the WS while crocheting the rest of the square.

Once the square is finished, insert the hook through the first st between color changes, pick up the yarn on the back and pull it to the RS (2). Work surface sl sts all the way around, ending in the last st. To finish the round seamlessly, cut the yarn and pull the tail out on RS. Thread a needle and pull it under two loops of the first st from side to side (3), then insert it through the center of your last st and pull all the way to the WS (4). Weave in the end.

Blocking

Blocking is not required but it may help you to keep your squares consistent in size. If you decide to block your squares, do it prior to adding the finishing details.

Simply soak them in warm water, squeeze out the excess moisture, and pin around the edges to the specified size using rust-resistant blocking pins. Leave your squares to dry.

Joining Squares

When it comes to joining squares into projects, choose one of the following techniques or use your own preferred method.

For instance, join as you go works best for joining the granny square edges of the pillow and blanket, while the mattress stitch and surface crochet joins can be used for any type of project.

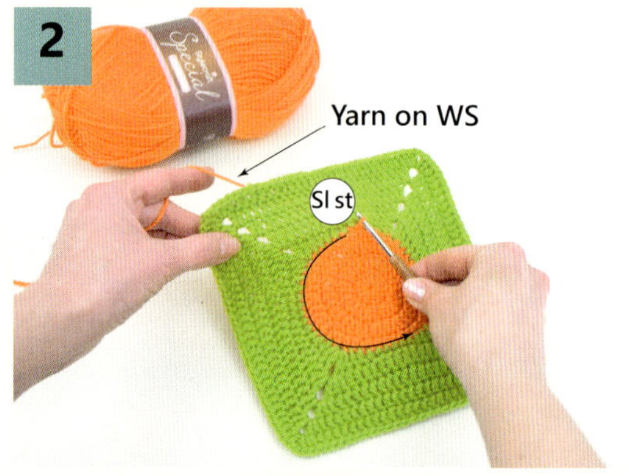

Mattress Stitch Join

Position the squares based on your project layout, and sew them together as follows:

Thread the tapestry needle with a coordinating color yarn and sew from corner to corner through the corresponding sts of the two squares. Insert the needle from back to front through the ch in the corner of the left square, then through the ch in the corner of the right square; *insert the needle from back to front under both loops of next st on the left, then under both loops of next st on the right; repeat from * ending in corner chs. Fasten off and weave in the end. Continue sewing the remaining edges in the same manner (5–7).

Surface Crochet Join

Position the squares based on your project layout, and join them together using any color of yarn and a 4mm (G/6) hook as follows:

Make a slip knot and keep the loop on the hook. Insert the hook through the corner chs of both squares and complete a sl st; with yarn in back, work in BLO—*sl st in next st of both pieces at the same time; repeat from * ending in corner chs. Fasten off and weave in the ends. Continue joining the remaining edges in the same manner (8–10).

Join As You Go

Finish your first square as usual. For the remaining squares, join them to the previously made squares as you go, while working the joining round as follows:

Begin the rnd as described and work to the corner where you need to start joining. In the corner, work 3 dc, *ch 1, sl st into corresponding corner of the previously made square, ch 1, 3 dc in same corner**; [sl st into corresponding sp of the previously made motif, skip 3 sts, 3 dc in next sp] to next corner; repeat from * to **. Continue to work around the remaining sides of the square in pattern as established, ending the rnd as described in the pattern (11–13).

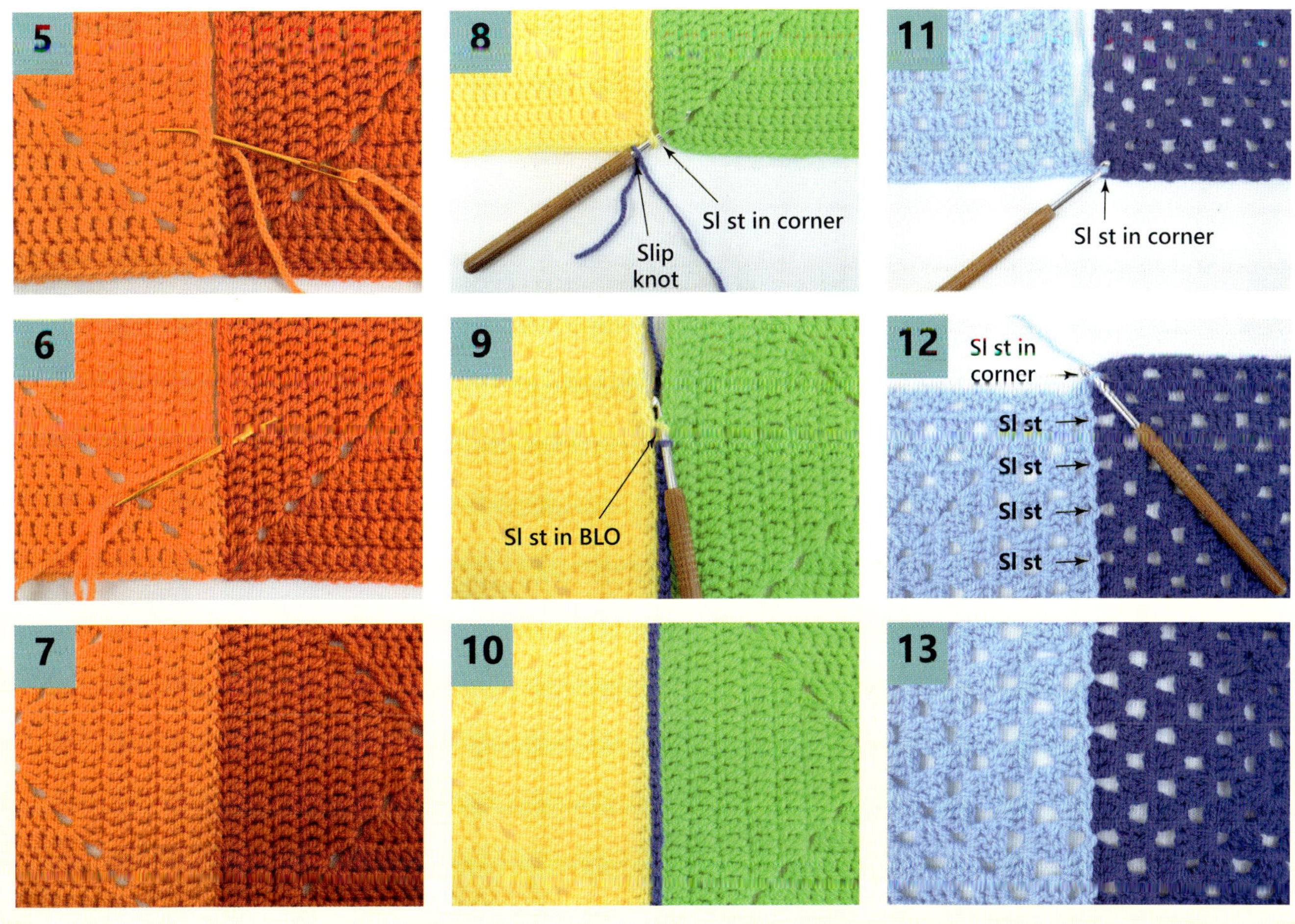

About the Author

Hi! I am a Canadian fiber artist, pattern designer, and author. Coming from a family of textile engineers, my childhood was filled with all things fiber, which ignited my passion for fiber art. Whether with my family or at school, I never passed up the chance to create something new from yarn. While I enjoy all kinds of textile art, there's a special place in my heart for crochet and it will always be my first love.

I discovered the joy of Pokémon a long time ago, and I've been hooked ever since. It has become a fun way to bond with our children and help us make new friends along the way, which has only added to the fun and excitement. I am deeply honored by the opportunity to incorporate my life's journey into this book through crochet art! I hope *Pokémon Crochet Squares* will help you create wonderful memories, spreading happiness and good vibes by showing off your projects.

Thanks

My testing team is simply the best! I'm so grateful for the time they spent testing my patterns, checking yarn requirements, and proofreading. Thanks a million to Cheryl McNichols, Courtney Knorr, Melinda Dickie, Ryan Nicole Hazeltine, Helen Hamilton, and Cynthia Fuller. I'd also like to give a shout-out to Stylecraft for their amazing Special DK and 4-ply yarns, which helped me finish all the Pokémon squares and projects featured in this book!

Suppliers

Yarn

Stylecraft Special DK and Special 4-ply: Stylecraft-Yarns.co.uk

Craft Felt

Wool Blend Felt Sheets: CanadianFeltShop.com

Additional Supplies

Quick Bond Fabric Fuse Adhesive: ThermOweb.com

DMC Floss: DMC.com

Mill Hill Glass Beads: MillHillBeads.com

Index

abbreviations 7

back loops 118
back post stitches 116–17
backstitch 121
Banner 104–5
beads, glass 4
beaks 17, 29, 69
Blanket, Lap 98–9
blocking 124
bows 69–70
Bulbasaur 92–3

chain 112
chain ring 112
Charmander [illegible]
cheeks 12, 87
Chespin 32–4
Chikorita 84–6
Chimchar 65–7
circles, basic 9
collars 52, 53
color changes 118
crochet hooks 4
Cyndaquil 22–3

decreases 114–15
double chain crochet cord 121
double crochet 113
double crochet 2 together 115

ears 13, 25, 39–40, 46–7, 52, 63–4,
  66, 72–5, 92–3
edging 98, 102, 104, 109
embroidery floss 4
ends, weaving in 120
eyes 17, 23, 42–3, 48–9, 78, 94–6

fastening off 120
feathers 82–3
felt, craft 4–5, 122–3
Fennekin 71–3
finishing work 120–1, 124–5
fins 21, 88
French knot 121
Froakie 42–3
front loops 118
front post stitches 116–17
Fuecoco 18–19

gauge (tension) 6
gills 21
glue, fabric 122–3
Great Ball 41
Grookey 38–40

hair 66–7
half double crochet 113
hats 29–30

join and fasten off 120
joining squares 124–5
joining yarn 118

large popcorn 114
leaves 33, 36, 39, 56, 81, 85
Litten 44–7

magic ring 113
Master Ball 31
materials 4–5, 122
mattress stitch join 125
mouths 49, 78–9
Mudkip 20–1
Mug Rug 106–7

noses 25, 43, 53

Oran Berry 26–7
Oshawott 24–5

patterns, reading 6
Pecha Berry 35–7
picot 114
Pikachu 12–13
Pillow 100–3
Piplup 16–17
Play Cubes 108–9
Poké Ball 14–15
Popplio 52–3
projects 97–111

Quaxly 28–30

Rowlet 68–70

safety issues 4
satin stitch 121
Scorbunny 74–6
sewing stitches 121
single crochet 113
single crochet 2 together 114
Sitrus Berry 50–1
skills levels 6
slip knot 112
slip stitch 112
Snivy 94–6
snouts 19, 22, 38–9, 53, 60, 77–8,
  87–8, 94–5
Sobble 87–9
Sprigatito 62–4
squares 10–96
  basic 8
Squirtle 58–9
standing stitches 119
stitches 7, 112–21
straight stitch 121
surface crochet 124
surface crochet join 125
surface slip stitch 120

Tamato Berry 80–1
templates 122–3
Tepig 60–1
tools 4, 122
Torchic 82–3
Totodile 77–9
treble crochet 113
treble crochet 3 together 115
Treecko 48–9
Turtwig 55–7

Ultra Ball 54

Wall Hanging 110–11
whipstitch 121
whiskers 46, 64, 74
work in the round 6, 119
work in rows 6

yarn 4, 5, 118

A DAVID AND CHARLES BOOK

David and Charles is an imprint of David and Charles, Ltd, Suite A, Tourism House, Pynes Hill, Exeter, EX2 5WS

EU GPSR Authorised Representative:
Logos Europe, 9 rue Nicolas Poussin,
17000, La Rochelle, France
Email: contact@logoseurope.eu

First published in the UK and USA in 2025

A catalogue record for this book is available from the British Library.

ISBN-13: 9781446315514 paperback
ISBN-13: 9781446315521 EPUB

This book has been printed on paper from approved suppliers and made from pulp from sustainable sources.

Printed in China through Asia Pacific Offset for:
David and Charles, Ltd
Suite A, Tourism House, Pynes Hill, Exeter, EX2 5WS

10 9 8 7 6 5 4

Publishing Director: Ame Verso
Publishing Manager: Jeni Chown
Project Editor: Lindsay Kaubi
Lead Designer: Sam Staddon
Designer: Maria Bowers
Pre-press Designer: Susan Reansbury
Illustrations: Kuo Kang Chen
Art Direction: Prudence Rogers
Photography: Jason Jenkins
Production Manager: Beverley Richardson

Full-size printable versions of the templates are available to download free from www.bookmarkedhub.com. Search for this book by the title or ISBN: the files can be found under 'Book Extras'. Membership of the Bookmarked online community is free.

Layout of the digital edition of this book may vary depending on reader hardware and display settings.